Canoeing
Louisiana

Canoeing Louisiana

Ernest Herndon

University Press of Mississippi
Jackson

www.upress.state.ms.us

The University Press of Mississippi is a member of the
Association of American University Presses.

Photos by Ernest Herndon
11 10 09 08 07 06 05 04 03   4 3 2 1
∞
Library of Congress Cataloging-in-Publication Data

Herndon, Ernest.
  Canoeing Louisiana / Ernest Herndon.
  p.   cm.
  Includes bibliographical references (p.) and index.
  ISBN 1-57806-425-2 (cloth : alk. paper) — ISBN 1-57806-426-0 (pbk. : alk. paper)
  1. Canoes and canoeing—Louisiana—Guidebooks. 2. Louisiana—Guidebooks. I. Title.
  GV776 .L68 2003
  796.1'22'09763—dc21   2002012148

British Library Cataloging-in-Publication Data available

This book is dedicated to my darling granddaughter
Ella Martin Coy.

Contents

Acknowledgments

Thanks to the following folks who helped me explore Louisiana waters: Greg Bond, Steve Cox, Andy Coy, Jack Curry, Travis Easley, Wyatt Emmerich, Walter Neil Ferguson, Bobby Funderburk, Billy Gibson, Angelyn Herndon, Maudie Herndon, Robert Herndon, Sam Hughes, Keith Hux, Eddie McCalip, Brian Moore, Kemal Sanli, Jimmie Van, and Scott Williams. Also thanks to James Brantley of Panther Creek Outfitters in Farmerville, Danny Rowzee of Tack-A-Paw Expeditions in Toro, James Proctor of Lafayette, and Jack Curry of New Orleans for proofreading portions of the manuscript; and to employees of the Louisiana Department of Wildlife and Fisheries, Louisiana Office of State Parks, U.S. Army Corps of Engineers, U.S. Fish and Wildlife Service, and U.S. Forest Service, who fielded my numerous queries with courtesy and helpfulness.

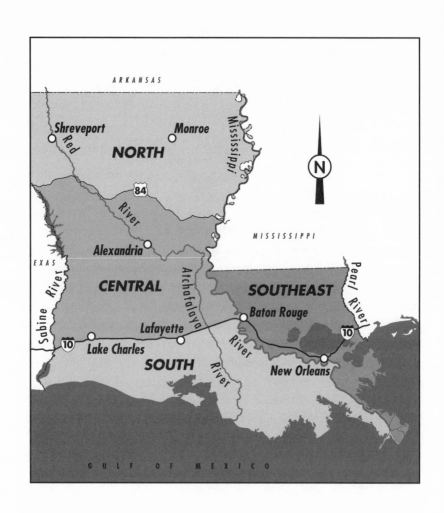

1. The Waters of Louisiana

In the late 1990s when I was finishing up my quest to canoe the state of Mississippi, I cast a curious eye toward Louisiana. Even though I had paddled in the Bayou State off and on for years, I still had no clear, overall concept of the lay of the land as far as rivers went. Little wonder: Louisiana literally swarms with waterways, nearly 3 million acres, in fact. That includes 40,300 miles of rivers, bayous, and creeks, plus half a million acres of backwaters and natural lakes and 245,000 acres of man-made lakes. And then there are 3.6 million acres of marsh. Nor do Louisiana's waters follow obvious patterns. Streams squiggle all over the place; lakes change in size drastically according to rainfall. But after considerable studying, driving, and paddling, I began to form a cohesive mental picture of this fascinating and complex region.

Picture the state as a clunky work boot, toe facing right. On most of the left, or western side, the state is bordered by the Sabine River. The right side of the boot shaft is edged by the Mississippi River. Slicing diagonally across the shaft, from northwest to southeast, is the Red River. When the Red touches the Mississippi, just above the top of the foot of the boot, it swings back south as the Atchafalaya River like a stirrup strap to the sole, which is the Gulf of Mexico. Meanwhile, the Pearl River rims the tip of the boot toe in the extreme southeast. Sabine, Red, Atchafalaya, Mississippi, Pearl: Those are the major defining rivers of Louisiana. Now let's fill in some details.

The Sabine doesn't border the entire west side, only the lower three-fourths, and the top 65 miles of the river takes the form of Toledo Bend, a vast reservoir created by damming the river. Below the dam, the river runs clear and mid-sized through big woods. North of Interstate 10 it splits to form a 9-mile-long "island" which has been set aside as a wildlife management area, providing some of the finest swamp paddling anywhere. Below I-10 the Sabine wends south through marsh and out to the Gulf.

The Red River begins in New Mexico, works eastward as the border between Texas and Oklahoma, clips the corner of Arkansas and dives south into Louisiana north of Shreveport. This wide, brown river has miles-long stretches running south and southeast into prevailing winds, and miles of slack water behind its five locks-and-dams, but it absorbs some fine tributaries from the piney woods of north and central Louisiana. For instance, northeast of Shreveport, Bodcau Bayou squirms through 20-mile long Bodcau Wildlife Management Area, one of the most intriguing pockets of wilderness in the state. Just east of Bodcau, scenic Bayou Dorcheat flows south into Lake Bistineau, which discharges into the Red as Loggy Bayou. Near Winnfield, Saline Bayou in the Kisatchie National Forest provides entrance to a dramatic cypress swamp. Northwest of Monroe, three bayous—Little D'Arbonne, Middle Fork, and Corney—come together into Bayou D'Arbonne Lake and emerge as Bayou D'Arbonne. Both D'Arbonne and neighboring Bayou de L'Outre flow into the Ouachita River, which slides south out of Arkansas, passing through a national wildlife refuge. Just east of the Ouachita, where the hills give way to Delta farmland, Chemin-A-Haut Creek and Bartholomew Bayou come together near Bastrop at Chemin-A-Haut State Park en route to the Ouachita. The Ouachita continues south, receiving Boeuf River near Harrisonburg, then meeting the Tensas and Little Rivers at Jonesville to form the Black River, which empties into Red River downstream from Marksville not far from the Mississippi. The upper Little River offers some interesting paddling, though the lower Little and surrounding waterways are wide agricultural rivers that tend to be more suitable for motorboats than canoes. However, there are some fine vestiges of Delta wildland in places like Boeuf River Wildlife Management Area, Tensas River and Bayou Cocodrie National Wildlife Refuges, and a cluster of wildlife management areas along the lower Red.

South of the Red's diagonal course, several streams flow down to the Gulf. Calcasieu River runs out of the piney hills into Lake Charles and Calcasieu Lake before meeting the brine. One of Calcasieu's tributaries, Whiskey Chitto, is that rare Louisiana phenomenon, a clear, swift, sandy stream, making it one of the most popular canoeing waterways in the state. East of the Calcasieu lies a long, barren stretch as far as paddling is concerned: a host of muddy farmland rivers like Bayou des Cannes, Bayou Nezpique, Bayou Queue de Tortue, Bayou Plaquemine Brule, and Mermentau River. Things become more interesting from a paddler's perspective north of Ville Platte at Chicot Lake and east of Lafayette at Bayou Teche. And prospects get downright awesome with the Atchafalaya Basin.

The Atchafalaya is touted as the largest river swamp in North America. The 15-by-100-mile swath of roadless swamp offers near-infinite paddling possibilities. The presence of camps, motorboats, and posted signs makes it less than perfect, but there is still much to enjoy. You can do a downstream trip on the river itself, spend days exploring the swampy backwaters, or make day trips from Lake Fausse Pointe State Park east of New Iberia. The area near Grand Isle State Park to the southeast provides sea kayaking opportunities, while Jean Lafitte National Historical Park and Preserve gives a glimpse of both cypress swamp and marsh not far from New Orleans.

Southeast Louisiana, on the east side of the Mississippi River, is characterized by piney woods and sometimes-clear rivers coursing south from the hills of southwest Mississippi: Amite, Tickfaw, Tangipahoa, and Bogue Chitto, plus the shorter Tchefuncte and Bogue Falaya. The Bogue Chitto empties into the Pearl River in a wild wetland known as Honey Island Swamp. South of these streams lie huge Lakes Maurepas, Pontchartrain, and Borgne, ringed by bayous and marsh, with several parks and wildlife refuges.

For the purposes of this book I've tried to simplify things by dividing the state into four broad swaths. The North Louisiana portion encompasses waters north of U.S. Highway 84: Bodcau, Dorcheat and Saline Bayous, the bayous in and around Bayou D'Arbonne Lake, Bayou Bartholomew, and Ouachita, Boeuf, and Tensas Rivers. (I profiled the Mississippi River in my book *Canoeing Mississippi*.) The Central Louisiana passage describes the area between Highway 84 and I-10: Sabine River, Whiskey Chitto Creek, Chicot Lake, upper Little River, Saline Bayou (different from the one in north Louisiana), Bayou Cocodrie (different from one in south Louisiana), and the lower Red River swamps. The South Louisiana section focuses on waters south of I-10 and west of the Mississippi River: Bayou Teche, Lake Fausse Pointe, the Atchafalaya Basin, Jean Lafitte Preserve, and Grand Isle. The Southeast Louisiana chapter encompasses the region east of the Mississippi River: Amite, Tickfaw, Tangipahoa, Bogue Falaya, Tchefuncte, Bogue Chitto, and Pearl Rivers, Manchac Swamp, and the Lake Pontchartrain area.

With its abundance of water, Louisiana was once eminently—you might say infinitely—canoeable. But that was in an era before motorboats, channelization, large-scale agriculture, and other changes. To enjoy Louisiana these days, it is important to find the choice spots. That brings the number of destinations down considerably, but there are still plenty. In selecting waters to describe for this book, I used two main criteria. First: aesthetics. My standards are broad and mainly require a natural environment. I don't mind muddy water and lack of current if they're couched in lush forest, for example. There's little whitewater in Louisiana, but plenty of paddlers don't require that if they have a deep-woods setting; witness Minnesota's famous Boundary Waters Canoe Area, which is a land of lakes and forest. My second criterion is the proximity of some sort of public land, so paddlers who must travel to get there have a place to camp. Shoreside camping is possible on some waters, but many Louisiana bayous are too muddy and mosquitoey for enjoyable overnighting. Swamp camping can be fun if you're prepared for it—and I describe how to do so in this book—but many paddlers appreciate a good campground where the land is semi-dry and the bugs not quite so bold. Private property is also an issue, judging by the number of posted signs along waterways. While it's possible to camp in places along some rivers with no problem, staying in a campground eliminates trespassing concerns. Fortunately, Louisiana abounds in public campgrounds, and they're often located near good canoeing waters. In particular, I've looked for destinations that are in or near state wildlife management areas, state parks, national forest, and in some cases national wildlife refuges, though the latter usually forbid camping. There's no shortage of options, from easy day jaunts to semi-wilderness expeditions. Incidentally, canoeing or camping within any state wildlife management area requires a hunting or fishing license or Louisiana Wild stamp, available in sporting goods and other stores. The stamp (ask for Code 73) is a good bit cheaper than hunting or fishing licenses ($5.50 at this writing). You can buy the stamps at department stores, sporting goods stores, and bait shops, or by calling 1-888-765-2602; however, buying over the phone adds a $3 processing fee. Visitors to wildlife management areas should fill out the cards at the self-serve check-in stations, not only because it's required but to let wildlife officials know that paddlers are using the areas. That way, planners may consider paddlers' interests and needs along with those of hunters and fishermen.

The key to canoeing Louisiana lies not just in where but how. That sometimes calls for dispensing with preconceived notions. Camping in a campground instead of on a riverbank is an example. Another is making round trips rather than downriver ones, which has the added benefit of eliminating the need to shuttle. A typical downriver float trip—requisite on swift streams that can't feasibly be paddled upstream—requires parking one vehicle at a lower bridge and driving a second one to the upper bridge, or else arranging for someone to pick you up at the end of the trip. That can be a hassle. Since many Louisiana bayous have little or no current and often spread out into large swamps, you can frequently put in and take out at the same spot. That's convenient for anyone, especially solo paddlers.

I have identified more than 30 waterways that meet the criteria of beautiful surroundings and nearby public lands. I've tried to keep my focus broad, covering the entire state in a way that anyone, local or visitor, day-floater or wilderness tripper, can enjoy. This book provides general descriptions and specific information on where to go and what to expect. I also discuss types of boats and gear most suited to Louisiana, as well as techniques for camping, navigation, and fishing. And I delve into relevant facets of history, ecology, folklore, and biology since I think most paddlers want to know more than just the logistics of a paddling destination.

As I learned in writing *Canoeing Mississippi*, the amount of detail in such an endeavor can be overwhelming. If any errors appear or if conditions change after this book is printed, please notify me care of University Press of Mississippi, 3825 Ridgewood Road, Jackson, MS 39211, and I'll try to make corrections in future editions.

2. Equipment and Techniques

Boats

It would seem sensible to believe pirogues, the quintessential Cajun vessels, are the perfect choice anywhere in the Bayou State. While they excel on creeks, small bayous, and swampy shallows, they don't suffice everywhere—as I found out on a trip into the Atchafalaya Swamp.

When two buddies with a 17-foot canoe and I with a 14-foot pirogue got ready to launch at Bayou Pigeon one morning, a line of hefty motorboats was already massed at the ramp. My pal Walter Neil Ferguson, watching the array of massive vessels with motors ranging from 85 Evinrudes to 150 Suzukis, shook his head doubtfully. I assured him there was nothing to it—then we launched just as a towboat pushed a line of barges up the canal. We made it across the canal and entered Little Bayou Pigeon. The motorboats were right behind us. One after another thundered past, en route to their fishing grounds in a big hurry. Most of them slowed down when they got to us, but a few paid us no mind. Their wakes resembled ocean swells, and I felt like I was riding a skateboard down the interstate. "Is there any *little* water out here?" Ferguson asked one boater who throttled down. The man shook his head, grimly eyeing our fragile vessels. "You're in the wrong place for those boats," he warned. "It's all big water down here." It was strange to be made to feel like a greenhorn for taking a pirogue to a Louisiana swamp. Fortunately we soon found a small slough—putting the lie to the man's claim that it was all big water down here—

Baton Rouge native Ken Kennedy displays handmade cypress pirogues made of white cypress.

and within moments our view of the Atchafalaya changed. As the woods closed behind us, we left the world of motorboats and entered forest primeval, perfect pirogue country. But I learned an important lesson: A pirogue is not at home everywhere, even in south Louisiana.

Pirogues are generally used in places where nearly no other boat can go. Some of those Atchafalaya motorboaters strap them to their big vessels for use in shallow fishing spots. Duck hunters zoom down canals in motorboats, then switch to pirogues on narrow ditches leading to blinds. Savvy paddlers take them down small, fast rivers like the Tangipahoa, weaving their way through tight squeezes and over shallows. But the pirogue is just one of many boats found on Louisiana waters. And that's been the case since the earliest settlers spread out across this watery state. Charles Cesar Robin, who traveled the region in 1804–5, described the situation in his book *Voyage to Louisiana*:

People in this country are so accustomed to travel by water that the generic term "voiture" (standard French for "carriage") is always applied to a boat. . . . These voitures in use on the river are extremely variable in size and shape. Many are made from a single tree trunk; others from two or three, firmly joined. Others are real skiffs made of planks of varying timbers in the European manner; some are flat-bottomed, some are rounded and some are provided with a keel like ships. Some can contain only two or three people;

others up to thirty or forty and can carry 100 barrels. Some are elongate and pointed at each end; others are broad and rectangular like those called chalans. Those made of a single tree trunk are called pirogues. Some of these are forty to fifty feet long by six feet wide and four to four and a half feet deep. . . . The diversity of shape of these boats comes from the diversity of their usage and in the places where they must go. Those that come from the far-off rivers that are wide and shallow are wide and flat in order to draw little water, while those that navigate the surface of the deep rivers and must overcome the swift current, are more elongate and draw more water and are heavier. Their thick, rounded bottoms glide over the snags and logs which are found in all parts of the river bed. The narrow bayous where the water sometimes rushes in torrents require boats that are shorter and lighter, whereas others still require very light skiffs in order to shoot the rapids or to be dragged over the river bed in low water.

Materials are different these days, but the variety remains. Self-propelled boats include canoes, pirogues, sea kayaks, river kayaks, and hybrid pirogue-kayaks. Canoes are the most versatile, but the others do well in their respective territories.

Like pirogues, nimble river kayaks and sit-on-tops are useful in tight quarters but do best on creeks with currents. Swift water gushing around fallen logs is the closest thing Louisiana has to whitewater. Yet even on small bayous with no current, river kayaks have the advantage of being easy to propel upstream with a double-bladed paddle.

Sea kayaks, meanwhile, do well on big water: offshore, on lakes and wide rivers, in the marsh. They can cover a greater distance than a canoe, and easily slice against a current or tide. One downside is that in the swamp, getting in and out means tracking mud into the cockpit, which can get messy. But when the wind and waves kick up, there is probably no better self-propelled vessel.

Many Louisianans go for hybrid vessels that offer a cross between pirogue and river kayak; there are several such hybrids on the market. (Some of them are made in Louisiana, such as Bobcat Boats of Gloster, near Shreveport.) Flat-bottomed, with a spacious cockpit and low profile, the typically fiberglass boats are handy for one person, or an adult and child. They range from 10 to 15 feet long, and some models even have an optional built-in electric motor. These boats are more stable and seaworthy than standard pirogues but slower since they're short and wide, and less useful for carrying camping gear. They're really geared toward fishermen, who use them in ponds, wooded lakes, and shallow water. Some people propel them with double-ended kayak paddles, others with plain canoe paddles. Some even use two ping-pong paddles, one on each side, tying them together with a length of cord so they're easy to keep up with.

A square-stern canoe with a small motor would be appropriate for many

David Landreneau of Pine Prairie puts a life vest on daughter Kaitlyn before setting out on Chicot Lake in a hybrid pirogue-kayak.

Louisiana waters. While I don't use one, there have been times when I could have. For instance, sometimes you have to get down a long body of open water to get to the good canoeing part, and you may be sharing the water with other motorboats. At such times a 3-horsepower outboard or a trolling motor wouldn't be out of place, at least to get you to the paddling waters.

For all-around use, though, it's hard to beat a standard canoe. You can take it across wide, windy waters where a pirogue would be in peril; down crooked creeks where sea kayaks can't maneuver; and all in between. There are countless shapes and sizes available. One of the most popular and practical styles these days is a 16-footer made of foam-core plastic that goes under brand names such as ABS Royalex. Sixteen feet is a good size for one person or two, even two people with a week's worth of camping gear. It's small enough to be easily carried; I just throw mine up in the bed of my long-wheel-base pickup truck. The hull—a stiff foam material sandwiched between layers of plastic—is nigh-indestructible and relatively inexpensive. This material has virtually replaced fiberglass in canoe manufacture, since the latter can crack on logs and rocks and deteriorate in sunlight over time. Most foam-core plastic canoes sell for less than $1,000, some considerably less. They come in a variety of shapes, from sleek and low-slung to traditional with curving, swept-back ends. Mine (a Buffalo) is the latter, its performance suggesting that while we've improved on materials since the days of birch bark, the classic design can't be beat.

Traditional beavertail-shaped wooden paddles are also unbeatable, in my opinion, and you don't have to spend a lot of money on them, either. Though canoe catalogs sell paddles ranging from $60 to $150 and up, your local hardware or department store may have serviceable wooden models for $15 or so. Try to find paddles made from one piece of wood rather than laminated strips since the

A 16-foot canoe made of foam-core plastic is a popular choice for exploring the waters of Louisiana.

latter can get waterlogged and split with extended use. There are also inexpensive plastic and aluminum paddles available; just don't get ones with bare aluminum shafts, as the metal will turn your hands black. Regardless of whether you buy plain or fancy, get them at least the height of your chin when standing.

It took me quite a few miles and years to arrive at these choices. I tried more expensive paddles and found no advantage over the cheaper ones. As for canoes, I owned several before settling on the 16-foot foam-core plastic model (actually, mine is 15½ feet). Having taken mine on trips ranging from twisty, loggy Bayou de L'Outre to the wide Atchafalaya River, I'm confident I made the right choice. I'm glad to notice that this boat is basically an updated version of the one favored by the late Canadian canoeing author, artist, and filmmaker Bill Mason. "If I could have only one canoe, it would be the original Chestnut wood-canvas 16 ft. (4.8 m) Prospector," Mason wrote in his book *Song of the*

Paddle. "There are faster, slower, tougher, less stable, more stable, more beautiful and less beautiful canoes than the Prospector, but none that do everything as well." Substitute foam-core plastic for wood-and-canvas, and a brand such as the Buffalo or the Old Town Camper for the Chestnut Prospector, and you've got essentially the same boat. There's even a foam-core plastic Prospector on the market. Now, I know there's an inherent elegance to wooden boats—I have one myself, and love it—but foam-core plastic is tough, cheap, practical, low-maintenance, and long-lasting.

I credit Mason in large part for the existence of this book. Mason, who died in 1988 at the age of 59, was known for his white beard, floppy canvas hat, red plaid shirt, old khakis or denim shorts, and red wood-and-canvas canoe. On his long, solitary camping trips, his supplies included an old canvas tent, a video camera, painting supplies, a journal, and a Bible. Though he isn't widely known in the South, in Canada he's a national icon. His nature films won all sorts of awards, including an Oscar nomination. The most famous was the 1973 *Cry of the Wild* about a man who lived with wolves. His masterpiece, *Waterwalker*, focused on the wonderful region around Lake Superior. One mark of an artist is that in describing his experiences he makes you think of your own, and in filming and writing about Canada, Mason turned my thoughts to Louisiana. When he chronicled paddling trips on Lake Superior and Hood River, I thought of Lake Pontchartrain and the Atchafalaya River. His vistas of granite and spruce correspond to our labyrinths of cypress and lily pad, his loons and bears to our egrets and alligators, his blue northers and black flies to our thunderstorms and cottonmouth snakes. While I've done some paddling up north and enjoyed it, I think it's important to adhere to the tradition of one's region. Mason's celebration of the Canadian backcountry helped me appreciate the sprawling wetlands of Louisiana.

Camping

Louisiana is a prime truck- or car-camping state. It's overflowing with public campgrounds, both primitive and developed, in beautiful places near canoeable waterways. In states with sandy or rocky rivers, paddlers often camp on the banks or sandbars. That's less feasible in Louisiana, where you can just about number the sand-and-gravel rivers on one hand. In most instances, the best option is to stay at a public campground and take day trips.

That conclusion didn't come easily for me. There was a time when I ranked campgrounds near the bottom rung of outdoors settings. If you weren't deep in a wilderness, miles from any road, with only a tent or the open sky overhead, you weren't really camping—that's how I figured it. I must be mellowing, because my campouts at public campgrounds in Louisiana have been as enjoyable as an outdoorsman could ask for. Whether the remote woods of Union Wildlife Management Area or the RV-lined lanes of Lake D'Arbonne State Park, I've found peace, quiet, and natural beauty, plus great paddling nearby.

Truck camping also allows considerable latitude in gear. You can take as heavy and spacious a tent as you like. Ice chests, double-burner campstoves, and beaucoup groceries make life easier. Guitar, lawn chairs, barbecue grill, screen house, lantern—why not? Add your own firewood in case there's not much around the campground, and maybe some citronella candles while you're at it.

Campgrounds can have disadvantages, of course. By being near other people, you're subject to obnoxious noise. Yet with a little planning, you can greatly increase your chances of avoiding crowds. On weekdays many campgrounds are deserted. They also get relatively little use during the off-season, from Labor Day at the beginning of September to Memorial Day at the end of May. Go on a weekday during the off-season and you may have the whole place to yourself. Other tips: If you have a choice between a campground near a body of water, such as a lake, and one that's not, choose the latter since most people gravitate toward water; you'll get plenty of water when you paddle. Look for hunter-type camps during nonhunting season. If you go to a wildlife management area primitive campground during deer season, for example, you can expect plenty of people and vehicles. Go after hunting season and there's liable to be no one but you and the deer. Generally speaking, state parks tend to be good settings because they're controlled and regulated. Their entry fees cut down on drive-throughs. Their gates typically close by 10 P.M., and there's a ranger on the premises. Unregulated campgrounds, such as some national forest primitive campgrounds, are subject to being hangouts for partiers, especially on warm-weather weekends if they're near bodies of water.

Louisiana also offers some unusual camping opportunities. Lake Fausse Pointe and Chicot State Parks have canoe-in campsites. Lake Bistineau State Park has lakeside campsites with canoe trails and rental canoes and kayaks. Attakapas Wildlife Management Area's primitive campground in the Atchafalaya Swamp is accessible only by boat. Some WMAs, like Bodcau and Boeuf, have campgrounds right beside a bayou.

Truck camping is not feasible in some situations, of course, such as a long downriver trip or extended swamp exploration. Such trips mean overnighting on a river bank or in the swamp. The former can be great, especially on a remote sandbar by clear, running water. The latter isn't nearly as bad as it sounds. For instance, it's a common misconception that swamp camping requires slinging a jungle hammock between two trees to stay above the water. Yet in 20-plus years of swamping I have never had to resort to a jungle hammock. There is virtually always some sort of high ground (not to say dry ground) in a swamp, typically identifiable by tree species such as oak or beech as opposed to cypress and tupelo gum. I do consider rubber boots a necessity for most of Louisiana, however. River sandals, so popular elsewhere, can mean mud-caked, mosquito-chewed, sun-scorched feet here. Good mosquito protection is also a necessity in a swamp. Bring thick, long clothing such as denim or khaki, and a cap or hat, to ward off the bugs. Apply strong spray repellent, such as Repel or Deep Woods Off, to clothing and hats, and gentler stuff, like Skintastic, on exposed skin. Mosquito coils or citronella candles won't drive away all the mosquitoes, but they help.

It's a pity so many Americans are introduced to camping as a summertime activity. Summer camping means sweaty days, muggy nights, and mosquitoes buzzing your ears. I pretty much hang up my tent in late May and leave it until late September. That way I avoid both heat and crowds. I try to wait for the off-season when nights tend to be cool. However, that's harder to do if you have school-age children who have summers free. By the same token, during the peak of hunting season—late November through January—it's wise to avoid popular hunting areas such as some wildlife management areas.

Regardless of when or where you go, packing for a campout needn't be a chore. It always grieves me when a paddling partner tells me he spent a day getting ready for a trip. With a bit of preplanning, it shouldn't take more than an hour or so. Here's how:

- Keep a knapsack loaded with everything you need for a day float: poncho, sun screen, insect repellent, compass, toilet paper, flashlight, plus a small waterproof bag for wallet, keys, camera, map, and lighters.
- Keep an old duffel bag stuffed with boat gear: life vests, optional seat backs, sponge, and bailer (the top half of a bleach bottle).
- Keep an extra-large duffel bag packed with the sort of camping equipment

that can get wet: tent, tarpaulin, machete, hammock, dish soap and scrub pad, campstove and fuel, utensils, trash bags.

When it's time for a trip, the day pack, boat gear duffel, and camping equipment bag are already ready. All you have to do is:

- Put items that mustn't get wet in a large waterproof dry bag: clothes, sleeping bag and pad, first-aid kit, toiletries, spare toilet paper.
- Fill a medium waterproof dry bag or a couple of plastic buckets with food. I keep it simple: instant oatmeal and tea bags for breakfast; sardines and crackers for lunch; rice, chili, cookies, and hot chocolate for supper; plus a big bag of fresh fruit. Take whatever you like—even an ice chest with steaks, eggs, bacon, milk, juice, and such.
- Fill jugs with fresh water (old bleach bottles are durable).

Grab a hat, rubber boots, paddles, optional fishing tackle, and you're set. Just don't forget the boat!

Navigation

I've been lost twice in Louisiana. The first time was deliberate, so it doesn't count. We were on a weeklong canoe trip and wanted to see the back-bayous of Honey Island Swamp. The second time was fully unintentional and stands as an object lesson in Louisiana swamp navigation.

Our first mistake was in even setting out. My buddy, Eddie McCalip, and I drove to north Louisiana despite 100 percent chance of rain and flash floods throughout the region. I was determined to go and wasn't going to let anything as paltry as weather stand in my way—though I must admit my mood didn't brighten when I heard "Oh Death" by Ralph Stanley and the Clinch Mountain Boys on the cassette player in my truck. When we pulled up at the old bridge at Dixie Inn, Bayou Dorcheat was swarming like a nest of eels, nipping at the underside of the concrete, just itching to wrap their tentacles around some foolish boaters' heads. We drove on to safer waters at Bayou Bodcau below the dam at Bodcau Wildlife Management Area. There, though the water was high, the dam slowed the current considerably.

We parked my truck at the Highway 157 bridge, drove back to the dam-side campground in Eddie's Jeep and launched our canoes. I already knew how difficult navigation can be on Bodcau Bayou, having recently paddled in the WMA, in normal water conditions. But this was a mere 4-mile downriver float, and I

Bayous like Bodcau can be deceiving when they spread out into the woods.

didn't even bother to bring a map—second mistake. Four miles of bayou paddling should take one and a half, maybe two, hours, I figured. It was 1:30 P.M., so we had ample time. The bayou was white with foam from the churning action of the spillway, but it quickly slowed as it passed between cypress woods swaddled in cottony Spanish moss. Then we rounded a bend and Bodcau spread out into the woods with no discernible channel. As we picked a route through the woods in a southerly direction, rain began to stipple the dark water. Nothing but trackless swamp spread in all directions, and there was no sign of the bayou. When we emerged onto a channel again, it took us nowhere. In fact, each time we found what appeared to be the bayou, it dead-ended in dense brush or high ground.

Finally, with the rain picking up, the temperature falling, and the daylight fading, I had to admit that I didn't have a clue where the bayou was. This was early March, hypothermia weather, and it looked like we might have to spend the night out here. That's a bad feeling, one that rattles like a coiled snake in the pit of the stomach. After weighing the alternatives, Eddie and I decided to hike out. We spotted some high ground and set out on foot into the woods. We found a deer hunter's ladder stand, and from its perch I took a compass bearing on a distant cutover. We located my truck about a mile and a half away. It was

5:30 P.M., not quite dark. We drove to the campground, and that night as rain tapped on my tent and the temperature dipped into the 40s, I felt mightily relieved we weren't having to bivouac in the swamp.

Our task next morning was to hike back in, locate our canoes, then find our way to the bridge. As I got into my truck and pushed in the Ralph Stanley tape, the first song that came on was "Jesus Savior, Pilot Me"—quite an improvement over "Oh Death." We left my truck at the bridge, parked Eddie's Jeep at the spot where we had emerged from the woods, hiked back to the boats, bailed out the rainwater, and started paddling. This time we knew which direction to go and had all day to allow for errors, plus I had a machete and Eddie had a big hunting knife in case brush blocked our way. But the going was easy. Rain murmured gently as we cruised through the eerily beautiful flooded forest. In an hour's time we were at the bridge, loading our boats onto our vehicles. The Clinch Mountain Boys sang "Traveling the Highway Home" as we headed out.

A glance at the Shreveport newspaper afterward made me realize how crazy it had been to go canoeing this particular weekend: "Rising water levels heighten concerns: More rain, flooding is forecast for the area"; "Homeowners are sandbagging, cattle are moving to higher ground, and the waters just keep rising"; "Officials work to shore up low-lying areas"; "High water halts barge navigation on Red River."

Though the high water was definitely a factor—turning the bayou into a mile-wide swamp—I attribute our getting lost mainly to my overconfidence. With many years of swamping under my belt, I casually disregarded the weather and the difficulty of this particular bayou. A simple map (not to mention a Global Positioning System [GPS]) would have reminded me that the bayou swung north and west before angling back to the south, and I could have relocated the channel once we lost it. I also didn't bother to bring a wool shirt, just a denim jacket and a poncho. If we had had to spend the night in the swamp, I would have been miserable.

Some good did come from the experience. First off, it reminded me not to treat the swamp cavalierly no matter how much experience I might like to claim. Also, by getting lost, I happened to find a magnificent thorn bush, with briars one to two inches long. My pastor had put me in charge of getting some thorns for a church Easter exhibit, and these fit the bill splendidly. So I emerged from the swamp with a tangible benefit, even something of a spiritual lesson: When you're lost is when you find the crown of thorns.

Make no mistake, navigation is serious business in Louisiana. While some states boast dangerous whitewater, Louisiana's perils are more subtle, and getting lost in the swamp is high on the list (as are cottonmouth snakes). But just as training equips a paddler to handle whitewater, so can some preparation negate the threat of getting lost. It's not necessary to become expert in orienteering, but it is important to acquire a decent compass and the basic ability to use it. Simply keeping up with the cardinal directions can enable you to travel in flooded forests where you can't see a shore.

As my Bodcau experience shows, however, a compass alone isn't always enough. After all, Eddie and I were going in the right direction, just a mile off to the side of where we needed to be. A GPS and/or a map would have corrected that. In this age of the Internet, good maps are more accessible than ever. Some Internet sites, such as www.mapquest.com or the U.S. Army Corps of Engineers website, provide topo maps for free: Just print them out on your own printer. There are CD-ROMs for sale, such as a set offered by DeLorme that provides detailed topo maps of the whole nation. Used to be if you wanted a good topographic map you automatically got a U.S. Geological Survey quadrangle map, and that's still a good choice. To get quad maps, call toll-free 1-888-ASK-USGS and request a free index map for the state of Louisiana. Then, when you plan a trip, identify the quadrangles for which you need maps and order them from the Survey for a few dollars apiece, or buy them in a map store. Good topo maps not only keep you on course but show you surrounding features you might otherwise never know about, such as Indian mounds or backwater lakes. Quad maps can be problematic since each covers a relatively small area, meaning you'll probably wind up with several, and since they come rolled they can be hard to handle, especially on the water. I know one paddler who cuts them into notebook size, laminates them and keeps them in a notebook. He stores it in a plastic tub in his canoe where it's easily accessible. Other government agencies offer useful maps as well. If you're floating a stream in Kisatchie National Forest, a U.S. Forest Service map may be all you need. If you're exploring a bayou in a state wildlife management area, the Louisiana Department of Wildlife and Fisheries can provide you with a map of the WMA. The Corps of Engineers has maps for some of the larger waterways such as Atchafalaya and Mississippi, ranging from simple brochures to detailed (and expensive) chart-books used by riverboat pilots. In this book I provide sources for relevant maps needed for each waterway.

One map set I wouldn't be without is *Louisiana Atlas & Gazetteer* (DeLorme, P.O. Box 298, Yarmouth, ME 04096, 207-846-7000, www.delorme.com, $16.95), a collection of topo maps of the entire state in handy atlas form. The maps aren't as detailed as U.S.G.S. quad maps, so don't rely on them for close work such as, say, picking out specific sloughs to explore in Manchac Swamp. But they give a good overview, and since they show every road and waterway in the state they're invaluable for finding put-ins and take-outs as well as remote campgrounds.

I have mixed feelings about maps, especially the extremely detailed ones. On the one hand, they are without doubt extremely helpful, showing you routes and features you might otherwise never know about—and, yes, obviating the danger of getting lost. On the other hand, they run the danger of eclipsing your own first-person observations. If you're floating down a river with a detailed map in your lap, you're likely to spend as much time studying it as your surroundings. It can get to where you only look at your surroundings to confirm where you are on the map. And that tends to defeat the purpose of being out on the water. It also prevents us from learning to read the lay of the land and the water. When we depend more on our own senses than on a map, we learn to take note of unusual features, such as a cypress tree full of heron nests, a submerged fence line, the sound of distant traffic, the presence of weeds in the water that indicate nearby high ground. But if we depend only on our senses, we're also more subject to getting lost. The conundrum reminds me of William Faulkner's great story "The Bear," where the boy finds out the only way he can meet the bear face-to-face is to leave behind the trappings of civilization: first his gun, then his compass. Unless you're on a spiritual quest, though, you may be content with just a fleeting glimpse of the allegorical bruin, in which case I recommend a compass and at least a basic topo map.

Fishing

I spoke at a Deep South canoe club one time and asked how many of the 35 people present like to fish. About five hands went up, and they seemed tentative. That confirmed an observation of mine, which is that most people who consider themselves paddlers do not consider themselves fishermen. Similarly, most fishermen aren't paddlers, though a minority will use canoes, pirogues, and kayaks when needed. There's a practical reason for this dichotomy: It's hard to

Paddling a motorless flatbottom boat, Nicky Dodd of D'Arbonne hoists crappie at Little Bayou D'Arbonne.

focus on both activities simultaneously. I learned the hard way over the years that if I want to catch fish, I should go specifically for that purpose. If I set out to go canoeing and plan to do a little fishing on the side, I'll probably come home empty-handed. Each activity demands concentration.

That being said, I agree with canoe author Robert Kimber in *A Canoeist's Sketchbook* when he points out that since paddlers spend so much time in prime fishing habitat, it seems almost foolish not to wet a hook. Louisiana, which calls itself "Sportsman's Paradise," offers particularly good habitat. From creeks to lakes to marsh to saltwater, it's a fisherman's state. Fishing in Louisiana is at least as complex and varied as canoeing in Louisiana, and I can't begin to cover it thoroughly here, even if I were qualified. But I can provide a few tips for paddlers who want to give it a try.

Louisiana paddlers face a wide variety of fishing options. They can angle for bass while drifting down clear rivers like Bogue Chitto, casting spinnerbaits and topwater lures in deep pockets beside swifts; or venture into cypress swamps like those off Sabine River, tossing crankbaits around tree trunks. Find a likely bend in a quiet bayou like Little D'Arbonne and use a jig pole for crappie with jigs, minnows, or a combination of the two. Or ease up a tree-crowded bayou like De L'Outre, tie up by a deep pool, and use fly rod, rod and reel with beetlespins, or cane pole with crickets to catch bream. Or set yo-yos: If you place the spring-loaded metal reels near camp, you can sit around the campfire at night and hear them go off as fish bite and get yanked to the surface. Since catfish are active at night, fish for them when you're camping by setting out limb lines or trotlines in the evening, using such bait as chicken liver, worms, or blood bait in still waters like Tickfaw or Little River. Check the hooks throughout the night if you're a night owl, or in the morning if you prefer a good night's sleep. In the marsh, such

Keith Hux, left, and Obie Simmons of southwest Mississippi hold catfish taken from a trotline on Tickfaw west of Ponchatoula.

as lower Pearl River, cast spoons for redfish and be prepared to be towed around until the fish tires out, or use spinnerbaits for feisty marsh bass. Regardless of where you go or what species you pursue, be sure to get a current copy of "Louisiana Recreational Fishing Regulations," a booklet with specific rules for all areas of the state as well as some good general information on fishing in Louisiana. Free copies are available in most sporting goods stores.

For people who can't decide if they're paddlers or fishermen, there is a way to combine the thrill of both: Handle the boat while your partner fishes. It takes finesse to put the boat in optimum position. If you're on a flowing stream, you must keep it within good casting distance of holes and dropoffs. If you get too close to the hole, the boat may spook the fish; too far, and casting is difficult. On a lake, it takes effort and skill to manage the wind and move the boat slowly along the tree line or submerged channel. Also, the boat-handler is in a better position to see promising spots and mention them to the angler. By doing a good job maneuvering the boat and advising where to cast now and then, you can claim partial credit for your partner's efforts—and hopefully some of the fish as well.

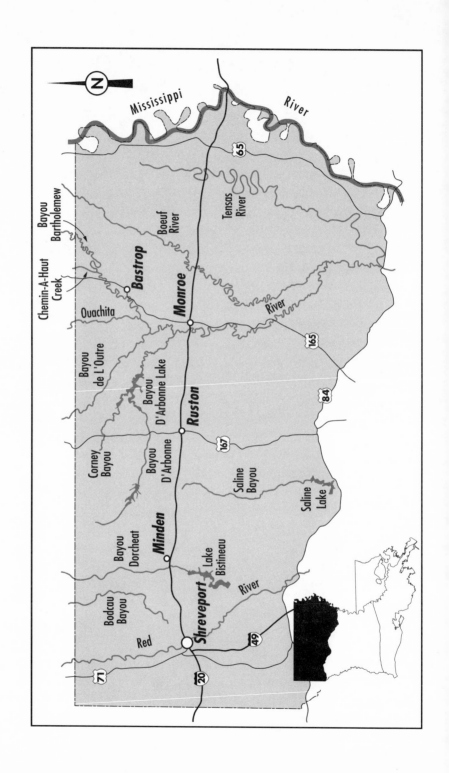

3. North

Bodcau Bayou

Northeast of Shreveport stretches one of the most intriguing—and challeng-ing—bayous in Louisiana. Though its floodplain is from 1 to 4 miles wide—small compared to some swamps—Bodcau is notoriously easy to get lost in. The bayou runs through a state wildlife management area, giving it a buffer zone of wildness. It continues to be interesting below a dam at the south end of Bodcau Wildlife Management Area. It turns into Red Chute Bayou as it angles south, merging with Loggy Bayou at Loggy Bayou WMA and emptying into the Red River between Shreveport and Coushatta.

The origins of the word "Bodcau" (BOD-caw) are unknown. The bayou starts in Arkansas and meanders into Louisiana near Springhill, a quaint logging town that is a case study of north Louisiana history and culture. Settled in the 1850s, the town has gone by several names: Sawmill Town, Piney Woods, Barefoot Sta-tion (due to the large number of local folks who went barefoot), and finally Springhill. The sawmill thrived from 1896 until 1933, when boom went bust. Then, in 1937, International Paper Company started a Kraft paper mill, and the town flourished again. In 1946 IP added a box plant. Next came Stauffer Chem-ical's aluminum sulfate plant in 1949 and Arizona Chemical Co. in 1960, fol-lowed by American Cyanamid. In 1978 IP closed its paper mill but later opened a wood products plant. So closely is the town tied to its logging heritage that it hosts a lumberjack festival the second weekend of each October. Springhill still retains its small-town charm, with attractive wooden houses and tree-lined streets.

For 20-plus miles below the Arkansas line, Bodcau Bayou lies within a Corps of Engineers-owned flood-control area managed for wildlife by the Louisiana Department of Wildlife and Fisheries—32,471 acres of bottomland woods edged by bluffs. There is a boat ramp on the northwest side of Highway 157 just west of Springhill, but it seems to provide access to nothing more than trees, bushes, and standing water—no bayou to be seen. An adventurous paddler can worm his or her way south through a quarter mile of flooded woods and come out onto open water, provided water levels are high enough.

At the ramp on Highway 2 west of Sarepta, Bodcau looks like a bayou proper, and this is a good place to launch and explore upstream or down. There is a current, but not enough to prevent fairly easy upstream paddling (except during flood). At the bridge, Bodcau seems to be a classic-looking corridor of smooth, dark water bordered by cypress trees. But when you round the first bend going upstream, a funny thing happens: It spreads out into flooded forest, with no discernible channel—just trees, and lots of them, growing all the way across. As you pick your way through the standing timber, you're likely to spook crowds of wood ducks, whose dragging feet silver the water as they rise squawking away. Such habitat provides important shelter for waterfowl, wading birds, and Neotropical songbirds, a fact appreciated by birders such as the Shreveport Society for Nature Study's Bird Study Group. Fishermen like the area too, judging by the occasional catfish lines hanging from limbs. When the water's falling out, the fishing is good for bass and crappie.

The water is fairly clear and tea-colored, shallow enough to require shoving the boat over shoals in places. After you paddle through the woods, the bayou opens out again into a street-straight channel. That pattern repeats itself: straight, open stretches alternating with tree-choked bends. The woods along the stream are a typical bottomland mix of cypress, tupelo, and oak, while in the background steep slopes rise to piney hills. About 5 miles above the Highway 2 bridge, private land comes down to the east side of the bayou—part of the big International Paper Company property at Springhill. Just out of sight of the bayou are huge mill ponds.

Paddlers who stop to explore the WMA on foot may run across arrowheads and shards of Native American pottery along the banks, all of it protected by federal law since this is Corps property. Caddo Indians were the predominant native people in north Louisiana at the time of European contact. The Caddo nation, which included a number of linguistically related tribes, were Mound Builders, corn farmers, hunters, and fishermen. Like other southeastern Indians, they hunted in the piney woods and cypress swamps, paddled dugout canoes, and lived in and around villages with 200–300 cabins. The Louisiana city of Natchitoches and the Texas city of Nacogdoches are reputedly of Caddo origin. According to one legend, an ancient Caddo chief had two wives, Natchitoches and Nacogdoches, who were jealous of each other, so he ordered Natchitoches to go east and Nacogdoches to go west. Another legend says Natchitoches, which means "pawpaw eaters" or "chinquapin eaters," and Nacogdoches, which means "persimmon eaters," were brothers, each with a village equidistant from Sabine River. In any event, the namesake settlements became towns in the early 1700s and are among the oldest in the region. Pronunciation of the towns is also interesting. Louisiana's Natchitoches is pronounced NAK-a-dish, while Texas's Nacogdoches sounds more like it looks, Nak-a-DO-shus.

If you paddle south from Highway 2, you'll immediately encounter a confusing, tree-choked stretch. But it's not as hard as it looks. Just follow the current and the easiest route and you'll make your way through. In fact, the 4-mile stretch from Highway 2 down to Wenks Landing is considered one of the best downriver floats on the bayou since it's generally open enough to travel all the way without undue hardship. Expect to take longer than a comparable float on open water due to the trickiness of navigating. Wenks Landing is located just west of Highway 371 about 2 miles south of Sarepta, on the east side of the bayou. If the water's high enough, you can float an additional 7 miles from Wenks to Highway 160. However, bear in mind that there are places where you can get off channel, even with aerial maps, and if the water is low, the logjams and shallows can be formidable. Below that, the going gets even tougher.

The next road crossing below Highway 160 is Duck Dam Road about 8 river miles south, then Bodcau Dam Road another 8 miles south and west. A good way to see the lower bayou within the WMA is to launch at the northeast side of the main dam on Bodcau Dam Road and explore the small lake, the surrounding swamp, and the bayou itself. Below the spillway and off Duck Dam Road are good bank-fishing areas.

The WMA has primitive campgrounds at every bridge crossing except Duck Dam Road and at several other spots too, plus improved campgrounds at Wenks

A confusing bayou like Bodcau can become even harder to navigate in high water.

Landing and at the main dam. That makes the area perfectly suited for paddlers to make a base camp and explore at will. Call before going to get a WMA map; it's well-detailed. Any way you slice it, Bodcau WMA is challenging. Yet its difficulties help keep it wild and mysterious. One Corps of Engineers official called it "the best-kept secret in northwest Louisiana."

The WMA ends a short distance below the dam, but the adventure doesn't. A 4-mile float from the campground on the southeast side of the dam down to Highway 157 near Bellevue can be challenging, especially in high water when navigation is difficult. Around a couple of bends, Bodcau spreads out into the woods with no noticeable channel—up to its same old tricks. In low water the bayou is logjammed, and in high water it spreads out through the woods with no apparent channel, rendering it extremely difficult to find your way. In high water such as in late winter and early spring it's even trickier because at times there's nothing but trackless swamp spreading in all directions with no sign of the bayou. Bringing a map or GPS will remind you that the generally southbound bayou actually swings north, then west, before going back south. Without such a reminder you may plunge south into flooded forest in search of the channel and wind up well off-course.

The land around this stretch below the dam has been targeted for possible purchase to expand the WMA. The 1990 Water Resources Development Act authorized the Corps of Engineers to acquire up to 12,000 more acres of wetlands, and this stretch is a likely area. The Red River Wetlands Coalition, a Shreveport-based conservation group, is pushing for the expansion "to preserve northwest Louisiana's largest contiguous block of interior wetlands," according to the coalition's Website, www.sportssouthinc.com/LAWetlands/. The coalition calls Bodcau "one of the most significant natural areas remaining in the northern part of the state," of use not only to outdoor enthusiasts but students learning about wetlands. For now, there's no question that you're passing through private land, as attested by posted signs and the word "no" painted on trees on high ground.

Below Highway 157, it's a long way before the bayou approaches any sort of public land again. About 4 miles below Highway 157, Bodcau Bayou widens into a small lake and emerges from the other side under the name Red Chute Bayou. It squiggles southwest past Shreveport subdivisions, south under Interstate 20, through Barksdale Air Force Base and back southeast along the edge of Red River valley farmland, where it crosses 157 again and merges with sluggish Flat River just west of Loggy Bayou WMA. Passage continues to be difficult along much of Red Chute, but it is navigable by the time it nears the WMA. You can launch on the northwest side of the lower 157 crossing and paddle 12 miles to U.S. 71. Flat River enters Red Chute from the west 7 miles below Highway 157. According to maps, the waterway is named Flat River below this point, but local folks call it Red Chute all the way to Loggy Bayou. Poole Road bridge crosses 2 miles below the juncture of Flat River and Red Chute, but access is steep and difficult there. Red Chute Bayou/Flat River enters Loggy Bayou about a quarter mile above Highway 71. The meeting of these streams is a good fishing hole.

Bodcau options

1. Launch at Highway 2, paddle upstream, and drift back down.

2. Paddle 4 miles from Highway 2 to Wenks Landing, located just west of Highway 371 about 2 miles south of Sarepta on the east side of the bayou. If the water's high enough, you can float an additional 7 miles from Wenks to Highway 160, a difficult passage.

3. Launch on the northeast side of the main dam on Bodcau Dam Road and explore the lake, swamp, and bayou.

4. Launch at the southeast side of the dam and paddle 4 miles to Highway 157 near Bellevue.

5. On lower Red Chute Bayou (which Bodcau becomes), launch on the northwest side of Louisiana 157 and paddle into Loggy Bayou and on to Highway 71, 12 miles.

Area campgrounds

Primitive campgrounds are located at numerous places throughout Bodcau WMA, including bridge crossings at Louisiana 157 west of Springhill, Louisiana 2 west of Sarepta, and Louisiana 160 west of Cotton Valley. Improved campgrounds are located at Wenks Landing and on the east side of the main dam on Bodcau Dam Road. Call 318-371-3050 or 318-949-1804.

Loggy Bayou WMA on Poole Road east of U.S. 71, primitive camping only, 318-371-3050.

Maps

For map of Bodcau WMA, call the Louisiana Department of Wildlife and Fisheries at 318-371-3050.

U.S.G.S. quad maps from north to south are Carterville, Cullen, Cotton Valley, Hortman, and Bodcau Lake; order from 1-888-ASK-USGS.

Outfitters

Norris Canoe Outfitters of Princeton, 318-949-9522, rents canoes and offers guided trips on the bayou.

High points

Remarkably wild and remote.

Low points

Tree-choked bayou is hard to negotiate.

Tips

This is a good place for a GPS.

Bayou Dorcheat and Lake Bistineau

An easier place to experience northwest Louisiana is Bayou Dorcheat and Lake Bistineau. The bayou offers a 6-mile easily navigable stretch, and there are several miles of well-marked canoe trails at Lake Bistineau State Park. The 26.9-square mile lake, which is full of cypress trees, offers as much swamp paddling as you could want—provided you're equipped with map and compass or, better yet, a GPS.

Bayou Dorcheat roughly parallels Bodcau Bayou from the Arkansas line east of Springhill down to Lake Bistineau south of Minden. According to one account, Dorcheat comes from the Caddo Indian word "datche," which means "the gap eaten by a bear in a log," based on a legend that the first Indian to come across the stream saw a bear gnawing a log there and named it to commemorate the sight. Above Highway 80 at Dixie Inn, Dorcheat can be as convoluted as Bodcau, but from Dixie Inn down it's open. There's a public boat ramp by a restaurant on the northwest side of the U.S. 80 bridge at this small town just west of Minden. From there it's 6 miles to a ramp on the southwest side of Louisiana 164 west of Sibley. Since 6 miles is pretty short—about three hours of paddling—it's worth taking the time to venture upstream from Dixie Inn, where the bayou is smaller and more wooded. Don't be fooled by a current; it may look swift but it's easily brooked, and the workout is pleasant. The bayou is open for about 3.5 miles above Dixie Inn, beyond which it gets choked with logs and trees, not to mention infested with cottonmouth snakes. Go upstream as far as you want or can, then turn and drift back down to the ramp.

Below Dixie Inn, in rapid succession, you'll float under Highway 80, a railroad bridge, and Interstate 20. Unfortunately, the sounds of I-20 follow nearly all the way down to Highway 164 on a still day. The bayou is fairly wide and slow, with a few narrow, swift stretches for variety. Occasional sandbars border the clear, dark water. To the east, mostly out of sight, lies a string of borrow pits from years of sand and gravel mining. In flood, the bayou can top its banks and flow into the huge pits. There are no borrow pits to the west, only a few backwater areas, so if in doubt, stick to the western bank. To the west, in addition to some hunting club property, lies 13,665-acre Camp Minden, a Louisiana Army National Guard training camp. Most of the time the current is gentle, but upstream rains can change that dramatically, so call either Lake Bistineau State Park or Norris Canoe Outfitters before going. Norris specializes in guided trips down Dorcheat, in-

Bayou Dorcheat provides good scenery and easy cruising below Dixie Inn.

cluding group floats in a 37-foot wooden canoe. Owner Mark Norris also has access to a private put-in a few miles above Dixie Inn, so his customers can get a look at that area as well. Motorboats are a certainty below Dixie Inn, but most are hunters or fishermen who automatically slow down to minimize their wakes. However, hot-rodding personal watercraft have been known to travel the bayou in summer.

Below Highway 164, Dorcheat meanders among some small islands as it widens into Lake Bistineau. The word "Bistineau" is said to be a derivative of the French for "big broth lake," perhaps because the water is clear and brown like broth. The lake was created by backwater flooding from a huge logjam in Red River, and steamboats once plied it. It drained when the logjam was removed in the 1800s, but an artificial dam was built across Loggy Bayou—lower Dorcheat—in 1935 to restore it. Lake Bistineau State Park was formed in 1938. From Highway 164 it's 8 miles to the park, which lies midway down the lake in a large bay on the west side. You can follow the channel, which takes about six hours, or hug the western shore, which can take up to nine hours, assuming you don't get lost in the tree-studded lake. People unused to these wooded waters of north Louisiana may be surprised by Bistineau, which is full of standing cypress trees, most of them rather small. A GPS or map and compass are essential for traversing this lake, which is 15 miles long by 1–2 miles wide. The channel is marked, but there is no sign showing where to turn west to go to the park. To get to the park from the channel, veer southwest at Diamond T Fish

Camp, which is easily visible on the east bank, and paddle to the Hay Meadow, which was actually a hay field before the lake was dammed. Then go due west to the ramp, which is about 2 miles from the east shore. There's also a park boat ramp on the west bank about 2 miles north of the main ramp, but it's sometimes closed, so check with the park before planning to take out there. There are problems with paddling the lake channel, not least of which is the fact that it's the main route for motorboats. Hugging the shore isn't as easy as it sounds, either, since wooded thickets reach well out from shore, obscuring visibility and requiring detours. Be sure to budget extra time to allow for losing your way. By the same token, it's virtually impossible to get truly lost, since if you paddle a mile east or west you'll come to a shore. Plus, passing boaters can give you directions.

An easier way to explore the lake is via the state park's canoe trails. From the main park boat ramp, you can take loops ranging from 2.1 to 5.1 miles. A park sign board and maps plainly show the way. The park also rents canoes and kayaks. Following the trails minimizes the chances of getting lost and takes you places that motorboats don't frequent. If you're comfortable with compass or GPS, you can branch off from the trail and explore a bit. If you're really adventurous, you can spend days probing this huge, bewitching lake. And it is tricky. On a cloudy day, it looks the same in every direction—water and trees. Stands of cypress range from a few scattered trees to deep, dark forest. The shore is rarely visible. Islands may even sport pine trees, so if you think you can find the shore by tree species, prepare to be mistaken. I paddled the lake on a gray, spooky December evening. We decided to abandon the canoe trail when we came across a batch of duck decoys—presumably someone was hunting over them—and we relied on map and compass to locate the nearby return trail. From there we ventured out to what we thought was the main lake, only to find more trees and more water. I loved it.

I also loved the park. It has a beautiful camping area near the lake, and the sight of those brooding cypress trees on a foggy dawn is reminiscent of Louisiana primeval. The park has hiking and biking trails as well. There's also public camping north of Minden just a few miles east of Bayou Dorcheat in the Caney Ranger District of the Kisatchie National Forest. Caney Lakes Recreation Area has improved campgrounds at two lakes, plus the 7.6-mile Sugar Cane National Recreation Trail around Upper Caney Lake for hiking and biking. Fishing in Dorcheat and Bistineau is great for crappie, with local anglers preferring chartreuse jigs or minnows. It's also good for bream, Kentucky redeye bass, and barfish on their springtime run. Some people hand-grab for catfish as well. Most of the grabbing takes place north of the bridge at Dixie Inn in hollow logs and bank holes.

Below Lake Bistineau, the bayou emerges under the name Loggy Bayou. It borders the east side of Loggy Bayou Wildlife Management Area and meets with Flat River (also called Red Chute Bayou there) before emptying into Red River. The low-lying, 4,211-acre Loggy Bayou WMA is popular with deer and rabbit hunters. It's possible to float Loggy Bayou if you're willing to do some work. Take Haughton Road south from Louisiana 154 east of the Lake Bistineau dam and turn right at the WMA sign. At the end of this gravel road—purportedly a primitive campground—you can portage about 100 yards south through the woods till the log-choked stream becomes a navigable bayou, or so I'm told. From there paddle 5 miles to the concrete boat ramp on the west side of the bayou, at the end of Poole Road east of U.S. 71. Continue 3 more miles to Highway 71, just past the juncture with Flat River. You can eliminate the portaging by launching at the Poole Road ramp and exploring up- and downstream. About 3 river miles north of the ramp lies a 2.5-square-mile "walk-in only" area; you can also reach the edge of this area by road from the southeast side of the Bistineau dam. Below the ramp, the juncture of Flat River and Loggy Bayou is an excellent fishing hole, especially for bass. Due to Red River dams, the water in Flat River and Loggy Bayou sometimes rushes downstream, sometimes upstream, and sometimes doesn't move at all. Such fickleness can play havoc with fishing and paddling.

Loggy Bayou WMA has two campgrounds, but the one on the north end, off Haughton Road, is nothing but a tiny gravel turnaround. The campground on the south end of the WMA, just east of Flat River, is better but nothing fancy: a grassy field, a row of garbage cans chained beneath a solitary tree, and two port-a-johns side by side. Several miles of trail wind around in the WMA; rubber boots are advisable.

Dorcheat and Lake Bistineau options

1. Paddle from U.S. 80 at Dixie Inn to Louisiana 164 west of Sibley, 6 miles.
2. Paddle from Highway 164 to Lake Bistineau State Park, 8 miles.
3. Paddle marked canoe trails of up to 5.1 miles at Lake Bistineau State Park.
4. Explore Lake Bistineau using map, compass, or GPS.

Area campgrounds

Lake Bistineau State Park off Louisiana 163 south of Doyline, developed campgrounds, 1-888-677-2478.

Caney Lakes Recreation Area in Kisatchie National Forest between Louisiana 3008 and 159 north of Minden, developed campgrounds, 318-473-7160.

Loggy Bayou WMA on Poole Road east of U.S. 71, primitive camping only, 318-371-3050.

Maps

For a map of Lake Bistineau, call the state park at 1-888-677-1400.

U.S.G.S. quad maps Minden South, Heflin, Koran, and Bossier Point cover the bayou from Minden south and the entire lake; order from 1-888-ASK-USGS.

For a map of Loggy Bayou WMA, call 318-371-3050.

Outfitters

Norris Canoe Outfitters of Princeton, 318-949-9522, rents canoes and offers guided trips on the bayou and lake.

Lake Bistineau State Park rents canoes and kayaks, 1-888-677-2478.

High points

Pleasant bayou, bewitching swamp lake.

Low points

Difficult to navigate lake.

Tips

Check out the marked canoe trails at Lake Bistineau State Park.

Saline Bayou (Kisatchie National Forest)

There are two Saline (pronounced Sa-LEEN) Bayous in Louisiana: a National Wild and Scenic River that passes through Kisatchie National Forest northeast of Natchitoches, and a Delta bayou that runs through Dewey Wills Wildlife Management Area south of Jonesville. The latter is profiled in the chapter on central Louisiana. The former begins near Arcadia, located between Ruston and Minden, and runs south, entering the Winn Ranger District of the Kisatchie National Forest near the town of Saline. For some 20 miles the bayou is bordered on both sides by national forest. It flows into Saline Lake near Goldonna, emerging to proceed south into Red River at the town of St. Maurice. Despite the National Wild and Scenic River status, most of the bayou isn't floatable without frequent pullovers, but the lake and the stretch of bayou flowing into it contain some of the best cypress swamp paddling I've found.

U.S. Forest Service workers used to travel the bayou in motorboats with chainsaws to keep it clear of logjams, but they tell me they haven't done that in years. Nevertheless, there's some paddling potential in the vicinity of Cloud Crossing, a national forest primitive campground on Forest Service Road 513 east of Highway 1233 north of Goldonna. It's worth acquiring a national forest map or taking a good road atlas along since the campground is remote and its sign likely to be missing—a not uncommon phenomenon in some national forests where local folks, perhaps, want to discourage tourists and keep the good places to themselves. The primitive campground sprawls along the west side of the bayou, which here seems little more than a muddy creek. One way to explore around Cloud Crossing is to paddle below the bridge (or above, logs permitting) as far as you choose, then return. The gentle current makes upstream paddling no problem—except in times of high water, of course. Call the Forest Service, 318-628-4664, for information on water conditions.

As you ease down the bayou from Cloud Crossing, you'll likely hear only the quiet dip of the paddle and the sigh of the wind. Massive cypress trees loom all around, ghosted with Spanish moss. Keep your eyes peeled and you may see a four-foot-long black racer stretched across a log, glossy as lacquer, or a cottonmouth swimming across the bayou, curling up defensively when you near. If the weather's warm, you may want to stop at a rare sandy point and slip in for a dip. The water is frigid, untouched by sunshine in these gloomy reaches. And the surroundings are spooky: Who's to say some big gator isn't lurking nearby? The bass fishing's not bad in the semi-clear water; the catfishing is better. You can choose how many logs you wish to cross before returning to the campground. You can also hike along the bayou here on the 2-mile Saline Bayou Hiking Trail from Cloud Crossing to Pearfield Launch. Apply mosquito repellent and take drinking water.

A boat ramp on Saline Lake leads to an impressive cypress swamp and provides access up Saline Bayou.

If you're willing to take on the logjams, you can paddle 2 miles from Cloud Crossing to Pearfield Launch at the end of Forest Service Road 507 on the east side of the bayou; 8 more miles to the old Salt Works on a road extending west from Highway 1233, 1.3 miles north of Highway 156; 2 more miles to Goldonna Launch at Highway 156; and 6 more to the Sand Point boat ramp on the east side of Saline Lake at the end of F.S. Road 592 south of Highway 156. The old Salt Works is a site of natural salt deposits used by Native Americans and later settlers. By the first half of the nineteenth century there was a large mine at the site, which is located over a salt dome. Up to 100 wells were in operation at a time, with brine brought up and boiled in huge kettles to evaporate the water and get to the salt. Winn Parish was a major source of salt for the Confederate army, with up to 1,000 men employed in the salt works during the Civil War. Saline means salty and that's how the bayou got its name, though the water itself isn't briny.

Better paddling prospects await at Sand Point at the upper end of Saline Lake. The instant you stop at Sand Point—once a Caddo Indian camp—you'll think you've taken a wrong turn and ended up in the Amazon rainforest. The lake is actually a flooded cypress forest, a mysterious and intriguing maze. A picturesquely ramshackle house nearby only adds to the sense of remoteness. From the ramp, strips of orange tape lead to a channel where canoe trail signs and red blazes mark the route (at least they did when I was there). A compass and map are advisable since it's easy to get off course—which need not be disastrous since the lake runs generally north-south and isn't that wide. As you head north up the lake it narrows into the bayou, which has an easily handled current. The channel curls like a snake disturbed in mid-swim. Huge cypress line both sides, their hoary trunks garnished with sprawling branches of bright green tupelo leaves.

If you travel in April or May, you may see reddish-pink mayhaw berries floating in the water. Common throughout Louisiana swamplands, mayhaws are oh so tart when eaten fresh, but the jelly is oh so sweet. The taste of the fresh fruit makes me think of green mangoes. Mayhaw trees, which belong to the hawthorn family, grow wild in low-lying areas but also do well in orchards. When ripe, the fruit is slightly larger than a large blueberry, and tangy as a crabapple but with a creamier texture. That tanginess is coveted by jelly-makers, some of whom maintain that the sourer the fruit, the sweeter the jelly. Savvy jelly-makers use a mix of 25 percent green fruit with the ripe. Some don't even use Sure-Jell, the store-bought additive that gives homemade jelly its consistency, since mayhaws contain a natural jelling agent. In the swamp, the berries are often harvested from a boat and scooped out of the water with a small-meshed dipnet. On dry ground they can be shaken from trees onto a sheet spread on the ground.

Out in the dark woods around the bayou, beaver-girdled tupelo trunks gleam bright as peeled bananas. A huge white form lurching through the gloom with a squawk turns out to be a heron. Cypress knees resemble hooded, robed medieval figures, chess pieces perhaps. If you accidentally bang the boat, you may hear a herd of deer bolt in a panic upstream, floundering through the flooded forest. That in turn may spook some ducks, which splash off squawking. Paddle as far as you like, or can, up this bayou; the return trip won't be dull, so complex and beautiful is the scenery.

Things are fascinating below the boat ramp as well. The trees are more widely spaced, with patches of open water fringed by black walls of tupelo gums. The lake runs south for some 10 miles, growing gradually wider until it's more than a mile across. At the bottom end it hooks west for another 3 miles in a section called Cheechee Bay. A bayou connects it with Clear Lake to the west.

Paddling isn't the only outdoor activity available in these parts. In addition to Saline Bayou Hiking Trail, there's the 1-mile Dogwood Hiking Trail off Highway 84 south of Saline Lake; and from Gum Springs Recreation Complex on Highway 84 east of the lake stretch a 1-mile hiking trail and 5.6- and 17-mile trails for horses, horse-drawn wagons, bicycles, and hiking, plus a horse camp and regular improved campground.

On Highway 9, 2 miles south of the town of Saline, is Briarwood Nature Preserve (318-576-3379), which honors the work of the late Louisiana naturalist Caroline Dormon. A Briarwood brochure refers to it as "the most complete botanical and wildlife sanctuary in Louisiana." The preserve is open every weekend in April, May, August, and November, and by appointment year-round. Dormon was a pioneer in conservation and believed to have been the first professional woman forester. She is credited with helping establish Kisatchie National Forest, which now comprises 604,000 acres across north and central Louisiana.

The infamous robbers Bonnie and Clyde—Bonnie Parker and Clyde Barrow— had a hideout west of the bayou, and it was near there that their bloody career came to an end at 9:15 A.M., May 23, 1934. Officers had tracked the Texas couple to the spot after a nationwide crime spree. They were waiting for them on Highway 154 between Gibsland and Sailes, and greeted the duo's car with a storm of bullets. There's now a historical marker by the highway. The town of Arcadia commemorates the couple with an appointment-only museum and a flea market called "Bonnie and Clyde Trade Days" held the weekend before the third Monday every month. Another local sight worth noting is Driskill Mountain, at 535 feet above sea level the highest point in Louisiana, located west of Highway 507 some 7 miles southeast of Arcadia.

If you see a roadside watermelon stand anywhere, stop and grab one or more melons. The Saline area is famous for its watermelons, and a few hours immersed in Saline Bayou should cool one off to perfect eating temperature. I can attest that they are sweet indeed, rivaling Mississippi's equally renowned Smith County watermelons. You might also stop at the old country store in Calvin for goodies like stage planks, peanuts, cream soda, and conversation with the old-timers out front. A possible topic? Try possums. In the book *Swapping Stories: Folktales from Louisiana*, folklorist C. Renee Harvison describes local folks' affection for the critters. "Arcadia resident Rodney Cook founded an organization dedicated to its preservation, Possum's (contraction for Possum Is) Unlimited, patterned after Ducks Unlimited," Harvison writes. "The lifetime membership fee to Possum's Unlimited is $2.89 and includes a subscription to *Tracks: The Official Newsletter of Possum's Unlimited*; a road kill body bag, in case any unfortunate possum is spotted along the highway; an official T-shirt; and a suitable-for-framing Honorary Degree of Possumcology." *Swapping Stories* doesn't give the address for Possum's Unlimited, probably because the editors knew the organization would be swamped with requests for membership. Such an elite group may not be ready for prime time.

Saline options

1. Paddle above and below Sand Point ramp on Saline Lake. The ramp is on the east side of the lake at the end of F.S. Road 592 south of Highway 156.

2. Paddle up- and/or downstream from Cloud Crossing, returning to the starting point. Current is usually slight. Cloud Crossing is located on Forest Service Road 513 west of Highway 1233 north of Goldonna.

If you're willing to take on numerous logjams, you can:

1. Paddle 2 miles from Cloud Crossing to Pearfield Launch. Pearfield is located at the end of F.S. Road 507 on the east side of the bayou.

2. Paddle 8 miles from Pearfield Launch to the old Salt Works. The Salt Works bridge is located on a road extending west from Highway 1233, 1.3 miles north of Highway 156.

3. Paddle 2 miles from Salt Works to Goldonna Launch at Highway 156.

4. Paddle 6 miles from Highway 156 to the Sand Point ramp.

Area campgrounds

Cloud Crossing Campground, F.S. Road 513 west of Highway 1233 north of Goldonna.

Gum Springs Campground, U.S. 84 west of Winnfield.

Maps

For Forest Service maps, call 318-628-4664. In addition to a map of Kisatchie National Forest, the Forest Service has a detailed map of the Winn Ranger District.

U.S.G.S. quad map Goldonna shows the bayou, Coup Point shows upper Saline Lake, and Saint Maurice shows the lower lake; order from 1-888-ASK-USGS.

High points

Saline Lake is magnificent cypress swamp.

Low points

The bayou itself is narrow and logjammed.

Tips

Launch at Sand Point on upper Saline Lake and explore from there.

Bayou D'Arbonne

I was tempted to include three bayous—D'Arbonne, Corney and De L'Outre—under the single heading of D'Arbonne, since they're all near the centerpiece of Bayou D'Arbonne Lake. The 15,250-acre lake is located near Farmerville northwest of Monroe in the extreme north and center of the state. Bayou D'Arbonne and Corney Bayou enter the lake from the west, emerging below the dam as Bayou D'Arbonne, which flows into Ouachita River near Monroe. Bayou de L'Outre parallels Bayou D'Arbonne just a few miles to the north. You can stay in a developed campground at Lake D'Arbonne State Park or a primitive campground at Union Wildlife Management Area and take day trips, doing some productive fishing as well. But though none of the bayous offers much more than a day float, each is interesting enough in its own right to merit a separate section.

It's necessary to note here that, while Louisiana is dotted with French names, unlike Cajun country to the south the pronunciations in the northern part of the state are rawboned English. It's as if Inspector Clouseau named the places and Gomer Pyle read them aloud. The French would pronounce D'Arbonne "dar-BUN," but here it's "dar-BONE." L'Outre in French is "LU-truh," but in north Louisiana it's "LU-ter."

Bayou D'Arbonne was originally spelled Derbonne or Derbanne, the name of an early settler. Locally referred to as Little Bayou D'Arbonne above Lake Bayou D'Arbonne, it begins far to the west, just south of Haynesville. It's impounded in Lake Claiborne at Homer, then continues for 28 miles to Bayou D'Arbonne Lake and another 25 to Ouachita River north of Monroe.

Below Lake Claiborne it's a narrow, loggy creek past Dubach. It becomes re-

Wyatt Emmerich, front, and Kemal Sanli canoe Little Bayou D'Arbonne above Bayou D'Arbonne Lake.

liably boatable at Highway 151, where there's a ramp, about 4 miles from the southwest corner of Bayou D'Arbonne Lake. With the exception of high-water time, the bayou has little or no current, and you can paddle upstream from the bridge beneath the forest canopy, though depending on the time of year and water level you may not get far. When I went in October we barely made it a mile before weeds blanketed the water and fallen logs crossed it. If you go downstream from the bridge, you'll find no obstacles but will likely encounter fishermen. Since the bayou is quiet and narrow, they're typically in slow-moving johnboats with small motors, or even pirogues of some type. The moss-draped bayou is classic Louisiana with a touch of Arkansas. It's barely 20 miles from the Arkansas line, and you may note a hint of Ouachita Mountains in the hilly terrain and abundant hardwood trees. Even with weekend fishermen present, wildlife abounds. Deer flash gray in the shadows. A cat squirrel scampers the bank. We saw an otter rolling in the leaves like a cat, and only when we came close did it slide in and swim away.

Middle Fork, a tributary, enters the bayou from the left just before it reaches the lake. Like Bayou D'Arbonne, Middle Fork too begins far to the west, near Haynesville, but remains a tiny creek until within a few miles of the lake. It expands into a mile-wide cove before meeting Bayou D'Arbonne, which makes for some good exploring and fishing. Paddle up Middle Fork and you're likely to see a swamp version of a chess game: a white egret stalking the shallows spearfishing while a black vulture paces a cypress limb. You can wend through the stump-strewn cove and up the bayou until it grows narrow and twisty.

From the juncture of the Middle Fork and Little D'Arbonne, it's about 7 miles across the lake to the state park. Bayou D'Arbonne Lake is not one mighty sheet of water but rather a 10-mile-long octopus with three major coves opening onto the main lake. There are plenty of submerged stumps, which cuts down on speedboating and makes for good fishing. The stretch leading from Bayou D'Arbonne to the state park is rarely more than a mile wide and dotted with islands. A feasible day trip would be to launch at Highway 151 and paddle the 11 miles to the park.

At the east end of the lake, Bayou D'Arbonne exits below the spillway and meanders through a low-lying floodplain, including 13 miles through 17,421-acre D'Arbonne National Wildlife Refuge (NWR), before entering the Ouachita River. This is motorboat-and-catfish water, wide and slow, but offers some exploring potential, especially in the 8-by-4-mile refuge. Water levels in the refuge vary widely across the year, based on amount of rainfall, which is usually heaviest from January through May. Water backs up from the Columbia Lock and Dam on the Ouachita River and at flood time may cover up to 87 percent of the refuge. Even in normal conditions the bayou sprawls all over the place into lakes and side-channels. The simplest strategy for exploring it is to get a refuge map, launch at a ramp, meander around, and return to the starting point. There's a ramp on the east side of the bayou off Highway 143, and two on a backwater lake on the west side off Highway 552.

Fishing is good in all these waters. A popular tactic is baiting yo-yos with shiners to catch crappie; the best time is in cooler weather, from late fall through early spring. Or tie up in a bend or other likely spot and fish with jigs or minnows. Bass lurk in these waters too. We were picnicking at the juncture of Little D'Arbonne and Middle Fork when a fisherman motored up, cast a spinner right off the point, and hauled in a thrashing bass. Underwater dropoffs are productive spots. Catfish action is great below the spillway on Bayou D'Arbonne, particularly in high water when shad swarm in the churning water and the big fish move in to dine. Live bait such as shiners and perch is best. You're also likely to catch a choupique, a fierce fighting fish, though not many fishermen like to eat them.

The 655-acre Lake D'Arbonne State Park, located off Highway 2 some 5 miles west of Farmerville, has 65 improved campsites near the lake. It lacks a separate tent area but is still a peaceful place to camp. I enjoyed the village feel of the place in the late evening with fires crackling, charcoal smoking, lights twinkling around RVs, kids playing, elders talking. Later the voices hushed, and from a pier near our tents we looked for constellations and listened to 10,000 crickets. Farmerville is a lovely town with impressive churches and an old-timey feel in its downtown business district. It was named for an early resident named Farmer, not for an agricultural heritage. Timber is the main resource in these parts. The D'Arbonne area is the very definition of Louisiana piney woods country.

In the old days, travelers either came by steamboat up the Red, Black, and Ouachita Rivers to the post of the Ouachita—now the city of Monroe—or they rode horse or wagon across the flat Delta country. Amos Parker rode a horse on his trip in the 1830s, as he described in his book, *Trip to the West and Texas,* about a journey from New Hampshire to Texas. He crossed the Ouachita and reached the piney woods, where settlers lived a pioneer lifestyle. Parker wrote:

At night, we came to the house of a planter, near a small river. He had a hundred acres cleared of river bottom land, which had been planted with cotton and corn; a large stock of cattle and hogs, which ranged in the woods. He had lived here 12 years, and was worth $20,000; yet still, lived in a log house with only two rooms, and without a window in it. Our supper was fried beef, fried greens, sweet potatoes, corn bread and a cup of coffee, without milk or sugar; which we ate by the light of the fire, as he had neither a candle or a lamp. Our fellow traveller told us, that we had now got out of the region of what we should call comfortable fare; and we might expect to find it worse, rather than better, all the way through Texas. Our lodging was on a comfortable bed made of Spanish moss; and our breakfast was exactly like our supper, which we ate with the doors open to give us light.

Parker had mixed feelings about the piney woods. "To ride a short distance in them, is not unpleasant; but to continue on, day after day, is too monotonous—there is no change of scenery," he wrote. However, "the pine woods are not without their use. Their resinous qualities give a salubrity to the air about them, and thereby render a situation in their neighborhood healthy; and the trees themselves furnish an inexhaustible supply of the first rate of timber."

Unfortunately, the notion that the virgin forest was inexhaustible led to its being exhausted in the Great Cut of the late 1800s and early 1900s, when the South was nearly denuded of timber. It greened again in the twentieth century, but the small to mid-sized pines that cover northern Louisiana today are a far cry from the towering trees of Parker's day.

By the time surveyor Samuel H. Lockett came along in the summers of 1869–72, there were still big woods aplenty. Lockett provided a "geographical and topographical description of the state" in his book *Louisiana As It Is*, when north Louisiana was still profoundly rural. Lockett surveyed the state parish by parish as part of his duties as professor of engineering. He came up with an interesting description of the types of lands in Louisiana: "good uplands" (mixed pine and hardwood); pine hills; bluff lands; pine flats; prairies; alluvial lands; wooded swamps; and coast marsh. Both he and Parker described the wide-open longleaf pine forest, where a traveler could see for a mile across the swards of broomsedge. But Lockett was decidedly unimpressed by the cuisine of the pinelanders.

"The greatest drawback to the people in the pine woods is the manner in which they live, I mean the food they eat," he wrote. "Three times a day for nearly 365 days of the year, their simple meal is coarse corn bread and fried bacon. At dinner there will be added perhaps `collards' or some other coarse vegetable. Even when they have fresh meat or venison, which they can obtain whenever they wish, it is always fried and comes to the table swimming in a sea of clear, melted lard."

Louisiana eateries still abound in fried food, but there are some fine banquets to be had—as I can attest after a post-campout breakfast of eggs, bacon, grits, and cat-head biscuits at Dubach Cafe in Dubach.

Bayou D'Arbonne options

1. Paddle above and below Highway 151, returning to starting point.

2. Paddle 11 miles from Highway 151 to Lake D'Arbonne State Park, which includes 4 miles down the bayou and 7 across the lake.

3. Paddle above and below one of three boat ramps in D'Arbonne National Wildlife Refuge, exploring backwaters and oxbow lakes. There's a ramp on the east side of the bayou off Highway 143, and two on the west side off Highway 552.

Area campgrounds

Lake D'Arbonne State Park, cabins and developed campground, located off Highway 2 some 5 miles west of Farmerville, 1-888-677-5200.

Maps

For a map of Union Parish, which includes the lake and surrounding bayous, call Lake D'Arbonne State Park, 1-888-677-5200.

For a map of D'Arbonne NWR, call 318-726-4222 or 726-4400.

The applicable U.S.G.S. quad map is Cedarton; order from 1-888-ASK-USGS.

Outfitters

Panther Creek Outfitters of Farmerville, 318-726-4371, leads guided canoe trips and rents canoes.

High points

Plenty of paddling options.

Low points

Popular with fishermen, so there will be motorboats.

Tips

Stay at D'Arbonne State Park and take day trips on different stretches of bayou. See Corney Bayou and Bayou de L'Outre, below, for more options.

Corney Bayou

At the northwest corner of Bayou D'Arbonne Lake, another fine bayou, Corney, enters. Corney begins in Arkansas and is impounded in Corney Lake in Louisiana's Kisatchie National Forest near Summerfield. It emerges as a swift, narrow, shady creek and remains tree-choked for most of the 12 miles to Highway 550 northeast of Bernice. It's open from Highway 550 down to the lake, 8 miles away, and in high water you can start even farther up.

People used to float the bayou as high up as Highway 167 north of Bernice regularly, but reportedly falling water levels coupled with increasing logjams have made that difficult. The town of Bernice has an annual Corney Creek Festival the first weekend in October with street dance, arts and crafts, foot races, and such. The festival used to feature canoe races from Highway 167 to High-

Great blue herons soar above a cluster of nests in and around a tall cypress tree on Corney Bayou.

way 550, but those were canceled when it got to be too hard to get through. However, in mid to high water, you can paddle the 7-mile stretch if you're willing to handle several pullovers. Expect to take a good five hours.

Highway 550 is an easier spot from which to explore Corney. You can launch at the ramp on the northwest side of the bridge and head upriver; the current is negligible. The channel soon fritters away into swamp forest, typical for these north Louisiana bayous. It's not hard to lose your way temporarily, especially in spring high water, but it's also not that hard to find it again since the backwaters don't spread out too far. Besides, losing your way is sometimes how you find good things, like a tall cypress tree Scott Williams and I saw that supported at least nine great blue heron nests, most of which had herons on them. The birds spooked and flew, but not far: This was springtime and they had nests to guard. They quickly returned and settled back down with huge, swooping wings as if held aloft on the strings of an unseen puppeteer. We left them alone and continued to play hide-and-seek with the channel. A big barred owl swooped into an oak and watched us with bottomless dark eyes as we stopped and stared.

In addition to exotic birds, I also discovered oil in these backwaters, or at least I think I did. With the swamp lapping at the edges of the hills, we paddled right up to a flooded strip of pasture, and there I saw oil glistening in the standing water. Best I could tell it was a natural seep (there was no other apparent source), and a good illustration of why oil and gas exploration is one of Louisiana's main industries. Seeps are places where natural deposits of oil rise to the surface. Native Americans used them for medicinal purposes, probably applying the oil to wounds and burns. In the 1540s, Hernando de Soto's men used such oil to seal their boats. People began drilling for oil in Louisiana in the late 1800s and finally hit it in 1901 near Jennings in the southwest part of the state. They turned to north Louisiana the following year and found the Monroe gas field in 1916. In the 1920s and 1930s, north Louisiana was the state's main source of oil; then offshore wells started producing and attention turned south.

When I told some oil men I know about the seep on Corney Bayou, they said that's the kind of place you're likely to find oil, along a fault line such as where hills meet a creek. In the early days oil men relied on "creekology," guessing at underground deposits based on surface formations. One man tasted sulfur in Red River and knew to drill nearby. Another saw a downward-sloping vein of chalk in an embankment cut by highway builders, calculated where the vein would intersect an oil-bearing formation, and drilled successfully. Louisiana's abundant salt domes are particularly conducive to the presence of oil. Since such domes tend to contain water, and oil floats on water, oil is often found near the crest of the underground domes.

Depending on the water levels, you can paddle upstream from Highway 550 for several miles, then drift back down, fishing if you like. Since Corney connects with the big lake, it has bass, bream, catfish, crappie, you name it. You can also paddle from 550 down to the lake 8 miles away. This stretch of bayou, while scenic, ranges from sluggish to currentless and is wide enough for motorboats, which travel to and from the main lake. There's a takeout on the lower bayou, a mile from the lake, at the end of Simmon Hole Road (Parish Road 4455). There are other takeouts on the lake, including a ramp at Highway 2 some 6 miles from the entrance to Corney Bayou. Paddling around to the state park involves a good 12 miles of open lake.

There's a developed campground at Lake D'Arbonne State Park and primitive campgrounds at Union Wildlife Management Area to the east and Corney Lake to the west. There's also a hunters' primitive camp, Sugar Creek Camp, in the national forest northwest of Corney Lake. Both Union WMA and Sugar Creek Camp are typically deserted when winter deer season is over. I like walking the lonely sand roads around these primitive camps in the pine-scented dusk. Loblollies and oaks tower over a jungle of possum grape, ash, wax myrtle, red maple, sweet gum, water oak, bluejack oak, dogwood, devil's walking stick, pawpaw, American holly, and sassafras, the ground alongside pocked with bobcat, turkey, and deer tracks. At dark return to camp, build a campfire in the Louisiana jungle, sleep hard, and wake at first light. As you sip black coffee in the gray dawn, you'll probably conclude, as I did, that this is truck camping at its finest.

Corney options

1. In mid to high water levels, paddle 7 miles from U.S. 167 to Louisiana 550.
2. Paddle upstream from Highway 550 and drift back down, exploring backwaters.
3. Paddle 7 miles from Highway 550 to takeout at end of Simmon Hole Road (Parish Road 4455). To get to Simmon Hole Road, follow Highway 2 west just over a mile from the state park turnoff, angle right onto Patrick Church Road (P.R. 4460), go 2 miles to Simmon Hole Road (the second road on the right), turn right, and go 2 miles to dead end at bayou.
4. Launch at Simmon Hole Road and explore up the bayou or down to the lake 1 mile away, returning to starting point.

Area campgrounds

Lake D'Arbonne State Park, cabins and developed campground, located off Highway 2 some 5 miles west of Farmerville, 1-888-677-5200.

Union Wildlife Management Area primitive campground, 318-343-4044. Take Highway 33 about 7 miles north of Farmerville, turn left on Highway 348, go 1 mile and turn right on Concord Road, go 2 miles and turn left on Tennessee Road, go 1 mile and turn right on Post Hill Road; campground is on the left.

Corney Lake primitive camping areas off Highway 9 north of Summerfield in the Kisatchie National Forest Caney Ranger District, 318-473-7160. Campsites are located along Corney Lake–Weldon Road on the south side of the lake and Forest Service Road 902 on the north side.

Sugar Creek Camp, a primitive hunters' camp on Forest Service Road 904 west of Highway 9 northwest of Corney Lake.

Maps

For a map of Union Parish, which shows Bayou D'Arbonne Lake and surrounding bayous, call Lake D'Arbonne State Park, 1-888-677-5200.

For the navigable part of Corney Bayou, the U.S.G.S. quad map is Shiloh; order from 1-888-ASK-USGS.

For a map of Union WMA, call 318-343-4044.

For a map of the Kisatchie National Forest Caney Ranger District, which shows Corney Lake, call the U.S. Forest Service, 318-473-7160.

Outfitters

Panther Creek Outfitters of Farmerville, 318-726-4371, leads guided canoe trips and rents canoes.

High points

Easily accessible swamp-bayou habitat.

Low points

Logs on upper bayou limit paddling possibilities.

Tips

Launch at Highway 550 and explore upstream.

Bayou de L'Outre

Bayou de L'Outre (pronounced de LU-ter) is French for Otter Bayou. As you paddle into this deep-woods, water-water-everywhere environment, you have to admit this is ideal habitat for the water-loving mammals, which can still be found here. Unfortunately, you have to be nearly as small as an otter to travel very far on this wooded little creek. De L'Outre angles southeast out of Arkansas, broadening into swampy lakes east of Farmerville before debouching into Ouachita River north of Monroe, 40 river miles from where it crossed the Arkansas line. This is a squiggly creek for most of its length. A canoe will suffice, but a river kayak, pirogue, or hybrid pirogue-kayak would be better since they maneuver well in tight places and can more easily go upstream. Due to tree-choked stretches between bridges and little public access, this is the kind of bayou where the best bet is to launch, explore the bayou up or down, and return to the starting point.

It's possible to do that at Louisiana 549 north of Farmerville, but the bayou is small and thick with trees and logs even near the bridge. Louisiana 33 northeast of Farmerville is a more reasonable point to begin explorations. From here you can easily paddle upstream against the slight current. You may pass a local person fishing for bream from the bank at a roadside launch just west of the bridge on the south side of the bayou—an alternate put-in, by the way. Trees canopy the stream, which spreads out among them with dark, clearish water. Even in spring high water you can barely go a mile before logs block your way. However, in a light boat you can get over or around them for a while. Or do like the bank fisherman and just tie up in one spot and fish. The action is good in De L'Outre, and it's not heavily fished, probably because it's so hard for boats to travel. Prime species are panfish, bass, and catfish.

In late April and early May, fringetrees, also known as Grancy graybeards, are in full bloom, glowing white on the banks in the otherwise dark woods. These native trees, which rarely grow higher than 20 or 30 feet, are popular ornamentals. The cream-colored, fringe-like flowers are incredibly lush and fragrant; I've never seen as many along a waterway as I did along De L'Outre.

Below Highway 33 the bayou is more open, at least for a couple of miles. Then De L'Outre does the usual north Louisiana vanishing trick and spreads out into the woods, virtually losing the channel. There is no good public takeout at rural Miller Bridge Road (also called Linville Fire Tower Road, or Parish Road 8702) 6 miles downstream, so when you've explored your fill, just paddle back up to Highway 33. The only time the current is noticeable is in the occasional sharp bends; otherwise the going is easy.

Below Miller Bridge Road there are a couple of rural roads that dead-end at the bayou—Clear Branch Road and Buffalo Hole Road—and provide launch sites for exploring. To get to the Clear Branch Road access point, turn northeast off Highway 828 at Antioch Church and go to a dirt landing on the southwest side of the bayou. To get to the ramp at Buffalo Hole, go east across the bayou on Miller Bridge Road—which runs northeast from Louisiana 828 east of Farmerville—turn right and keep bearing right till you get to Buffalo Hole Road, which dead-ends on the northeast side of the bayou. These are remote put-ins, so don't blame me if you get lost. Panther Creek Outfitters has access to private land near Miller Bridge Road and offers a downriver day trip to Buffalo Hole Road, so if you want to try this stretch you might give them a call. You can also explore Phillips Ferry Lake, a cypress swamp that the bayou broadens into above Highway 2, from ramps on either side of the lake north of Highway 2 or from the Highway 2 bridge. The lake has some fine cypress trees.

Nearby 13,390-acre Union WMA west of Marion is a good base camp. This popular hunting area is usually deserted after deer season is over. You can pitch a tent in the primitive camping area, an expanse of ryegrass beneath towering loblolly pines. When we stayed there, not a vehicle passed in the night, unless you count a local man on horseback.

In addition to the otters for which the bayou is named, local people have reported seeing cougars along Bayou De L'Outre as well as in the area around Corney Lake on upper Corney Bayou. Panther Creek Outfitters of Farmerville, which leads guided canoe trips in the area, got its name from owner James Brantley's memories of his grandmother's panther tales. Even now, reports of the big cats aren't uncommon throughout the more remote regions of the Deep South. I've talked to plenty of rural southern residents who claim to have seen them. One gentleman in a piney woods section of Mississippi, now deceased, told me about seeing one that "was so black he was blue." He measured footprints at 4 inches across, just over 4 inches long, with a distance of about 5 feet between front and rear tracks.

Virtually every wildlife official I've talked to smirk at such claims. While Eastern cougars were once widespread, they're now considered virtually extinct east of the Mississippi River—and they're brown, not black. Even the Florida panther, which still holds out in extreme southern Florida, is barely making it. If there are any panthers, officials say, they're no doubt someone's released pet. Or they may be a mistaken sighting of another large animal such as a bobcat, coyote, or dog. Besides, officials say, where's the proof—the photograph, the videotape, the panther caught in a trap or hit by a car, the plaster of paris cast of a footprint?

Good points. People do tend to misidentify wild animals. More than once I've gone to check a "panther" track that turned out to have come from a large dog (if the track shows claw marks it's not from a cat since most cats retract their claws when walking). I've also talked to many people who mistake coyotes and coyote-dog hybrids for wolves (the only wolves in the South are isolated populations of extremely rare red wolves, which aren't much bigger than coyotes). There may be a reason for the lack of documented panther tracks, however. Elizabeth Marshall Thomas in her book *Tribe of the Tiger* recalls a friend who kept a panther in a fenced-in yard. The friend moved the cat out for a spell and Thomas inspected the yard. To her surprise, she found not a single track, even though the animal lived there—it was that cautious about where it walked. She believes panthers are so elusive that they have been able to avoid being documented. Others too believe the cats' presence is feasible. The Eastern Puma Research Network, a Baltimore-based organization, said it received 385 reports of sightings from 24 states in the year 2000. Having canoed, hiked, and camped in the piney woods of the Deep South, I can only say that if no panthers live there, they're missing a good opportunity. The deep woods and intricate swamps of places like Bayou De L'Outre would make a good hideout for any wild and secretive creature.

De L'Outre options

1. Launch at Highway 33 and explore up and/or down the bayou, returning to the bridge.

2. At Phillips Ferry Lake, launch at a dirt ramp at the end of Ferry Road (Parish Road 8842) on the west side of the lake, or a concrete ramp at the end of P.R. 8844 on the east side. The roads run north of Louisiana 2 from either side of the bridge. Or launch at the bridge itself.

Area campgrounds

Union Wildlife Management Area primitive campground, 318-343-4044. From the Highway 33 bridge over the bayou, go 3 miles north, turn left on Highway 348, go 1 mile and turn right on Concord Road, go 2 miles and turn left on Tennessee Road, go 1 mile and turn right on Post Hill Road; campground is on the left.

Lake D'Arbonne State Park, 1-888-677-5200, cabins and developed campground, located off Highway 2 some 5 miles west of Farmerville.

Outfitters

Panther Creek Outfitters of Farmerville, 318-726-4371, leads guided canoe trips and rents canoes.

Maps

For a map of Union Parish, which includes Bayou de L'Outre, call Lake D'Arbonne State Park, 1-888-677-5200.

For a map of Union WMA, call 318-343-4044.

Applicable U.S.G.S. quad maps are De Loutre, Haile and Rocky Branch; order from 1-888-ASK-USGS.

High points

Just right for a small boat like pirogue or kayak.

Low points

Only select stretches are passable due to logs and trees.

Tips

Ease along quietly; you may see a namesake otter—or even a panther.

Ouachita River

I almost didn't include Ouachita River in this book. The river is large, slow, and heavily traveled by hunters and fishermen in motorboats. Nor is the scenery spectacular, at least not in the 40,000-acre Upper Ouachita National Wildlife Refuge, where I focused my attention. But there are factors that may entice determined paddlers, in particular the presence of bald eagles and huge numbers of waterfowl in late fall and winter. Serious birders will find that the river gives access to an astonishing leveed area known as the Mollicy Unit, where as many as 100,000 ducks and geese gather in the winter. And there are enough eagles to merit an official count by wildlife officials each year in mid-January.

The 510-mile-long Ouachita starts in western Arkansas, where it's a fine canoeing stream. Well before it reaches Louisiana, it's wide and slow, plied by barges and strapped with locks and dams. At Jonesville, Louisiana, it connects with the Tensas and Little Rivers to form the Black. Perhaps the most interesting stretch to an outdoorsman is the approximately 20 miles bordering the wildlife refuge. Part of that is on the 18-mile segment between Felsenthal Lock and Dam in Arkansas to Finch Bayou Recreation Area in Louisiana. Five miles below the

Travis Easley checks out backwaters of Ouachita River near Mollicy Unit during high water.

lock and dam, the river enters Louisiana and begins touching the refuge on the west bank. A few miles farther down, refuge lands begin on the east bank, and except for occasional inholdings of private land, the refuge borders both sides of the river all the way to Finch Bayou and beyond.

But 18 miles can be slow going on a river that at times has no current. The Ouachita also runs south, into prevailing winds, so headwinds are likely. A sea kayak is a good choice for this stretch since it will easily handle the distance. Regardless of type of boat, expect to paddle continuously except after recent rains, when the current is pleasant if not swift. What with commercial fishing, plus sport fishing for catfish, bass, and crappie, and hunting for deer and waterfowl in the winter, the river sees plenty of johnboat traffic, even on weekdays.

There are plenty of camp houses and houseboats along the Ouachita. Where the refuge lines both banks, floating camps are not permitted, but when it borders just one, camps may moor to the other side. And there are usually camps at privately owned inholdings. Low-lying hardwood forest lines both banks until the Mollicy Unit starts on the east bank about 8 miles below Felsenthal. Massive levees rise from the bank to encircle 13,000 acres of what was once a rice farm but is now the largest bottomland hardwood restoration project in the nation. A local fisherman recalled seeing 40–50 bulldozers and 30 or so belly-loaders at work building the massive levee, which lines the east bank for miles. The U.S. Fish and Wildlife Service is planting hardwood trees on the unit, which one wildlife official called "a prime example of man at his best"—devoting prime farmland to wildlife. The unit is generally off-limits to hunting, so paddle as close as you can get and climb up it. In winter you may see masses of waterfowl on the watery plain. Even early in the season when they're just arriving, you'll probably hear plenty of honking and quacking. But the unit is impressive even when empty, a perfectly flat expanse reaching to the horizon.

A few bayous run into the Ouachita and provide opportunities for exploring, but keep in mind that motorboats tend to travel these narrow bayous at top speed. On the wide river, when a motorboat roars past, its wake poses little problem. About half a mile above Finch Bayou, the community of Alabama Landing borders the west bank. There's a ramp here plus a large gathering of camp houses. The Corps of Engineers ramp is just past Finch Bayou itself, which enters on the west. Although a sign identifies Finch Bayou Recreation Area as a day-use area, the Corps allows tent camping at the end of the road behind the rest rooms. It's an attractive area located beneath massive trees, but the limbs are prone to break off and crash to the ground in the middle of the night, so be careful where you pitch a tent. Unfortunately, camp houses are located just across the bayou from the camping area, so if the inhabitants decide to make a lot of noise, you'll be privy to it. Finch Bayou is a popular launching spot for motorboats as well, which tend to start arriving well before daylight. And there is no drinking water available. Despite all that, I thoroughly enjoyed camping there. The spot is secluded, there's plenty of firewood, and earplugs take care of the noise. No camping is allowed anywhere else in the national wildlife refuge, including along the river.

From Finch Bayou to Sterlington is another 15 miles, with only 1 mile of refuge frontage on the west bank, and 6 miles of Mollicy Unit on the east. More camps and houses appear on this stretch, especially as it approaches Sterlington.

If you do canoe the Ouachita in winter in hopes of seeing birdlife, dress warm. A wide river funnels wind much like a football stadium. A mild day in camp can seem freezing on the water. I suggest several layers of clothing with plenty of wool, which retains insulating qualities when wet. Carry a dry bag with a change of clothes. This is a remote area, and a capsize in cold weather can be disastrous if you're not prepared.

Farther downriver, there are some canoeing opportunities at Black Bayou Lake National Wildlife Refuge (318-726-4400) near Monroe, and at adjacent Bayou de Siard. Both lie just east of U.S. 165 about 5 miles north of Monroe. Unfortunately, you're never beyond the reach of highway sounds on either the lake or bayou. Established in 1998, the 4,000-acre Black Bayou Lake refuge consists mainly of a lake and surrounding wetlands. It has a single boat ramp—signs mark the way from 165—providing access onto a tree-dotted lake. Paddle south from the ramp and round a peninsula to the east to explore the remote northern end. Spring high water is a good time to go since backwaters are more accessible and the birding is great. Camping is not allowed in the refuge, but there's a primitive campground at Russell Sage Wildlife Management Area on U.S. 80 east of Monroe. On Bayou de Siard you can float 6 miles from a ramp off Highway 165 to a ramp behind the Louisiana Department of Wildlife and Fisheries office on the highway. Panther Creek Outfitters of Farmerville offers guided canoe trips on this slow-moving, little-traveled river. Bayou de Siard empties into the Ouachita in north Monroe. Ouachita was the name of an Indian tribe that lived along the river. The late Louisiana linguist William A. Read researched the word and concluded that its origin is obscure. However, legend has it that Ouachita means "sparkling silver waters." I confess I chuckled at that legend—until I saw the Ouachita under a full moon on a crisp November night. The sight was magical and convinced me that, despite its difficulties, the Ouachita River is a special place.

Ouachita options

1. Launch at Felsenthal Lock and Dam in Arkansas and paddle 18 miles to Finch Bayou Recreation Area in Louisiana on the west bank. It's 5 river miles from Felsenthal to the Louisiana state line. To get to Felsenthal, take Arkansas 129-A east to downtown Huttig, Arkansas, and follow signs to the lock and dam; the ramp is on a canal leading to the river on the west side of the lock. (There's another ramp farther on at Felsenthal Lake, above the dam.) To get to Finch Bayou, take Louisiana 827 east of Marion, Louisiana, and follow signs to the public ramp.

2. Launch at Finch Bayou and paddle 15 miles to Sterlington Recreation Area on the east bank just north of Louisiana 2 in Sterlington.

Area campgrounds

Finch Bayou Recreation Area east of Louisiana 143, primitive camping only, 318-322-7880.

Maps

For map of Upper Ouachita National Wildlife Refuge, call 318-726-4222.
For Corps of Engineers map "Ouachita and Black Rivers," call 318-322-7880 or 601-631-5000.

Outfitters

Panther Creek Outfitters of Farmerville, 318-726-4371, leads guided canoe trips and rents canoes.

High points

In late fall and winter, bald eagles and waterfowl nest along the river and backwaters.

Low points

Day trips of 18 and 15 miles may seem long if you're not used to steady paddling, particularly since there may be little current plus headwinds out of the south.

Tips

Start early in the day.

Bayou Bartholomew

If there's a prettier place in north Louisiana than Bayou Bartholomew, I haven't found it—unless it's Bayou Chemin-A-Haut. And since they run together north of Bastrop, the combination is superlative. You wouldn't expect woodland beauty on the drive there, though—at least, not if you're approaching from the south or east, where highways lead across endlessly flat cotton fields around towns like Rayville, Oak Ridge, and Mer Rouge. Cotton fields are scenic in their own right, especially in the fall when they're white as if dusted with snow. But only when you approach Bastrop does the land rise ever so slightly and pine trees appear. The pines are processed as efficiently as cotton in Bastrop, a paper mill town whose towering smokestacks and pervasive scent leave no mystery as to the main industry. U.S. 425 north of town, not far from the Arkansas line, crosses Bayou Bartholomew, a mid-sized, nicely flowing stream that meanders southwest between fields and hills from Pine Bluff, Arkansas, to the Ouachita River near Sterlington, Louisiana. Bayou Chemin-A-Haut, a creeklike tributary, squiggles south out of Arkansas, joining Bartholomew east of Chemin-A-Haut State Park. Chemin-A-Haut is French for high road, named for an ancient Indian trail that followed the edge of the hills. In French it would be pronounced che-MIN-ah-HOTE, but in north Louisiana it's pronounced che-MAN-ah-HALT. Regardless, the park makes an excellent base camp for exploring the two bayous. Its 503 acres contain a secluded campground—no separate tent area—and cabins, plus a trail along Bartholomew, although no boat access. The one downside to the park is its proximity to two heavily traveled highways. On a breezy night it's no problem, but on still nights the traffic sounds never seem to stop. The noise has good competition from the owls, which love the park's tall trees and keep up a steady hooting all night.

It's possible to launch at Bayou Chemin-A-Haut from its southernmost bridge on a gravel road east of the park, but access is poor and you'll have to battle a mile or so of logs and thickets before it widens for its final mile to Bayou Bartholomew. An easier method is to float Bayou Bartholomew from Louisiana 591 to a ramp at U.S. 425 and explore Chemin-A-Haut upstream. It's about 7 miles between Highways 591 and 425, and in normal water you can paddle about a mile up Chemin-A-Haut before it gets clogged, making for a 9-mile journey, a leisurely day float. This is a prime stretch since it's mostly away from roads, whereas roads line other stretches of Bartholomew.

At Highway 591 you can get to Bartholomew on the northwest side of the bridge, parking on the grassy right-of-way and launching in the weeds—not great, but no serious difficulty either. You might be surprised by the pleasant current in this mid-sized stream. Although it flows through flat farmland, it normally has a good flow and in high water can be pretty stout.

You may see a coyote at the water's edge dart into the woods, its fur a lustrous blend of brown, gray, red, and gold, its tail thick and long. Vultures soar overhead and, when they find a banquet like the floating carcass of a wild hog,

Eddie McCalip paddles down Bayou Bartholomew near Chemin-A-Haut State Park.

are reluctant to move even when you're just feet away. Whistling hawks sail the sunshine air while brave squirrels gather nuts in the shadows. In the fall, leaves whisper past on the cool breeze like chords strummed on a harp. Heaps of possum grapes dangle from vines draped across tree limbs; they taste sweet and musky and stain your fingers red. Leaning swamp hickories offer foursome clusters of iron-hard nuts in soft green husks.

Two miles downstream from Highway 591, Bayou Chemin-A-Haut enters on the right. It has a noticeable current but not enough to pose a problem when you paddle upstream. The payoff is worth any extra effort as you soon realize you're in a veritable gallery of cypress trees. Specimens of every size and shape rise from the water. Scaly-barked trunks flow smooth and sculpted in knobs and scoops. Several maintain impressive diameters far overhead. Some tops flare wide and horizontal like Japanese bonsai trees; others form round, fluffy domes. The grandest cypress tree we saw flared 20 feet wide at the water line. I backed the canoe into its hollow trunk and looked up through a tunnel to blue sky. Beside me an ingrown cypress knee stood like a stalagmite in a cave. About a mile upstream from the mouth, the creek begins to narrow, and you'll soon find yourself forcing a way through bushes and over downed logs. When you get enough, you can drift back to Bayou Bartholomew.

Chemin-A-Haut is dark and relatively clear compared to Bartholomew, which vacuums up tons of silt on its farmland passage. The contrasting waters flow side by side for hundreds of yards before finally mingling. From the mouth of Chemin-A-Haut you have a languorous 5 miles or so to the takeout. Bartholomew winds past woods, occasional cotton fields, and then up against the high bluffs of state park property on the right. In bends the current runs nicely, but on long straight stretches it can disappear altogether.

A park official told me the two bayous are good for catfish, bream, and white perch fishing. Chemin-A-Haut's relatively clear, dark water looked especially good for bass. There's more angling action at Bussy Brake, a 2,000-acre wide-open reservoir just west of Highway 425. There's hunting for deer and small game at adjacent 28,000-acre Georgia-Pacific Wildlife Management Area (318-343-4044). And there's wildlife viewing from an observation tower at Handy Brake National Wildlife Refuge on Cooper Lake Road 6 miles north of Bastrop.

Bayou Bartholomew is the only major stream in the area that hasn't been dammed or channelized. Compare that with ditch-straight Bayou Lafourche to the southeast. Bartholomew harbors more than 100 species of fish and 40 species of mussels, including seven found nowhere else in the state and one, the pink mucket, on the endangered species list. Mussels act as filters and provide food for some mammals, but they're sensitive and subject to die from pollution or drought. In recent decades the bayou has suffered from increased logging and farming, which makes it muddy and adds pesticides, herbicides, and fertilizer. In dry years farmers use so much water from the river that at times it's just inches deep. Scientists from the University of Louisiana-Monroe are studying the river in hopes of staving off further degradation.

My first planned trip to Bayou Bartholomew was canceled due to a phenomenon once rampant in Louisiana: mosquito-borne illness. It was September 2001, and north-central Louisiana was in the grip of an encephalitis outbreak. Sixty-nine people were hospitalized with the disease between early August and mid-October, with at least three fatalities. Mosquitoes I can stand, but mosquito-borne illness is something else. I postponed the trip until late October, by which time cold snaps had knocked the mosquitoes back and the outbreak was over. Generations ago it was common knowledge that to travel in Louisiana during warm weather was to risk fever. Yellow fever was a recurrent fear in the 1700s and 1800s, while malaria, also known as the ague, was common. Most of the bad mosquito-borne diseases have been virtually eradicated in the United

States, but now and then we get outbreaks of encephalitis, a swelling of the brain caused by viruses spread by mosquitoes. The main virus causing problems in Louisiana was St. Louis encephalitis; cases of West Nile and LaCrosse viral infections were also reported. Symptoms include fever, dizziness, and impairment of speech or balance. While most people infected have no problems, some get ill and may even die. Health officials point out that people are most likely to contract the virus by sitting on their porches, walking, or jogging in the evening, so there's nothing exceptionally dangerous about canoeing. Except for such outbreaks, mosquitoes in north-central Louisiana are more nuisance than threat, controllable by wearing long sleeves and using repellent.

Mosquito-borne fevers were definitely a danger when Baron de Bastrop, for whom the town of Bastrop is named, arrived in the area in 1795. He was actually a Dutch official named Philip Hendrik Nering Bogel, who fled to America in 1793 under suspicion of embezzlement and changed his name. He received a Spanish land grant at modern-day Bastrop. A condition of the grant was that he bring in 500 families, but he failed to do that and moved on to Kentucky, where he sold part of the grant to Abraham Morehouse, for whom Morehouse Parish is named. Bastrop later moved to Texas, which also has a town named after him.

Bartholomew options

1. Launch at Louisiana 591 and paddle 7 miles to ramp at U.S. 425, exploring a mile or so up the mouth of Bayou Chemin-A-Haut along the way for a total of about 9 miles.

Area campgrounds

Chemin-A-Haut State Park off U.S. 425 north of Bastrop, 1-888-677-2436.

Maps

The applicable U.S.G.S. quad map is Twin Oaks; order from 1-888-ASK-USGS.

Outfitters

Panther Creek Outfitters of Farmerville, 318-726-4371, leads guided canoe trips and rents canoes.

High points

Remarkably scenic; nice current.

Low points

Muddy water due to farmland.

Tips

Be sure and paddle up Bayou Chemin-A-Haut to check out the cypress trees.

Boeuf River

Boeuf is French for buffalo, and northeast Louisiana's Boeuf River presumably got its name for the herds that once roamed the region. Though the river now winds mainly through cotton fields, when it reaches 50,000-acre Boeuf Wildlife Management Area, the surroundings start to look wild enough for buffalo again. The French pronounced it "buff," but local folks now call it "beff." The river actually rises in southeast Arkansas and worms its way south by southeast over the flattest, muddiest terrain imaginable. It's little more than a creek for most of the way, but west of Winnsboro it joins the channelized Bayou Lafourche to form a river. The Boeuf forms the eastern border of the WMA for some 45 miles before entering the Ouachita River west of Sicily Island. While it's wider and slower than most paddlers are used to, it passes through wild and lonely country that's worth seeing.

In dry conditions you can drive to the northern part of the WMA and float 7 miles from Gunby Dam to Cross Bayou Road and 10 miles from Cross Bayou to Highway 4. However, both roads are seasonal and may require four-wheel drive. A more reliable put-in is at Fort Necessity Recreation Area on Highway 4 west of Winnsboro. It provides a boat ramp and a U.S. Army Corps of Engineers primitive campground. From there it's 13 miles to the gravel-surfaced Pipeline Road on the west bank. River levels fluctuate wildly, and it's wise to call ahead to make sure the access roads aren't underwater. In late winter and early spring, the river may sprawl deep into the WMA, flooding woods and fields. Inches of rain in Arkansas can mean feet of high water in the Boeuf. We arrived after one of those Arkansas rains, and a pair of local fishermen raved about the strong cur-

Eddie McCalip gazes out across muddy Boeuf River from the shore of the Boeuf Wildlife Management Area.

rent. But when we launched, we barely noticed it, which reminded me that current is a relative thing in Louisiana. Since Boeuf is barely moving most of the time, even a slight increase in velocity is something to get excited about.

I admit I had qualms about tackling such a wide, muddy, slow river in a canoe. Would it be worth the effort to paddle it? In no time at all we were glad we came. The fishing couple were the only people we saw. The current kept us moving, albeit slowly. There were tributaries to explore. And the silence was immense. Silence is a rare commodity these days. It's a pleasure to find a place where, when you cease your activities and open your ears, you hear precisely nothing. But wait. There's the low hum of crickets, chirruping sleepily in the willows. The rustle of cottonwood leaves. The whisper of water around a downed tree. The plop-plop of turtles dropping off logs. The shrill of a hawk high overhead. Those are sounds our souls need to hear.

The west bank, which is wildlife management area, is mainly woods, with some fields maintained for wildlife. The east bank, which is private land, has been cleared and is grown up in brush; our map showed it to be interlaced with sloughs and oxbows. Both sides looked like prime wildlife territory, the very sort of place a shaggy bison might emerge with steaming nostrils. Bison, commonly known as buffalo, originally roamed as far east as Georgia and northern Florida. They lived throughout Louisiana, growing 5 to 6 feet tall and weighing 900 to 2,000 pounds. Bison may be out of the question here now, but there is an occasional bear in the area, probably a traveler from Tensas National Wildlife Refuge to the east, which has a couple hundred or more. Boeuf WMA also abounds in waterfowl in the winter and in deer year-round. And there are plenty of raccoons and squirrels, among other creatures.

Boeuf River is good for white perch fishing in the low water of late summer and fall, especially in a dry year. It's mainly a channel catfish river, though. Fishermen tightline, trotline, and jugfish with all variety of bait: cut bait, shiners, crawfish in spring, nightcrawlers in summer. The fishermen we saw caught three blue catfish totaling 55 pounds on cut shad in a morning's outing. Commercial fishermen work the river too.

There are other interesting forms of wildlife. While Eddie McCalip and I floated, I noticed that he was trailing a long spider web from his seat in the bow. He brushed it away and kept paddling. But soon there was another. And another. What were spider webs doing out here in the middle of a wide river? At first I thought the wind had blown a few hapless spiders from the bushes out onto the water. But gradually it dawned on us that there might be more involved. Spiders apparently were casting themselves off tree limbs into the wind, which carried them far downstream. We probably saw 100 such one-strand webs, enough to suspect it was no accident. "They're fly fishing," Eddie said. I later checked with an entomologist, who agreed with Eddie's assessment. The spiders—which were brown and about the diameter of a quarter with legs outstretched—appear to be in the genus *Dolomedes*, commonly known as fishing spiders. They can scurry across the surface of the water and push themselves under to catch tiny prey such as mosquito fish.

From Pipeline Road it's possible to paddle another 23 miles to Harrisonburg on the Ouachita River, but that's a rather long stretch for a day paddle on slow water, and the muddy, weedy banks detract from the appeal of riverside camping—not to mention the fact that it's against WMA regulations to camp anywhere other than a designated camping area. It's easier to camp at Highway 4 or one of the WMA campgrounds and take the 13-mile stretch, or the northern segments if roads are passable.

Boeuf options

1. Launch at Gunby Dam at the north end of Boeuf WMA and paddle to Cross Bayou Road, 7 miles. Cross Bayou Road leads east from Louisiana 848, and the road to Gunby Dam branches north off that. Four-wheel-drive may be required.

2. Paddle 10 miles from Cross Bayou to Fort Necessity Recreation Area ramp at Louisiana 4.

3. Launch at Highway 4 and paddle 13 miles to gravel landing at Pipeline Road on west bank. To get to the Pipeline landing, take Louisiana 559 south from Highway 4. At the Ouachita River ferry at Duty go left on a gravel road for 1.5 miles and turn left at the WMA sign. Follow the gravel road 4 miles to the river.

4. Launch at Pipeline Road and paddle 15 miles to Ouachita River and 8 more miles to ramp at Harrisonburg, 23 miles total.

Area campgrounds

Fort Necessity Recreation Area on the northwest side of the river at Highway 4.

WMA campgrounds at Morengo Lake, Duncan Bend, and Sawyer Pond. WMA map shows locations.

Maps

For map of Boeuf WMA, call 318-757-4571.

High points

Wild and remote.

Low points

Sluggish current.

Tips

Before going, call the Department of Wildlife and Fisheries (318-757-4571) to check river levels and road conditions.

Tensas River

The Tensas River starts near Lake Providence, and by Interstate 20 west of Tal-
lulah it's little more than a tree-lined ditch in a cotton field. At Louisiana 4, some
25 air miles to the south, it's a broad, brown, often-stagnant river, also in a cotton field. A view of the river at either place would leave most paddlers decidedly
uninterested. But in the middle, the Tensas passes through a vast area of woods
that includes the 64,000-acre Tensas River National Wildlife Refuge, 19,000-
acre Big Lake Wildlife Management Area, 9,000-acre Buckhorn WMA, and
some adjacent stands of privately owned forest that bring the total to well over
100,000 acres. That's enough to harbor a couple hundred bear, dozens of
gators, and untold numbers of deer. These woods alone make the Tensas worth
tackling. The Tensas refuge was formed in 1980 from the largest privately
owned tract of bottomland hardwood forest in the Mississippi River valley. Tensas, pronounced TEN-saw, was the name of an Indian tribe, but the meaning of
the word is unknown.

   While there are several possible floats on the Tensas, one stands out because
of its passage through the center of the national wildlife refuge: the 13 miles
from Fool Lake boat ramp to Ben Lilly boat ramp just west of Louisiana 888. Located in Big Lake WMA, Fool Lake is semi-clear and bordered by hardwood trees
that glow with luxurious colors in the fall. The lake curves east and narrows into
Fool River, a currentless bayou that connects with the Tensas. All this is alligator
habitat, Fool Lake especially. We spooked a massive gator, which hit the water
with all the subtlety of a pickup truck going off a bridge. It and two smaller ones
then swam near a muddy, marshy strip of beach in a scene reminiscent of Nile
River crocodiles. As I paddled toward them, my partner Wyatt Emmerich, in the
front of the canoe, questioned the prudence of approaching. "Do gators eat canoes?" he asked. I assured him they don't—but of course, being in the rear of a
17-foot boat, I had a pretty good margin for error. The gators didn't bother us,
and as we continued on down the narrowing lake, we passed several more
swimming warily.

   Fool River passes from the state-run Big Lake WMA into the federally run
Tensas River NWR. Although having two government agencies administer tracts
of land side by side may seem an example of bureaucratic overkill, in fact the
two areas serve different purposes. Put simply, a national wildlife refuge is designed for wildlife first and people second. A wildlife management area is de-

Wyatt Emmerich enjoys woodland scenery — and looks for bears — on Tensas River in the Tensas River National Wildlife Refuge.

signed for people to hunt and otherwise enjoy wildlife. As an illustration, hunting in the refuge is far more limited than in the wildlife management area. The silence and majesty of the refuge quells any doubts about the wisdom of putting wildlife first. This is their kingdom; we are privileged to pass through it. Considering how little habitat they have elsewhere in the mainly agricultural Mississippi valley, refuge is a more accurate term than kingdom.

As you cruise past towering hickories, oaks, pecan, and cypress, Fool River gets shallow as it joins Tensas. In winter and spring the Tensas may be deep and relatively swift, in summer and fall so shallow not even a pirogue can get down it without portaging over shallow mussel beds. That's especially true above the juncture with Fool River. Below Fool River, the creek-sized Tensas stretches lazily beneath princely nuttall and overcup oaks, elms, and shagbark hickories. There are occasional camps on small, privately owned inholdings, but the view is mainly forest. Floods keep the banks clear and parklike, and there are some fine groves of trees, such as honey locusts, whose silky bark is guarded by clusters of thorns protruding from the trunks. The forest is pretty, but if you get out of the boat to take a stroll, mosquitoes are likely to chase you back to the river in all but the coldest weather.

We didn't see any bears, but local hunters tell us they're here in abundance—though not the abundance they once had. Louisiana black bears, a subspecies of American black bears, once roamed throughout the state. Now several hundred remain. Males typically reach 300–400 pounds, but their dark coat and wary nature make them hard to spot. Deer are more visible, springing up the banks from thickets. You're also likely to see squirrels and perhaps raccoons climbing the tall trees. The final few miles of this float border highway, houses, and cotton fields on the left. Leaving the solace of the refuge is depressing, as people have thrown old appliances, tin, lumber, barrels, and tires off the bank—all the more reason for wildlife refuges. The water quality of the muddy Tensas also leaves much to be desired. It receives so many cotton farming chemicals that it's been called one of the most polluted rivers in the nation.

There are other possible floats, but they are more problematic. Upstream, you can launch at a canoe landing on Mill Road, which runs east from Louisiana 603 at Englewood a mile south of I-20. The put-in is by the refuge maintenance shop north of headquarters. From here you can paddle 4 miles to refuge headquarters (which has a museum and hiking trail), where there's no launch but it is possible to put in or take out across the road. From the headquarters it's 17 miles to a takeout by the hunters' check station in Hunter's Bend on Louisiana 884. And from there it's 7 miles to the mouth of Fool River, where you can turn right and paddle 3 miles up Fool River to the Fool Lake ramp. All of these stretches border fields and in some cases roads. They're also prone to be shallow and logjammed, requiring frequent towing. Downstream from the Ben Lilly ramp, you can paddle 15 miles to a rough-access takeout on Highway 4, but cotton fields border most of the east side and part of the west. The Tensas makes long, sweeping bends, not short squiggly ones, and each bend has a name. From I-20 south to Fool River they are Greenleaf, Andrews, Disharoon, Hunters, McGill, and Ridge Lake Bends.

Neither the refuge nor the two wildlife management areas allow camping, but there are private campgrounds in the area, and Lake Bruin State Park is 20 miles to the southeast near St. Joseph. This is a beautiful park along a Mississippi River oxbow lake with magnificent cypress and hackberry trees. It's just over the levee from the Mississippi River, so you're likely to hear barges when you're sitting around the campfire. Lake Bruin lacks coves and is more suited for motorboating than canoeing, but the park is a fine place to camp. The lake provides good crappie fishing and is normally a good bass lake, though it was hit by largemouth bass virus in 2000 and 2001.

The Ben Lilly boat ramp on Tensas River was named for an outdoorsman who has been ranked with the likes of Kit Carson, Jim Bridger, and Davy Crockett. Lilly was born in Alabama in 1856 and achieved national renown after serving as a hunting guide for President Theodore Roosevelt on the Tensas. He lived for years on a farm near Mer Rouge on Bayou Bonne Idee, a tributary of upper Boeuf River in northeast Louisiana. He reveled in hunting, especially bear, panther, and alligators, and his feats were legendary. There is considerable irony in commemorating him, however. Lilly reported slaying more than 100 bears in Louisiana and Mississippi before moving out west, where he pursued mountain lions and grizzlies, paid by ranchers or the government. Yet he personified the old-style backwoodsman in an era when predators were considered varmints whose extinction was desirable.

In a photo taken when he was 50 and printed in the 1950 biography *The Ben Lilly Legend* by J. Frank Dobie, Lilly looks as tough as the bears he hunted. He sported a chest-length black beard and wore outrageously tattered clothes and a hillbilly hat. Though he wasn't that big—5 feet 9 inches, 180 pounds—he looks strong enough to merit claims that he could hoist a 100-pound anvil in one hand or sink a pair of cotton hooks into a 500-pound bale of cotton and sling it over his back. Lilly supposedly could execute a standing long jump surpassing the then national record of 11 feet, 4⅞ inches, and stand in a barrel and leap clear out without touching the sides. He was expert with rifle, knife, and cow whip, though he mainly took out his aggressions on beasts, not men, being reportedly of a "mild, Christianlike" temperament, as one observer put it. He disappeared on hunting sojourns for months at a time, which cost him a pair of marriages. Or maybe it was his hygiene that did it. Rather than a coat, in winter Lilly wore several wool shirts, and when the inner one got filthy, he moved it to the outside so the elements would cleanse it. He often went for days without food, except perhaps a handful of parched corn. But when he ate, he did so prodigiously. He slept outdoors even in bad weather, typically with a blanket and maybe a scrap of canvas, and seemed impervious to cold and wet conditions. Lilly was religious in his own way. He would not work or hunt on a Sunday, when he preferred to rest and read his Bible. On more than one occasion, his dogs treed something on a Saturday night and Lilly called them off, resuming the hunt on Monday morning even though the trail had gone cold.

In 1907 he served as Roosevelt's guide on bear hunts in the Tensas River swamps. The attendant reporters were fascinated with the grizzled swamper and made him famous. For decades thereafter Lilly was the topic of articles in newspapers and magazines, including *Sports Afield*, *Field & Stream*, and *Outdoor Life*. The rough-riding Roosevelt was impressed as well. Here is what he had to say about Lilly:

I never met any other man so indifferent to fatigue and hardship. He equaled [James Fenimore] Cooper's Deerslayer in woodcraft, in hardihood, in simplicity—and also in loquacity. The morning he joined us in camp, he had come on foot through the thick woods, followed by his two dogs, and had neither eaten nor drunk for 24 hours; for he did not like to drink the swamp water. It had rained hard throughout the night and he had no shelter, no rubber coat, nothing but the clothes he was wearing, and the ground was too wet for him to lie on; so he perched in a crooked tree in the beating rain, much as if he had been a wild turkey. But he was not in the least tired when he struck camp; and, though he slept an hour after breakfast, it was chiefly because he had nothing else to do, inasmuch as it was Sunday, on which day he never hunted or labored. He could run through the woods like a buck, was far more enduring, and was quite as indifferent to weather, though he was over 50 years old. He had trapped and hunted throughout almost all the half century of his life, and on trail of game he was as sure as his own hounds. His observations on wild creatures were singularly close and accurate. He was particularly fond of the chase of the bear, which he followed by himself, with one or two dogs; often he would be on the trail of his quarry for days at a time, lying down to sleep whenever night overtook him; and he had killed over 120 bears.

Lilly died in 1936.

Hunters like Lilly weren't the only cause of the bears' demise. Disappearing habitat played a huge role as woods gave way to farm fields, leaving the big creatures with few places to hide and little room to ramble. A residual population survived in places like the Tensas refuge, but numbers dwindled, and in 1992 Louisiana officials listed the subspecies as threatened under the Endangered Species Act. Fearing the possible extinction of the Louisiana black bear, in 1990 various conservation groups, industries, government agencies, and landowners formed the Black Bear Conservation Committee—trapping, studying, and monitoring the bears, occasionally transplanting them to other areas. Remnant populations remain in the Tensas refuge, the upper Atchafalaya Basin, and in Iberia and St. Mary parishes along the coast. Bayou Cocodrie National Wildlife Refuge along with Red River and Three Rivers Wildlife Management Areas form important stepping stones between such sanctuaries with small, often transitory populations. Wildlife officials are trying to link at least two of the main areas by acquiring private land to serve as forested corridors so the bears have more space to roam.

Such refuges not only protect bears, they attempt to recapture in a small way the pristine ecosystem that once existed here. It's hard to imagine now, but in the early 1900s the Tensas River ran clear. Back then there were more woods and aquatic growth to filter the water and less farm fields to silt it up and kill the vegetation with herbicides. Charles Sharp, who grew up near the Tensas in the 1930s and '40s, told me about sitting on the bank near underwater springs in the river and peering down at bass and catfish in clear water several feet deep. In those days loggers used 9-foot crosscut saws to tackle the big timber. To cut the giant cypress, they'd notch the buttresses and wedge planks in to stand on until they could get high enough for the saw to fit the tree. One cypress log could make a load for a single-axle log truck. The Tensas was floatable from Old Highway 80 (now I-20) to the mouth of Fool River—a stretch now too shallow and logjammed to negotiate without frequent portaging, due to siltation from clearing of woods for farm fields. Sharp told me he wishes he'd had a video camera in those days, "just to take shots of different views. People just wouldn't believe the difference," he said. "It's unbelievable the changes that's been made since 1935 in that country."

Tensas options

1. Launch at Fool Lake boat ramp in Big Lake WMA and paddle 3 miles to Tensas River and 10 miles to Ben Lilly boat ramp just west of Louisiana 888. To get to Ben Lilly ramp, from U.S. 65 at Somerset go west on Louisiana 575, then 888. Turn right on road that leads across the river and into the refuge about 8 miles from Highway 65. Ramp is on southwest side of bridge and is marked with a sign. To get to Fool Lake ramp, continue driving past Ben Lilly ramp about 6 miles; turn right just after leaving Tensas NWR and entering Big Lake WMA. (If you reach Big Lake Campground, you've gone too far.) Ramp is at end of first road to left. Paddle north on Fool Lake, which curves east into Fool River and enters the Tensas.

Area campgrounds

Lake Bruin State Park, off Louisiana 604 north of St. Joseph, 1-888-677-2784. There are also private campgrounds near the refuge.

Maps

For map of Tensas NWR, call 318-574-2664.
For map of Big Lake WMA, call 318-757-4571.

High points

Bear country.

Low points

Shallow spots.

Tips

Travel in silence to increase chances of seeing wildlife.

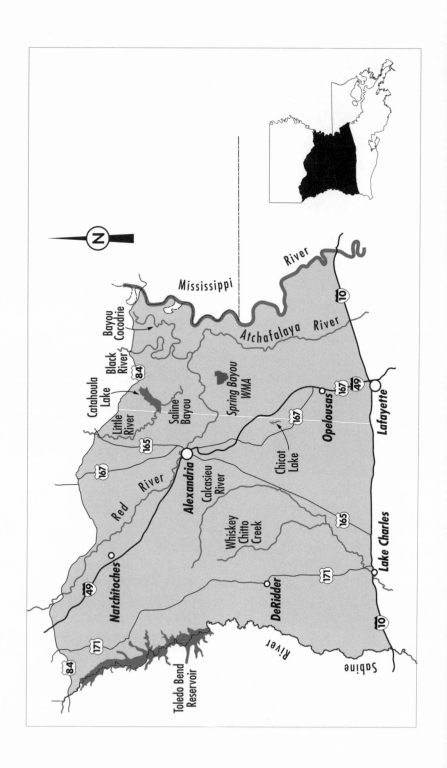

4. Central

Toledo Bend

Shortly after the Sabine River enters Louisiana from Texas, it's captured in 182,000-acre Toledo Bend, the fifth largest man-made reservoir in the nation at roughly 65 miles long by 5 miles wide. Most people don't associate such big, open water with canoeing, but Toledo Bend offers some good paddling potential. Constructed between 1961 and 1969, it offers a taste of the big-lake canoeing found in the North Woods. With 1,200 miles of shoreline, it's lined on much of the west side by Texas's 188,000-acre Sabine National Forest. The Louisiana side boasts six Sabine River Authority campgrounds and a state park. There are numerous other launches, both public ramps and commercial marinas, all around the lake. And if the reservoir is too huge for your tastes, there's a picture-perfect 225-acre canoeing lake at nearby Hodges Gardens, with campgrounds and cabin rentals to boot.

The biggest problem with canoeing Toledo Bend, or any large body of water, is wind. When I arrived at a campground with my canoe one afternoon, a pleasant breeze was gusting off the lake. I quickly unloaded my boat and launched. The breeze quickly turned mean as waves slammed the hull and gusts shoved me sideways. A few fishing boats bounced offshore; when they throttled up I could hear them slapped around by the whitecaps. Daunted, I returned to shore, slung a hammock and read the passage in Mark 6 where Jesus takes a walk on

A canoe lies ready at Toledo Bend Reservoir. The big lake can get windy fast.

a windy lake, something I could easily picture as I glanced up at the choppy water and the headlands receding into the haze. But at dusk the waves slacked up so I tried again. I was able to explore quiet coves until nearly dark with no problem. At dawn the lake was still smooth so I went again. But the wind picked up even then, bouncing my boat as I rounded a point. I ducked into coves big and small, enjoying close-up views of forest and longer views of great blue herons in orange shallows beside emerald thickets.

In strong wind, it's best to meet the waves at a quartering angle if possible. If a big wave catches a canoe broadside it can roll it; head-on, it can splash into the boat. But the best tactic for handling bad conditions is knowing when to get off the water. Go when the wind is mild—typically dusk and dawn—unless you're prepared for a struggle, and always wear a life vest. A sea kayak is better suited for big-lake conditions since it can handle waves and wind comfortably. The design makes it seaworthy; the spray skirt keeps waves out; a rudder helps brook the wind; the double-bladed paddle provides more power. I'm a canoer, not a sea kayaker, but it strikes me that a sea kayak journey from one end of Toledo Bend to the other could make for a magnificent expedition.

There's a long list of privately operated campgrounds, from primitive to resort-quality, along the Louisiana side of the lake, plus rental cabins and motels.

Most are located west of Highway 191, which parallels the lake. Louisiana's North Toledo Bend State Park also offers a good base camp for exploring by canoe. The 63-campsite park is located 9 miles southwest of Zwolle off Highway 3229 on a peninsula, with the main lake on one side and a large cove known as Bayou San Miguel on the other. The cove has a number of small inlets for exploring and getting out of the wind, while the main lake there is dotted with islands to duck behind. The park lacks a tent-only campground, but there's a primitive campground at nearby 14,880-acre Sabine Wildlife Management Area (distinct from Sabine Island WMA) 5 miles south of Zwolle on Highway 191. The WMA offers no access to the lake, but you can camp there and launch elsewhere.

Fishing such a huge body of water is a complex topic. The lake is legendary for its fishing, but with such a vast area to cover, it takes considerable skill and local information to know where to go—especially if you're in a canoe and can't zoom from one spot to another, guided by depth-finders, fish-locators, or a professional guide. One of the best ways to get up-to-date information is to stop at a bait shop or marina and ask. Such places usually stock the most appropriate lures and bait as well. If you do happen to tie into a big Toledo Bend bass, you may be surprised at the difference between it and the feisty but small creek bass to which paddlers are more accustomed. Here are some tips:

- When the fish takes the lure, pull the hook toward the heaviest cover, which will make the fish go the other way. When a fish gets into cover, its chances of escaping are magnified.
- Change the line drag according to conditions. Most fishermen adjust their drag once—when they buy the reel. It's wiser to change it frequently. If there's not much cover nearby, keep a light drag so the fish can run a bit. The heavier the cover, the stiffer the drag should be.
- If there's not much cover around, play the fish. If it heads toward an open area place, let it run. But don't let the line go slack.
- Try not to let the bass jump or it may throw off the lure. If the fish appears about to jump, put the rod tip in the water and pull it back down.
- Use extreme care in landing the fish. Don't let a buddy grab the line, which may provide just the amount of pressure needed to snap it. Reach down and grab the fish by the lower lip. If using a dip net, consider painting the metal rim black so it won't startle the fish, and be careful to slip the net well under

the bass to avoid bumping the line or spooking the fish. Many big fish get away right at the boat.

- Use quality tackle and keep it up to snuff. One Toledo Bend veteran I know favors a limber-tipped rod with 12-pound line. He prefers green line so the fish won't see it. He changes his line completely every three months, and says even casual fishermen shouldn't go longer than six months without a change. He constantly watches for nicks in the line and runs a cotton swab through the rod eyes to check for snags, filing them down or replacing the eye when needed.

If Toledo Bend is too big for your tastes, a much smaller lake is located nearby, every bit as beautiful, if not more so, at Hodges Gardens and Wilderness Park. Located south of Many on U.S. Highway 171, it features a 225-acre lake, vast areas of well-kept pine forest, rustic cabins, lodge, campground, trails, greenhouse, gift shop—and the centerpiece, the 70-acre formal gardens. Bluegill bream and bass flutter in the clear water along the lakeshore, and fishing is permitted. Rental boats are available, and guests may bring nonmotorized craft of their own. Admission to the gardens is $6.50 for adults, $5.50 senior citizens, $5 per person in groups of 20 or more, $3 for youths, and children 5 and under admitted free. Camping is $16 per night in an improved site, $10 in an unimproved site, and $7 for a primitive site. Cabin rentals range from $45 a night for a bunkhouse to $500 for a 42-person lodge. A comfortable two-person duplex goes for $75, complete with a kitchen and sitting area; guests need only bring food and clothing. It's hard to say which is more impressive: Hodges Gardens' Eden-like beauty, or the fact that it was built on a former cutover and rock quarry. In the 1930s, pioneer timberman A. J. Hodges bought a 4,700-acre tract south of Many. In addition to having been stripped of its magnificent longleaf pine forest, the land had been mined for its sandstone, which was used to build jetties. Hodges, a founder of the Louisiana Forestry Association, saw the acreage as a place to experiment with pine tree hybrids for regional reforestation. That alone was visionary enough. But it took a woman's touch, that of his wife, Nona, to carry things a step farther by creating a magnificent ornamental garden. Hodges Gardens opened to the public in 1956.

While many Deep South gardens rely mainly on the springtime glory of azaleas, camellias, and dogwoods, Hodges has a huge variety of plants so there are always colors galore. Set on the banks overlooking the breeze-cooled, forest-rimmed lake, the gardens offer breathtaking sights at every turn. There's a modern rose garden and an old-fashioned one, a camellia area and a swamp garden, waterfalls and running streams, statues and benches, lookout tower and manicured lawns, wildflowers and petrified logs, mid-lake geyser and small-scale lighthouse, giant cross and display of flags. Log cabins nestle on a peninsula with high porches looking out onto the lake. Trails network the forest for hiking, biking, or horseback riding. Guests may bring their own horses and tack, bicycles, or hiking boots. A 5.4-mile scenic drive around the lake passes fields with animals such as buffalo and burros, not to mention plenty of free-roaming whitetailed deer. For visitors who covet the gardens' gorgeous plants, the greenhouses have plenty for sale.

Toledo Bend options

1. Launch from North Toledo Bend State Park or one of numerous other campgrounds and explore coves and lakeshore.

2. Paddle down the lake, preferably in a sea kayak, from campground to campground.

Area campgrounds

Numerous privately operated campgrounds off Highway 191. Call the Sabine River Authority, 318-256-4112, for a list.

North Toledo Bend State Park, 63 improved campsites 9 miles southwest of Zwolle off Highway 3229, 1-888-677-6400.

Sabine Wildlife Management Area primitive campground 5 miles south of Zwolle on Highway 191, 318-487-5885. The WMA offers no access to the lake.

Hodges Gardens, Highway 171 south of Many, primitive and developed sites, 1-800-354-3523.

Maps

For map of the lake and campgrounds, call the Sabine River Authority, 318-256-4112.

High points

The kind of vistas you'd expect in North Woods lake country.

Low points

Wind and waves.

Tips

Paddle in late evening or early morning when the wind is likely to be calm.

Sabine River

The Sabine River heads up near Dallas, Texas, and enters Louisiana at Logansport. It forms the state boundary for the remaining two-thirds of Louisiana's western border, including Toledo Bend Reservoir. The Sabine (pronounced sah-BEAN or SA-bean as in salve) provides good downriver canoeing with clear water, a decent current, and big woods. The 54 miles from the dam to Merryville are the most appealing to paddlers because there are plenty of sandbars for camping. Sandbars become scarce below Merryville, making riverside camping more difficult.

The water is unusually clear because it's coming out of Toledo Bend Reservoir. Size-wise, the Sabine is larger than the canoe-perfect Whiskey Chitto but smaller than the barge-laden Atchafalaya. Because it's a tad large, it probably doesn't get as much attention from paddlers as it deserves. True, there are occasional motorized johnboats, but the infrequent access keeps crowds away, so the river is serene and quiet.

A 14-mile float starts just south of the dam at the canal off Louisiana 191. A number of fossils, including dinosaur bones, have been found on the Texas side of the canal here. It's about a mile down the canal to the main river. At the confluence of the old river bed and the canal, rapids can pose a danger within an hour after the dam starts generating. Call 337-286-5253 for a recording that gives the daily generating schedule. Some 5 miles farther down the Sabine, paddlers encounter a fun stretch of swift water. From there it's 8 miles to Louisiana 8 at Burr Ferry. There are plenty of sandbars along the way too. (Danny Rowzee of Tack-A-Paw Expeditions at Toro told me about a nifty afternoon round-trip below the dam. When the dam is generating, you can launch at the generator canal, ride the current down to the flood canal and back up to the dam. When it's not generating, make the trip in reverse. The float is 5.5 miles, and the boat ramps are a mile apart, walking distance, eliminating the need for a shuttle. Call him at the number below for details.)

It's 40 miles between the bridges at Burr Ferry and U.S. 190 west of Merryville. Paddlers can shorten the trip by taking out at a boat ramp below Anacoco Creek about 28 miles down. Pine trees predominate on this stretch, including pine plantations and pine-hardwood forest. "This is a sweet-smelling river," my canoeing buddy Steve Cox remarked, and the scent of resin does linger in the air. The word "Sabine" comes from the Spanish "Rio Sabinas" for river of cedars, but I wonder if the Spaniards had pine trees in mind when they named it.

Anacoco Bayou, which comes in from the Louisiana side about two-thirds of the way between Burr Ferry and Merryville, is discolored and sometimes slightly bad-smelling, reportedly due to a paper mill upstream. The word "Anacoco" is said to be from the Spanish "llana cucu." Llana means plain or prairie, and cucu means either raincrow or nutgrass. I don't know what a raincrow is, but crows abound on the river, their calls supplying a frequent background noise. About 2 river miles below the mouth of Anacoco Bayou is a boat ramp on the Louisiana side. There are numerous camps in this vicinity, many of them less than attractive. Some camp owners have adopted the practice of throwing rubbish off the bank purportedly to slow erosion, a real eyesore. After several miles, though, the camps give way to fine, lonely woods again. At Merryville there's a boat ramp on the Texas shore on the northwest side of the bridge.

It's 56 miles from Merryville to Louisiana 12. The river remains much the same until the mouth of Big Cow Creek on the Texas side about 21 miles downstream. Here sandbars begin to give way to swampy banks with lots of cypress trees. On the Texas side, a dirt road east of Texas 87 provides access at Big Cow Creek. A few miles below Highway 12, an old channel branches off to the southeast to form a 9-by-2-mile "island" laced with bayous and hidden lakes. This swamp, which has all kinds of paddling possibilities, lies within the Sabine Island WMA and is described in a separate section below. It's 20 miles down the river from Highway 12 past Interstate 10 to Orange, Texas. Below I-10 the river is wide and deep enough for oceangoing vessels. It flows into Sabine Lake bordering the oil refinery city of Port Arthur, Texas, then out through Sabine Pass into the Gulf of Mexico.

Based on our experience with my niece Maudie Herndon, the Sabine is a good river to take a child down. Make sure children wear life vests at all times in the boat, of course. Maudie helped pitch and take down tents, lay out sleeping bags, wash dishes, clean boats, build fires, and prepare snacks. She fished con-

Robert Herndon and daughter Maudie try out the fishing on Sabine River below Toledo Bend Reservoir.

stantly, learned how to identify trees, and imitated bird calls. The sandbars make for pleasant camping, and you can sit around the campfire singing such ditties as "There's a Hole in the Bottom of the Sea," "Row, Row, Row Your Boat," and "Are You Sleeping, Brother John?"

In normal conditions the fishing is good. When the water is low and clear in late summer and fall, try a variety of bass lures or live bait at creek mouths and along the bank. In higher water, use live bait for catfish. A prime-looking fishing spot is at the mouth of Little Cow Creek on the Texas side about halfway between Burr Ferry and Merryville. It's a slow, muddy creek, and fish gather where it meets the faster Sabine.

Since river levels are subject to fluctuation according to release from Toledo Bend Reservoir, it's not a bad idea to call either a canoe rental or the Sabine River Authority and check conditions before going. I didn't, and a few days before departure ran across a news item saying the authority was lowering water levels in the reservoir to work on the dam, which would mean high water on the river. I made some calls and found out that the Sabine indeed was unusually high and fast. We came up with a fall-back plan—if the river looked too dangerous, we would spend our time exploring Sabine Island Wildlife Management Area farther south—but the quickened current turned out to be just right for a down-river trip.

Additional paddling possibilities exist on Bayou Toro, a tributary to the Sabine on the southeast side of Toledo Bend. This stream offers Class I whitewater during spring high water, including an 8-mile stretch from Louisiana 473 to the Iron Bridge on a rural road south of the community of Toro, and 5.5 miles from there to Louisiana 392. Bayou Toro empties into the old Sabine River bed a short distance below there. Tack-A-Paw Expeditions keeps logs out of the lower part, but some logs may be encountered on the upper segment.

The Sabine has a wild history. In the early 1800s it was part of a "neutral ground" disputed by Spaniards and Americans—a haunt for outlaws, escaped slaves, and American adventurers seeking to take over Texas. When you read accounts of those days, several things stand out: the beauty of the wilderness, the hardships, the dangers—and the absence of game laws. "Alligators are so numerous in the uncultivated places that I happened to shoot at 40 in one hour," wrote Theodore Pavie about his travels in Louisiana. Back then there were no restrictions on the taking of game and fish, all of which seemed infinite. But then, there weren't many laws of any kind. Pavie was around 18 when he traveled into the hinterlands of Louisiana and Texas. His writings are preserved in the book *Pavie in the Borderlands: The Journey of Theodore Pavie to Louisiana and Texas, 1829–1830*, by Betje Black Klier. Leaving aside the slaughter, his descriptions of hunting trips are inspiring. Example:

Two canoes formed the entire fleet. This is another delicious way to travel that is unknown in Europe: to row this way for eight hours, a month, to camp in the evenings, light a fire which shines in the thick darkness like a torch and around which gather hungry vultures that fight over the scraps from our hunt, to sleep without fear, care, or worries on a bearskin, head on the trunk of a tree that stretches across the camp and serves as a common pillow and, when it rains, to gather under the tent, plunge into the ground a burning pine branch which furnishes light, and there, well hidden, smoke cigars with our arms crossed, waiting for the return of the sunshine while the rain runs in torrents around the stakes and floods the countryside. Could there be a sweeter life, more picturesque, more adventurous, more exempt from political troubles, in a word, freer?

Pavie wrote in an era of verbose romanticism. He admired authors like Chateaubriand and James Fenimore Cooper, who wrote about virgin forests, noble savages, buckskinned heroes, and beautiful maidens. But there was much that was unromantic about the frontier. "It so happened that we found ourselves eating at the very table of a man known throughout the country as a murderer forced into exile in Texas," Pavie wrote. "While shaking his hand in the American way, I experienced an almost uncontrollable repugnance; his stare, falling on me, made me shiver, and his shiny carbine mounted above the chimney seemed haughtily to proclaim the blood it once caused to flow." Historians believe he was referring to the notorious outlaw John Murel, who was something of a frontier Jeffrey Dahmer, murdering and mutilating unsuspecting victims from Tennessee to Texas.

And then there were sometimes-hostile Indians. Pavie tells the story of a pair of travelers forced to wait several days in the woods on the west bank of the Sabine River with their horses and cargo while the rain-swollen river subsided. "Suddenly chants arose from downriver and a rapid beat marked the cadence of a thousand paddles beating the water in unison," Pavie wrote.

A slender pirogue emerged from under the trees, then a second, then a multitude of others in single file, rowing with frightful speed, each powered by eight Indians leaning forward, heads immobile, eyes fixed on the prow. . . . Their tattooed heads, red as the lava of a volcano, made their thousand sparkling feathers stand up on the water, and a cry of joy rose up from the first canoe, repeated by this long parade of boats snaking its way along the meandering of the river.

These were valiant Coushatta warriors returning from hunting buffalo in the prairies dominated by the Rocky Mountains. Each pirogue moved under the weight of rich furs, as rowers celebrated their happy excursion with victory chants. Joyously, they moved down the river toward their village of pyramidal huts, still standing today at the place where the Opelousas trail crosses the Sabine.

Then a horse whinnied and the Indians spied the two men, who bolted, leaving their cargo. The Indians raced to shore to steal the goods, but their chief arrived and stopped them, and the white men nervously returned. Next day the two travelers built a raft and ferried their horses and goods across, then "remounted their impatient horses and galloped back into the heart of the beautiful forests of Louisiana."

Even after national boundaries were resolved, the Sabine bottomlands served as a hideout for outlaws such as "Leather Britches Smith," a killer who was gunned down at Merryville in 1912. The story of Leather Britches particularly interested me since "Leather Britches" has long been my own nickname as an outdoors columnist. Moreover, the outlaw was written about in the Beaumont, Texas, *Enterprise-Journal*, while the newspaper I write for is the McComb, Mississippi, *Enterprise-Journal*. And both of us spent a lot of time in the swamps. Back in 1979 when I became outdoors editor at the *Enterprise-Journal*, I chose the name of the old fiddle tune "Leather Britches" for my weekly outdoors column. The outlaw apparently did the same thing when he needed an alias after murdering his wife and a neighbor in Robertson County, Texas, west of Huntsville around 1910. After all, he was a fiddler and no doubt familiar with the tune. According to Ralph Ramos, writing in the Beaumont paper in a pair of historical articles in October 1972, Leather Britches was an alias for Ben Myatt, a violent drunk. After the murders, Myatt was captured, and a mob wanted to lynch him because of the heinousness of the crime. Lawmen spirited him to another county, where he was tried, convicted, and sentenced to death. But Myatt managed to escape to Louisiana. Ramos said Myatt assumed the name Leather Britches Smith and turned up in the DeRidder area around 1912. Strikers were listening to a speech at a sawmill when hidden gunmen opened fire. Leather Britches was one of the few men who were armed. He had a pistol and a .30-30-caliber rifle. He and a man named Chapman, who managed to get hold of a shotgun, returned fire until most of the sawmill workers got away. But at least six men died in the fracas. Leather Britches and 64 other men were indicted in the incident. Ultimately nine went to trial, and all were acquitted. "Leather Britches was never served," wrote Ramos. "He continued his hideaway in the Sabine River bottomland." Thus Leather Britches gained local renown. "Little did they know or did survivors of that troublesome era in 1912 realize their hero was, according to research, a vicious murderer," wrote Ramos. After the sawmill gunfight, "an overbearing wood's boss named Sterling who worked for the Merryville mill . . . bragged a lot about what he'd do if Leather Britches came his way," Ramos quoted an old-timer as saying. "One day while Sterling sat on a log ordering his crew about, Leather Britches stepped out of the brush and sat down beside Sterling. The way I heard it, Leather Britches pulled out his pistol, pointed it at a tree and cut the letter 'S' with his bullets. Then without saying a word he disappeared back into the brush." Ramos continued: "It was just a matter of time now for Leather Britches. On Sept. 25, 1912, he was killed in an ambush at Merryville." People were so afraid of him they left his body in a cabin for three days before they were bold enough to approach. A small, crude marker with the words "Smith, 'Leather Britches,' Slain 1912" still stands in Merryville Cemetery on Louisiana 110 just south of town. If you face the cemetery, it's on the left-hand side, not too far back.

The Sabine bottomlands also provide good hideouts for wildlife. Floating down the river one morning, we spotted a massive osprey—we thought it was an eagle at first due to its heft—standing in a dead tree close to the trunk. Vultures, both black and turkey, soared continuously on the updrafts over the river. A nonpoisonous brown snake lay curled in the grass when Maudie and I took a lunchtime walk on the back side of a sandbar. In camp, as I lay in a hammock reading about Sabine River history, a doe bounded out of the woods and stood browsing on vines 15 feet away. She only spooked when she heard my brother clang a pot as he prepared supper. Later, we watched a kingfisher rise above the river, hover, then plunge. It did this repeatedly until it had caught enough sardines. At night the cries of barred owls ricocheted through the black woods. All along the way, squirrels chattered, crows called, hawks squealed, egrets soared, turtles plopped. For folks who like downriver floating in a deep-woods setting, the Sabine is hard to beat.

Sabine River options

1. Paddle from Toledo Bend Dam to Highway 8 at Burr Ferry, 14 miles. Launch at the man-made channel below the Toledo Bend Reservoir dam off Louisiana 191. At Burr Ferry, there's a road under the bridge on the Texas side.

2. Paddle from Burr Ferry to a boat ramp near the mouth of Anacoco Creek, 28 miles. Ramp is located on Louisiana side 2 river miles below creek. It's at the end of Mouth of the Creek Road off Louisiana 111 a half mile north of U.S. 190.

3. Paddle from Anacoco Creek to ramp on Texas side at U.S. 190 at Merryville, 12 miles.

4. Paddle from Merryville to Louisiana 12 at Starks, 56 miles. West of Starks there's a ramp on the Texas side. There's also a takeout 21 miles below Merryville at Big Cow Creek on the Texas side, where a dirt road east of Texas 87 provides access.

Area campgrounds

Pleasure Point Campground on Toledo Bend west of Highway 191 south of Toro, 318-565-4235, tent and RV areas.

Boise-Vernon Wildlife Management Area on Louisiana 464 east of Burr Ferry, 318-487-5885.

Niblett Bluff Park on Niblett Bluff Road west of Highway 109 west of Vinton, improved and primitive campsites, 318-589-7117.

Outfitters

Sabine Canoes Inc., 1278 Don Plush Road, Merryville, 337-462-1924. Rents canoes for stretch above Highway 190.

Tack-A-Paw Expeditions, Toro, Louisiana 392, 2 miles from Toledo Bend Dam, 337-238-0821, 337-286-9337 or 1-800-256-9337, rents canoes for river from Toledo Bend to Highway 190 and on seasonal tributary Bayou Toro.

Maps

U.S.G.S. Texas/Louisiana topographical maps for Toledo Bend to Merryville are Haddens, Wiergate SE, Evans, Merryville N, Merryville S, and Bon Wier. Call 1-888-ASK-USGS.

U.S.G.S. Texas/Louisiana topo maps for Merryville to Starks are: Merryville S, Bon Wier, Bancroft, Shoats Creek, Suddeth Bluff, Hartburg, and Starks.

High points

Long, lonely stretches between bridges.

Low points

Wide, usually slow river.

Tips

Before going, check with a canoe rental company or the Sabine River Authority about the amount of water being released from Toledo Bend (337-286-5244 or 337-286-5253).

Sabine Island

I might as well say up front that Sabine Island Wildlife Management Area in western Louisiana is probably my favorite canoeing destination in the state—and that's saying a lot. Yet few people canoe there. Stretched along the Texas border north of Interstate 10, Sabine Island WMA isn't necessarily more beautiful than other Louisiana swamps. It's just that the layout is perfectly suited for paddling. The 8,700-acre "island"—devoid of roads, accessible only by boat—is bordered on the west by the Sabine River and on the east by Old Sabine River, called Old River for short, with the waterways connecting on the north and south ends. Roughly 9 miles long by 2 miles wide, the area is laced with bayous and hidden lakes. You can explore to your heart's content, going beyond the reach of motorboats or anyone else, for that matter.

Since no camping is allowed within the WMA, campers stay at Niblett Bluff (also called Niblett's Bluff), where there's a locally run park. Niblett Bluff is located on the east bank of the old river at the midsection of the WMA, so from there you can go north or south, taking bayous into the interior. There are also two other boat ramps on the east side, both of them north of the park off Green Moore Road, which loops from Highway 191 north to Highway 12. You could easily spend a week here, planning a different route each day. The Department of Wildlife and Fisheries puts out a detailed map of the WMA, and from that you can plan your forays. Here are just a few examples of the many possible itineraries:

Head south from the park down the Old Sabine, which is wide and slow. You'll see some camps on your left, and on your right the swamp. Turn right on Watson Branch, a lakelike bayou a mile below the park. You may see bass fishermen casting spinnerbaits against cypress knees. A bass club holds tournaments regularly, angling for largemouth and Kentucky redeye, or smallmouth as local folks call them. Anglers also catch bream—locally called perch—and crappie. Plus catfishermen run trotlines and limb-hooks. Watson Bayou narrows and twists as you paddle up it, bordered with many-kneed cypress and fat-boled tupelo gum trees. Channels cut across bends in the serpentine bayou, providing shortcuts but increasing the chances of becoming disoriented. Getting lost is a possibility in Sabine Island, especially in high water when large areas go under. Both a wildlife biologist and a park official cautioned me about the danger of losing my way in the swamp. I suspect it's harder to get lost in a canoe than in a motorboat because you're feeling your way along slowly, with time to study and assess the maze of branching waterways. If you pay attention, you can distinguish shortcuts from side branches that lead away from the main waterway. Those side branches rarely go far anyway before clogging up with trees, at least during normal water levels. Logs finally block your way on upper Watson. You can explore on foot but won't get far without hip boots, chest waders, or wet britches. Squirrels bark in the woods, and deer prints mark the mud—the two top hunting species in the WMA. In a day's time you can trace out every navigable tributary to Watson, stopping to watch wildlife such as a mink emerging from a hollow tupelo root, eat lunch and snooze in the shade, and chat with a trotliner hauling fish from the water.

For another option on another day, paddle 2 miles south of the park to Brenam Bayou, the second sizable bayou that enters from the west. Narrower and swifter than Watson, Brenam runs like a brook, clear and swift, beneath tall trees and tropical-looking palmetto fronds. A few miles of pleasant muscling against the current and hauling over a log or two brings you to Lost Lake, a small oxbow off Sabine River. A 25-yard hike through the

Robert Herndon peers from a hollow tupelo gum tree in Sabine Island Wildlife Management Area.

woods will bring you to the Sabine. Here you will face a dilemma: whether to take a leisurely float back down Brenam or portage through the woods and launch in the river, float down, and turn up Old River and back to the campground. If you choose the latter, you'll find the Sabine flows through lonely forest before a motley assortment of camps appears on the Texas side, ranging from elaborate floating houses to trailers on stilts guarded by dogs and geese. In 3.5 miles you're at the mouth of the Old Sabine. Turn northeast up it, pushing against its negligible current, and make your way 4 miles back to the park—a good day's paddle.

By far the most ambitious trip would be to circumnavigate the island. Unfortunately, there's a major obstacle for paddlers in the form of Dynamite Slough, a long, swift stretch on Old River a couple miles north of the park. Some people like to launch at one of the ramps north of the park and paddle down to the park just to ride the swifts down Dynamite Slough. You can get around that if you have two vehicles by leaving one at the park, then driving the other to launch your boat at one of the two ramps north of the park, thus missing the slough and shaving a few miles off the journey. About 6.5 miles north of the park, take milelong Cutoff Bayou over to the main Sabine. Then paddle south for a mile and a half, at which point the river forks; take the right fork, which is the main channel even though it's called Indian Bayou, and follow it 5 miles till it reenters the Sabine at Swift Lake. Continue 6 miles down the Sabine to the mouth of Old River, then turn back north and paddle 4 miles to the park. I haven't done this circuit, but I'm told it's doable, and it's easy enough to trace out on a map.

There are several other bayous that lead into the interior of the island. If you're willing to cross logs and beaver dams, you can get back to some remote lakes.

Niblett Bluff Park itself is interesting. There's a marker commemorating a Confederate cemetery; this was a major camp with a military hospital during the Civil War. The park also contains a menagerie with exotic animals, plus boardwalks, piers, and benches along the river. The local folks are friendly, and the smells of camp cooking in the late evening rival those in the French Quarter. The riverside benches are a great place to sit in the late evening or early morning, looking out to the wall of forest just across the water.

Sabine Island options

1. Paddle 1 mile south of Niblett Bluff and turn right on Watson Branch, exploring to the headwaters.

2. Paddle 2 miles south of Niblett and turn right on Brenam Bayou. Explore to the headwaters at Lost Lake and either return the way you came or portage 25 yards through the woods to Sabine River and float 3.5 miles south to Old Sabine River and 4 miles northeast back to Niblett Bluff.

3. Launch at Salter Bluff, paddle half a mile north to Cutoff Bayou, which forks northwest for a mile over to the Sabine, then float 12 miles south to the mouth of Old River and back northeast 4 miles to the park. Salter Bluff is located off Green Moore Road, which loops from Highway 191 north to Highway 12.

4. Launch at Salter Bluff and paddle 7 miles south on Old River to Niblett Bluff. There's also a ramp off Green Moore Road 3 river miles south of Salter Bluff.

Area campgrounds

Niblett Bluff Park on Niblett Bluff Road west of Highway 109 west of Vinton, improved and primitive campsites, 337-589-7117.

Maps

For map of the WMA and details on fishing and hunting regulations, call the Department of Wildlife and Fisheries office in Lake Charles at 337-491-2580.

High points

Numerous options for exploring.

Low points

Camping is not allowed in the WMA.

Tips

Be imaginative and adventurous in planning your routes, and you'll find some good places in this fine swamp.

Whiskey Chitto

The town of Mittie northeast of Lake Charles bills itself as the canoe capital of Louisiana, and that may well be true, for it's located on what has to be the most popular paddling stream in the state. If you like clear water under your hull, enough current to make paddling optional, and squeaky white sand between your toes, Whiskey Chitto Creek is the place. There are 29 miles of good floating and eight outfitters to rent canoes and provide shuttles—more than any other stream in Louisiana. (Bogue Chitto River has about the same number of outfitters, but most of them are in Mississippi.)

Heading up on the Fort Polk Military Reservation in the Kisatchie National Forest east of Leesville, Whiskey Chitto is nourished by pretty streams like Sixmile, Tenmile, and Bundick Creeks en route to its entry into Calcasieu River just north of U.S. Highway 190 near Kinder. The best canoeing is the 29 miles from Highway 26 at Mittie down to Indian Village on the east bank of Calcasieu River. The 9 miles from Mittie to rural Carpenter's Bridge are the most popular. There are 13 more miles to Highway 190, and 7 more to a boat ramp at Indian Village off Highway 383.

You've got to admit Whiskey Chitto is a poetic name for a Deep South stream. Chitto is an Indian word for big that is often applied to creeks. Whiskey conjures images of moonshine and sour mash. Actually, though, Whiskey is an anglicized version of an Indian word, Ouiska, which means cane—hence, big cane creek. Maps list the creek as Ouiska, Whisky, or Whiskey.

The creek has a good current, and after a rain it's even faster. When Billy Gibson and I launched at Highway 26 after a spring downpour, we covered the 9 miles to Carpenter's Bridge in just 2½ hours and barely got our paddles wet. Unfortunately, rain tends to muddy up the crystal water and submerge the sandbars. But if high water obscures some of the creek's attractions, it opens up others, providing entrance into mysterious backwaters. If you want to find some little-seen wonders of the creek, or simply slow your pace, try detouring into every slough and creek that catches your eye and holds your boat. I call that the mink style of traveling. When a mink roams a creek bank at night it pokes its head into every hole, tributary, and hollow log. Not everyone is enthusiastic about nosing into dark cypress swamps, especially when they have to duck to avoid vines while gar stir the water near the boat. But adventurous paddlers soon discover the appeal of these quiet backwaters: A big nutria rat watches sleepily from a log before sliding into the water and swimming off lazily; a great blue heron launches itself with 6-foot wingspread across the green-shaded sanctuary; a huge owl, perched on a low limb just 20 feet away, regards intruders with deep black eyes that suggest the essence of mystery. When you ease along silently in a nonmotorized boat, the creatures are not spooked. Maybe they think you're a floating log or some sort of oversized beaver. Only when you get within a few yards do they react to your impertinence and move off into the gloom.

The white sandbars and clear water are the most popular aspects of Whiskey Chitto, however, conducive for picnicking, swimming, and playing. The sandbars are accessible to the public for camping or picnicking, according to the Department of Wildlife and Fisheries. Campers should be alert to the possibility of flash floods, pitching tents well above the water line and tying canoes at night.

For all its attractions, the Whiskey Chitto has a depressing side: It's too popular. Hundreds of canoes take to the river during the summer. As a result, landowners are territorial, no doubt sick of litter and trespassing. Their response is to tack up posted signs or, worse, to write the word "No" on tree trunks. Other problems can result among paddlers themselves. In the summer of 1999, an argument between two groups of paddlers led to a brawl involving more than 100 people. Four were injured, one was arrested for aggravated battery, and lawmen issued 23 citations.

How does this happen? Isn't canoeing supposed to be a quiet, back-to-nature pursuit? The first problem is timing. Most people go on summer weekends. While many of these folks no doubt want a quiet, peaceful experience, some want to party. This may mean overindulging in alcohol, which fuels rude behavior, profanity, and combativeness, setting the stage for conflict. I avoid summer weekends, especially on popular streams. Another way to escape the crowd is to float a stretch of river less heavily traveled, such as below Carpenter's Bridge.

Such commotions are rare, of course, and everyone we encountered was friendly. One elderly gentleman on the bank hailed us over for some storytelling and advice about river conditions. He recalled the days when loggers cut virgin pine trees and floated them down Whiskey Chitto Creek and Calcasieu River to Lake Charles. Then the men would paddle canoes made of hollowed-out cypress logs back upriver, sometimes stretching their slickers onto makeshift masts to catch a south wind. He remembered his father's story of setting a personal record by chopping down 18 huge pine trees in a day. He also talked about the fishing; local fishermen use worms, crawfish, or chicken hearts to catch catfish and gasper gou, artificial lures to catch bass.

After Whiskey Chitto enters Calcasieu River, it's less than a mile to the Highway 190 bridge. Upstream from the juncture, the Calcasieu is similar to Whiskey Chitto but smaller and more prone to logjams. Some canoe outfitters have tried to run trips on it but couldn't deal with the shallows and logjams and gave up on it. Below the juncture of the two streams, Calcasieu is wide enough for motorboats, and you may encounter fishermen running trotlines. The ramp at Indian Village is a good place to take out; there's a primitive campground there owned by Allen Parish. The parish is home to the Coushatta Indian Tribe, which has a museum near Elton, holds a powwow each October, and operates a summer camp, Camp Coushatta.

Calcasieu River continues southwest, widening to lake size as it approaches the city of Lake Charles. At the north end of town it meets the West Fork of Calcasieu River, which is also wide and slow. Sam Houston Jones State Park off Highway 378 west of Moss Bluff is located where Houston River meets Indian Bayou to form the West Fork of Calcasieu. The park area provides some pleasant flatwater paddling alongside woods, farms, camps, and houses.

Whiskey Chitto options

1. Highway 26 to Carpenter's Bridge, 9 miles. Carpenter's Bridge is on Highway 1147 between two rural roads that parallel the creek. Take 410 south of Mittie, turn left on 1155, then left on 1147.

2. Carpenter's Bridge to Highway 190, 13 miles.

3. Highway 190 to ramp at Old Ferry Road west of Highway 383 at Indian Village, 7 miles.

Area campgrounds

West Bay Wildlife Management Area, Highway 26 east of Mittie, three primitive campgrounds, 337-491-2575. The 62,115-acre WMA is not located on the creek but provides a place for a nearby base camp.

Indian Village Park, small parish-owned primitive campground west of Indian Village on Old Ferry Road off Highway 383 on the east bank of Calcasieu River.

Sam Houston Jones State Park off Highway 378 west of Moss Bluff, on the West Fork of the Calcasieu River, improved campsites, 1-888-677-7264.

Outfitters

Ace Canoeing in Mittie, 1-800-311-1943.

Deep Woods Adventure Canoeing & Outfitters in LeBlanc, 337-463-3606, 337-738-3050.

Arrowhead Canoe Rentals in Mittie, 1-800-637-2086, 337-639-2086.

Campbell's Canoes in Mittie, 337-328-7121.

Riverfront Canoe Rental in Mittie, 1-888-419-0362, 337-639-2710.

T&J Canoe Rentals in Mittie, 337-639-2186, 877-TJCANOE.

Whiskey Chitto Canoe Rentals in Mittie, 337-639-4959.

White Sand Canoe Rentals in Mittie, 1-800-621-9306, 337-639-2740.

Maps

For a map of the creek, call Allen Parish Tourist Commission, 1-888-639-4868.

U.S.G.S. quad maps are, from Highway 26 south, Mittie, Le Blanc, Indian Village.

High points

Clear water, good current, white sandbars.

Low points

Crowds, posted signs.

Tips

Go during the off-season.

Chicot Lake

Lakes cover Louisiana like spots on a jaguar. They range from seasonal waters that are full only during winter and spring high water to vast permanent lakes big enough for barges. There are swamp lakes and reservoirs, places trafficked by roaring speedboats and by small johnboats. This book does not pretend to be a guide to the lakes of Louisiana—that would require a book of its own—but I do call special attention to several in this book, including one that is near ideal from a paddler's perspective: Chicot. It's long and narrow, almost like a wide river; it's chockful of trees so there's plenty of sheltered paddling and little room for speedboats; it's surrounded by state park land with no private development; and it has canoe-in primitive campsites. Put all this together and this lake is hard to beat.

The 2,000-acre Chicot Lake is embedded in a 6,400-acre state park on Highway 3042 north of Ville Platte, La., off Interstate 49 south of Alexandria. It's surrounded by a backpacking trail with hike-in campsites in addition to developed sites, cabins, and an Olympic-size pool. And it's just up the road from the Louisiana State Arboretum, a 300-plus-acre tract of some of the finest woods in the state.

The shape of this man-made lake is partly what drew me. It's around 7 miles long but just a quarter- to a half-mile wide, the shores crinkled with small coves—not your typical reservoir. Much of the time you can't even see the shore since cypress and tupelo trees march out from the high ground, ringing the lake with swamp. Other groves of trees stand in mid-lake like islands, favorite haunts of fishermen. Chicot was a sixteenth-century French word for stump. But since there was little logging in Louisiana that early, the word may have referred to cypress knees, which were and are abundant. Chicot combines the clean state park look of a small reservoir with the wild, cypress look of an oxbow.

Among anglers the lake is best known for its bream and white perch. It also has big bass, but they're hard to catch if you don't know the lake. Walker Branch Cove is a good bassing spot, I'm told. One bream fisherman I encountered had hooked a 16-inch bass along with his mess of bream. "I tried to stretch him," he lamented in a Cajun accent, referring to the 14–17-inch slot limit. "I had to put him back." Some fishermen use pirogue-kayak hybrids to paddle into stands of timber, while others prefer large motorboats in more open waters, though they have to pick their way slowly through most of the lake. A marked channel runs two-thirds the length of the lake, providing motorboats with a route for fast travel. Everywhere else requires caution, since you never know where a stump might appear beneath the dark water.

The lake has three boat ramps. The South Landing is located via the main park entrance on Highway 3042. This is where the bulk of the park accommodations are, including 100 campsites, 27 cabins, a group camp, lodge, picnic areas, pool, fishing pier, and dock with rental flatbottom boats (but no canoes, unfortunately). The North Landing off Highway 106 has 100 more campsites, dock, pier, primitive group camp, and lodge. The East Landing is the least developed with dock, lodge, picnic area, and bathrooms.

The lake is well designed for exploring by canoe, either poking around in coves or circumnavigating the whole thing in a 15–20-mile paddle. It tapers down to a snake's tail in the south, shaded by deep green tupelo forest. Pierced by shafts of golden light, this swamp spreads mysterious and brooding all around. Tupelo, also known as tupelo gum and water tupelo, is almost identical to swamp tupelo and black tupelo, both of which also go by the name black gum. Tupelo gum grows in the same watery habitat as cypress and is sometimes confused with the more familiar tree due to its flaring trunk. However, while cypress has small, fringed, needlelike leaves, tupelo's are more the shape and color of limes, 5–10 inches long and 2–4 inches wide. The trunks swell to a dome shape, unlike cypress trees' winglike buttresses. The wood of tupelo and black gum trees has almost no grain so is nearly impossible to split, as I discovered once when I foolishly cut a straight-trunked hill-country black gum for firewood. A neighbor laughed when he saw the pieces of log in my yard waiting to be split. I quickly found out why when my maul either bounced off or stuck in the wood

Chicot Lake tupelo swamp shows eerie mixture of light and dark.

without the slightest split in the grain. Because of this characteristic, old-timers used black gum for water well windlasses, around which the bucket rope was wrapped. Craftsmen also make broad, beautiful mixing bowls from slabs of tupelo trunk. In the swamp, the trunks can swell to amazing size and are often hollow. Bees like to nest in them, producing the namesake tupelo honey.

In the flooded forest at Chicot, navigation can get a bit dicey if you're not careful. The trick is to pay attention to the slope of high ground off through the shadows. Since the lake isn't wide, it's not hard to get reoriented. Paddle in any direction and you'll soon come either to high ground or open water. A compass and state park lake map will preclude problems.

The flooded forest thins out a bit as you paddle back to the north, though it extends outward from shore and forms islands in mid-lake for an enchanting woodsy feeling. The lake widens near East Landing and feels like a real lake rather than flooded forest. Forest resumes in Walker Branch Cove on the west and at the north end of the lake as well as in other spots. This mixture of woods and open water is popular with birds, such as anhingas, which soar so low their broad black tails brush the water. The bird's white head and neck stretch thin as a snake from its black body. It likes to perch on a tree limb and spread its wings to cool off on warm days. Herons—great blue, little blue, green-backed—and egrets also abound on the lake. The park puts out a checklist for birds found in the park.

The Chicot swamp is also a good place for owls. Most of the half a dozen owl species found in the area are nocturnal, so you're more likely to hear them than see them. Still, there's a good chance of spotting one. We saw a barred owl in the late afternoon on the west side of the lake not far from South Landing. The barred owl is known for its "Who cooks for you, who cooks for you-all" sounds. When several of these characters get together, their calls can escalate until they sound like a monkey house. Barred owls are grayish brown, with no ear tufts. They may stand 20 inches tall with a 44-inch wingspread, and prefer swampy forest like Chicot. Also fairly common are screech owls, though it was years before I realized they were responsible for the eerie whinnying cries at dusk and in the night. I used to fancy those noises came from gnomes or leprechauns blowing miniature hunting horns. Screech owls stand only about 10 inches tall and sport small yellow ear tufts. Great horned owls, on the other hand, may loom more than 2 feet tall with a wingspread of 4½ feet. They have big ear tufts and piercing yellow eyes and look like the classic wise old owl of storybooks. They produce five or six deep, ghostly hoots, the rhythm of which sounds roughly like, "Who's awake? Me too." Barn owls are easily identifiable by their heart-shaped white faces, like the Phantom of the Opera with wings. They typically reach about 18 inches in height with a 44-inch wingspan. Their calls, described as "weird" by The Audubon Society Field Guide to North American Birds, include hisses, clicks, screams, and grunts. Seldom heard are the short-eared and the long-eared owls, which only visit here during the winter.

Circling the lake is a 22-mile trail used by hikers and bikers. The trail has six primitive campsites not accessible by road, so paddlers, hikers, and bikers can really get away from it all for a mere $1 per night camping fee. Get a map and directions at the park entrance. The regular campground is relatively quiet and secluded if you prefer to car-camp. Though the land around the lake is hilly, mosquitoes breed in the swampy areas, so citronella candles, mosquito coils, repellent, and long sleeves are advisable. Some campers use screen houses, though the bugs didn't seem quite that bad to me.

Just north of the park on Highway 3042 is one of the most wonderful places in Louisiana: the state arboretum. I highly recommend a visit for anyone who loves the woods. It features 3 miles of interconnected trails, and you can walk them all with some doubling back. The arboretum is classified as a beech/magnolia climax forest. Those and other massive hardwood trees tower overhead to a height not often seen in the much-logged South, in places reminiscent of virgin tropical rain forest. In one place a beech had fallen across the trail and a section of trunk removed; I counted 125 rings, which means it's that many years old, and this was just a mid-sized tree, relatively. The terrain is gently rolling, located at the intersection of the coastal plain and the north Louisiana hills. "Due to this great variation in topography, almost every type of Louisiana vegetation, except coastal marsh and prairie, is represented on the site," says an arboretum brochure. The arboretum publishes a tree species guide that describes not only the better-known varieties like American beech, Southern magnolia, and various oaks, but lesser-known plants like bigleaf magnolia (leaves can reach 2½ feet long and a foot wide), blue beech (often confused with hophornbeam and called ironwood and hornbeam), beechdrops (a small plant that grows under beech trees), parsley hawthorn (a small tree with leaves shaped like parsley), strawberry bush (a shrub, not the same as wild strawberry plants), and witch hazel (a small tree used to make astringent; its forked branches are used as divining rods to find water). You'll walk in a state of awe through this forest, pausing to peer upward into the green mansions. These woods will make you marvel at what Louisiana once was, and still is in places.

Chicot Lake options

1. Launch at any of the three landings and explore the wooded coves and shoreline.
2. Circumnavigate the lake, 15–20 miles, for a solid day's paddle.

Area campgrounds

Chicot Lake State Park has several backcountry campsites accessible to paddlers, plus two campgrounds: at South Landing off Highway 3042 and North Landing off Highway 106.

Maps

For map of lake and park, plus other information on the park and arboretum, call 1-888-677-2442.

High points

Long, narrow lake with lots of flooded forest makes for secluded exploring.

Low points

No rental canoes.

Tips

Hike the 3 miles of trail at the nearby arboretum.

Little River

Probably few people associate Little River with canoeing. That's because for much of its 60-odd-mile existence, it's precisely the sort of slow, muddy, agricultural waterway paddlers tend to avoid. But the upper river passes alongside Little River Wildlife Management Area, which boasts deep woods full of wildlife, even if there's virtually no current. And if it's current you want, there's a lively tributary, Big Creek, south of the WMA, which is popular with paddlers.

Little River starts where Castor Creek and Dugdemona River join, just west of U.S. Highway 165 a couple miles southwest of its juncture with U.S. 84 at Tullos. There's no good access to the river at 165, and the next put-in is from Highway 500 at Zenoria 5 miles downstream, where a dirt track leads beneath the bridge on the southeast side.

About 4 miles below Highway 500, the 4,164-acre Little River WMA begins, stretching intermittently along roughly 10 river miles of the west bank. These are wonderful woods, with high bluffs and hidden oxbow lakes. South of the WMA, the river leaves the piney hills and flows southeast into the lower end of Catahoula Lake. The lake has two outlets that join at Highway 84, then parallel the highway eastward across flat farmland to Black River at Jonesville. Glimpses of the lower river from Highway 124 at Jonesville and Highway 84 west of Archie show it to be pretty but lined with levees and traveled by motorboats—not the best canoeing water. For that go to the WMA.

There are two primitive campgrounds in the WMA. The more northerly one at Doughty Bluff is positioned midway in the WMA and makes a good base camp for exploring up and down river. It's located off Lincecum Road east of

Highway 165. A more popular campground is due east of WMA headquarters to the south. You can launch at either place. A Louisiana Department of Wildlife and Fisheries map of the WMA makes the spots easy to find.

About 2.5 miles upriver from Doughty Bluff, a small tributary, Bayou Funny Louis, comes in from the east. Although it sounds like the bayou was named after some madcap Frenchman, the name actually comes from Choctaw "fani" for squirrel and "lusa" for black—Black Squirrel Bayou. Less than a mile farther up, the even smaller Lincecum Branch runs in from the east. Two more miles up Little River, some good backwaters lie to the west: Pine Lake and Nugent Brake. In this vicinity reportedly stand some tupelo gums 18 feet wide at the base. On the last piece of WMA property, 7.5 miles north of Doughty Bluff, a large oxbow lake stretches off to the west. Exploring downriver from Doughty, you'll find camps on stilts on patches of private land 1.5 mile down, just above the next campground. A few motorboats travel the river, mainly johnboats with fishermen. Local anglers also use kayaks and pirogue-kayak hybrids. This is primarily a crappie and bream stream. When I was there in the fall, crappie fishermen were reporting success with white-tailed jigs with blue heads. During higher water, fishermen set trotlines and limb lines for catfish.

Water levels vary drastically on Little River. In spring high water, backwater from Catahoula Lake can submerge most of the WMA, and you can paddle into the woods, exploring swamps and oxbows, glimpsing alligators and wood ducks. The roofs of stilted camps have been known to go under during severe floods. In low water, such as late summer or fall, you can hike up the shriveled tributaries. You may find dry lake beds aglow with waist-high bunches of purple cleomes, stretches of water impounded between beaver dams and bordered by hog wallows, and stands of thick-trunked, bark-peeling cottonwood trees. In such conditions the muddy river boasts high white sandbars and gravel shoals, and local arrowhead hunters squat on their haunches on gravel bars searching for artifacts.

Chances are excellent that you'll see wildlife on Little River. One of the most abundant species, though not easily spotted, is the hog, wild or semiwild. There's no shortage of free-roaming porkers throughout the South these days, but I've never seen anywhere hoggier than Little River WMA. On a fall campout there, Greg Bond and I saw the rounded prints of their hooves on seemingly every inch of riverbank, plus droppings, rootings, and an occasional whiff. Not all of these hogs are technically wild. Parts of Louisiana still allow livestock to

Greg Bond holds a Louisiana painted turtle at Little River.

range free, and that's the case in the portions of Grant Parish that include Little River WMA. Landowners trap the hogs, or catch them with hog dogs and horses, mark them with a notch on the ear, and register the mark in the parish courthouse. They turn them loose with the admonition to root, hog, or die, and they capture them later as needed. In LaSalle (pronounced La-SALL) Parish on the east bank of Little River, however, a parish ordinance requires livestock to be fenced, so farmers there can't turn their hogs loose. Of course, hogs don't know about parish boundaries and run loose like gangbusters around Little River. And there are plenty with no marks or other hint of domesticity. Whether wild or semi-so, the hogs are incredibly alert, and you're only likely to see one if you're quiet. Paddling beside a steep bank thick with mayhaw bushes, we heard footsteps as a black boar, maybe 100 pounds with a pair of white 2-inch tusks, came down to drink. It didn't notice us until I reached for my camera (the usual pattern). At the click of my camera bag latch the boar looked up, then sprinted up the bank, grunting to its companions. Hog hunting is not permitted in the WMA. There is deer hunting, but the most popular game is squirrel. The banks of Little River are topped with gorgeous forest of cypress, oak, wild pecan, and pine behind a thick screen of mayhaw bushes, which in May litter the ground and water with tart red fruit that no doubt drive the hogs and other creatures wild.

A sight perhaps rarer than hogs was the otter we glimpsed rambling along a log. It slipped into the water, swam toward us, then suddenly stopped, stared, and dove. We tracked its underwater movement by bubbles as it raced upstream like a nuclear sub. In the fall it also pays to look up now and then, to watch waterfowl migrating. If you don't remember to do so, cantankerous voices will remind you as flocks of geese wing across the sky. Some fly in proper V formation, while others may form a ragged W as the birds argue and tussle over who will take the lead. I guess more than one species can behave hoggishly at times.

For a downriver trip on Little River, you can launch at Louisiana Highway 500 and float 13 miles to Doughty Bluff or 2 miles farther to the next campground, keeping in mind there's not likely to be much if any current to help you on your way. You can also explore upriver from Highway 500, paddling the 5 miles to U.S. 165 and, just above there, the juncture of Dugdemona and Castor. The former, which runs southeast from the Winnfield area, is murky and contains paper mill outflow, which has been blamed on fish kills in the past. The latter, flowing south from Chatham and Olla, is clearer and prettier, though in low water may be too shallow to navigate.

For an experience markedly different from Little River, check out Big Creek, a tributary about 12 miles south of the WMA. For the record, Big Creek is little, and Little River is big. I suppose the names are meant to be relative, the former being large for a creek, the latter small for a river. Big Creek is clear and sandy, gushing eastward through Kisatchie National Forest past Pollock and into Little River. The creek is curvy and swift, with reportedly the highest elevation drop in the state at 7 feet per mile. It's about 30 feet wide, and logjams could be a problem were it not for the efforts of Big Creek Outfitters & Expeditions Inc., which runs 7-mile trips on the creek. If you have your own boat and prefer to do your own shuttling, you can canoe the 6 miles from Mary Barron Road to U.S. 165. You can continue 5 miles from Highway 165 down to Highway 8 at Fishville, but this section is not kept cleared so you'll likely encounter logs.

Little River options

1. Launch at either of the two campgrounds in Little River WMA and explore up and down the river.

2. Paddle 13 miles from Highway 500 at Zenoria to Doughty Bluff campground, and 2 miles farther to the campground east of WMA headquarters.

3. From Highway 500, paddle 5 miles upstream to U.S. 165 and, just above there, fork right onto Castor Creek or left onto Dugdemona River.

4. On tributary Big Creek, paddle 6 miles from Mary Barron Road to U.S. Highway 165. Mary Barron Road runs north off Parish Road 110 between Pollock and Dry Prong.

Area campgrounds

Little River WMA has two campgrounds: one at Doughty Bluff off Lincecum Road east of Highway 165, and one due east of WMA headquarters to the south, 318-487-5885.

Maps

Call 318-487-5885 for a WMA map.

Outfitters

Big Creek Outfitters & Expeditions Inc. at Pollock, 318-765-3060, rents canoes for Big Creek, a tributary to Little River.

High points

Abundant wildlife including hogs, otters, alligators, ducks, squirrels, beaver.

Low points

Slow and muddy.

Tips

Proceed slowly and quietly, stopping at times, to increase chances of seeing wildlife.

Spring Bayou

In Louisiana there are two Spring Creeks, a Spring Branch, Spring Gully, Spring Lake, and Spring Bayou, but only the latter has its own wildlife management area. And it's a gem. Spring Bayou WMA, a network of bayous and lakes just east of Marksville, is popular with hunters and fishermen, but a canoe has the advantage in many parts of the area due to shallow waters and thick aquatic vegetation. The 12,000-acre WMA is a good example of Red River swamps, or what's left of them. It's little over 5 miles south of the big waterway, which is leveed, locked, and dammed, its floodplain drained and converted mainly to farmland. Farm fields extend all around the WMA except for the west side, where the town of Marksville encroaches. That makes this area all the more valuable.

The best place to launch is a boat ramp near headquarters on Boggy Bayou. Getting there is a bit tricky, however. From either Louisiana 452 or 115 in Marksville, go east on Louisiana 1190, which is also known as Spring Bayou Road. Little over a mile outside town, the road forks, and Spring Bayou Road branches off to the right and meanders a few more miles. When it enters the WMA, notable by a large sign, bear left to get to Boggy Bayou. The road to the right leads to Grand Lake.

The Boggy Bayou put-in is a beautiful, deep-woods setting, with a fenced campground near the ramp. From there, paddle southeast down the bayou. This is one of those places where I was thinking a motor would be handy as I moseyed down the relatively straight 1-mile stretch to the main swamp. Then I glanced up and saw a doe studying me from deep grass just a few yards away. There are advantages to a slow, quiet boat. The scenery is lovely, with thick, marshy grasses and buttonbush thickets extending out from oak, pecan, and willow woods. Motorboaters may pass by, but they usually slow down to minimize their wake or even chat. One hunter, noticing my guide stroke, which keeps the canoe straight, asked me if I had a specially designed canoe that snaps back in position after each stroke. I explained that just flicking the blade away from the gunwale after each stroke does the trick.

The WMA is shaped like an Indian's headdress, with more than a dozen curving feathers protruding from the headband. In this case the feathers are bayous and finger lakes leading west from a swampy aggregation of lakes that are thick with weeds and dotted with islands and woods. The islands are spoil banks caused by dredging to keep a channel open through the swamp. Since the WMA is cut off from Red River by levees, there is no longer the natural flooding and "dewatering" of the swamp, which has resulted in siltation, increased aquatic vegetation, and decline in fishing.

When you arrive at the open water from Boggy Bayou, the first impression is utter confusion as waters branch off in every direction with no apparent order. This is a good place to stop and study your WMA map and compass to get your bearings. When I was there, orange marking tape dangled from trees at the entrance to Boggy Bayou, which leads back to the boat ramp. That's useful, though many of the other bayous are too choked with hydrilla and buttonbush to get far. This is where a canoe—or kayak, pirogue, or hybrid vessel—comes into its own, for it can go in shallows where most motorboats can't, the exception being airboats and vessels equipped with angled motors designed for shallows. The numerous bays and sloughs give the effect of rooms, which, as landscapers and horticulturalists know, add visual interest to an area. These rooms range from small, hydrilla-choked inlets to large open areas like Coulee Noir on the northeast, a lake 1.5 miles long by half a mile wide. Ringed with marsh and forest, it looks utterly lonely, like something out of northern Canada. I half-expected to see a moose feeding in the shallows. There are no moose, of course, but there are deer, alligators, and, in the winter, waterfowl. In fact, paddlers might consider not going during duck season—typically in December and January—since hunters fan out into the swamp, hiding in blinds to shoot ducks, not a great time to be paddling around.

There are boat ramps at Grand Lake on the west side of the area and Old River on the southeast side off Louisiana 451, but they have less appeal for paddlers. Both are long and fairly straight with little opportunity to explore and more access for motorboats. Their primitive campgrounds tend to be hangouts for teenagers seeking a place to party. The Boggy Bayou campground is more regulated and secluded.

On a bluff overlooking Old River just west of the WMA and east of Highway 452 is the Marksville State Historic Site (1-888-253-8954), the 2,000-year-old location of an Indian village. There are several mounds and other earthworks here, plus a museum with classes in flint knapping, pottery making, and basket weaving, and a nature trail. It's intriguing to reflect that when you paddle the waters of Spring Bayou WMA, you're doing just as the inhabitants of the nearby Indian village did for centuries. Then as now this area offers prime hunting and fishing habitat. Hunters still go after deer, waterfowl, and small game. Commercial fishermen catch catfish, buffalo, drum, and gar. And sport fishermen find the clear water makes for good bass and crappie habitat.

Spring Bayou WMA options

1. Launch at ramp on Boggy Bayou, paddle 1 mile southeast to open water and explore in all directions. Boggy Bayou is at the end of Spring Bayou Road off Louisiana 1190, which runs east of Louisiana 452 and 115 in Marksville.

Area campgrounds

Developed campground by Boggy Bayou and primitive camping areas at Old River and Grand Lake boat ramps.

Maps

For map of Spring Bayou WMA, call 337-948-0255.

High points

Lots of backwaters to explore.

Low points

Popular with hunters and fishermen.

Tips

Avoid duck season.

Saline Bayou
(Dewey Wills Wildlife Management Area)

The flat, agricultural region of eastern Louisiana along the Mississippi River does not seem particularly conducive to canoeing. The area is best known for its many oxbow lakes, which mainly appeal to fishermen with motorboats. Nevertheless, there are pockets here and there with big woods and sinuous bayous, a good example being Dewey Wills Wildlife Management Area between Alexandria and Jonesville. Actually, at 60,276 acres, Dewey Wills feels like more than a "pocket." When you turn off Highway 28 into the WMA, the sudden immersion into miles of woods is startling—especially if a bobcat darts across the road in front of you, as one did when I visited. The WMA is a huge floodplain along Saline Bayou, Big Saline Bayou, Saline Lake (a different Saline Bayou and lake than the ones in northern Louisiana), Larto Lake, and other waters. It's obvious from the mud marks along tree trunks that vast areas go under during spring high water.

In *Trip to the West and Texas*, author Amos A. Parker described how hard travel was through this country in the 1830s, when it was still raw wilderness.

Since the steamboat that ran from Natchez down to the Red River and up to Alexandria had already departed, Parker crossed the Mississippi on a ferry and set out on horseback.

"Our route now lay through a dense forest—and the ground generally so miry that we could only ride on a walk," he wrote. "Sometimes we came to the thick cane-brakes, about 20 feet high, and overhanging our narrow path. Sometimes, we found the palmetto, which exactly resembles a large green, open fan, standing on a stem a foot high, and so thick that we could hardly ride through them, or see any path at all. Sometimes we came to a sheet of water 100 yards wide, in which a horse would plunge to the saddle skirts, and for awhile, become stuck fast; and again, we would find a cypress swamp, full of cypress knees and mud. Indeed it is the worst swamp I ever travelled over, before or since; and sometimes, I thought our horses were stuck too fast ever to move again."

That area west of Vidalia is mostly farmland now, but you can get a glimpse of the jungle Parker saw in places like Dewey Wills, which is bordered and spliced by waterways. Saline Bayou meanders along the southeast side of the WMA. Big Saline Bayou, which is actually smaller than Saline Bayou, forms the southwest boundary. Both run into opposite sides of 5-mile-long Saline Lake. Larto Lake, a classic horseshoe-shaped oxbow, touches the southeast edge of the WMA, while huge Catahoula Lake stretches along the northwest side. Other, smaller lakes, bayous, and drainage canals crisscross the WMA as well. There are three good spots to start your canoe explorations: Saline Point Camping Area on Saline Bayou, Larto Camping Area at Larto Lake, and a U.S. Bureau of Land Management boat ramp on Big Saline Bayou.

Most BLM land is out west, but Louisiana has a 160-acre parcel along the southwest side of the WMA. This parcel includes a bridge across Big Saline Bayou on Paul Road east of Highway 1206 leading into the WMA. There is a boat ramp at the bridge and another nearby, both on BLM property. On the clear, dark-water bayou you can paddle north as it narrows toward Catahoula Lake, or south as it opens onto Saline Lake about 3 miles away. Clay Moore of the BLM office in Jackson, Mississippi, a former forester and a kayaker, said the cypress trees there are some of the biggest he's seen anywhere, with diameters that he estimated to be up to 20 feet at chest height. With branching bayous and flooded forest, a compass, map, and/or GPS is recommended. Because of the trees and stobs, most motorboats using this bayou are small. Camping is allowed on the BLM land, though there are no facilities, and teenagers reportedly use the bridge area as a hangout.

A second canoeing area is on the west side of Larto Lake, a 5-mile-long, half-mile-wide oxbow on the east side of the WMA popular among fishermen. The primitive campground is located where a branch of Saline Bayou connects with the lake. Just up the bayou from the boat launch, an offshoot leads north to Shad Lake. Other channels enter the bayou as well. A state WMA map provides good detail of the waterways. Larto Landing is not easy to get to, however. You have to follow Highway 124 south from Jonesville, take 3102 along the inside curve of the lake and Youngblood Road up to the campground.

Saline Point is a bit easier to drive to, located off Hunt Road east of Highway 28. The WMA map makes it simple to find. Primitive campsites are scattered along Saline Bayou here, and there's a boat ramp. It's about 2 miles south and west to Saline Lake; paddle north and east and waterways connect to Larto Lake. However, large motorboats travel the wide bayou, while smaller sloughs branching off in all directions allow for quiet canoe explorations. And there's no telling what you might find on these backwaters.

Scott Williams and I were paddling up a muddy, canoe-wide slough off Saline Bayou when we entered a stretch of crystal-clear water, evidently fed by underground springs. I just knew there had to be a fish in that clear water, so I rigged a weedless spoon to handle the thick grass. On the second cast, Moby-Dick struck. It was too heavy and strong to be a bass, and I knew my 8-pound test would never hold. I glimpsed the back of the fish when it rolled, then my line snapped. It was almost certainly a bowfin, also known by such names as choupique (pronounced "shoepick" in non-French Louisiana), grennel, cypress trout, mudfish, and dogfish. Bowfins are a top-level predator on a par with bass, but their thick bodies give them more fighting strength than bass, so when you tie onto one you're in for a battle. Like bass they're sight feeders and prefer water clear enough to see their prey. Biologists consider them primitive fish. They have strange fleshy protrusions from their nostrils, sharp little teeth and rounded scales. They're widely scattered but not as common as most fish and so are not often caught. Though they're not considered good to eat, the State of Louisiana put a season on them since people catch them for the roe, known as "Cajun caviar." Bowfins can get pretty big. The all-tackle sportfishing record is 21 pounds, 8 ounces, caught in Forest Lake, South Carolina, in January 1980, according to the National Fresh Water Fishing Hall of Fame. The Louisiana record was exactly 1 pound lighter, caught by Brian Fant in Toledo Bend in 1976. Dewey Wills WMA waters also harbor catfish, bass, bream, and crappie; Larto is particularly known for its bream fishing.

The WMA connects on the west to Catahoula National Wildlife Refuge (318-992-5261). The 6,535-acre refuge is located on the northeast side of Catahoula Lake off U.S. 84 between Jena and Jonesville. A ditch-straight diversion canal through the WMA connects Catahoula Lake to Black River on the east. Catahoula is an Indian word for clear water or beloved lake. The lake is roughly 13 miles long and 3 miles wide and averages 26,000 acres, but water levels vary drastically according to season. In summer the lake is lowered to 5,000 acres to grow vegetation for waterfowl. Shortly before duck season, the water level is raised 2 feet to provide waterfowl habitat. After the hunting season it's raised another 4.5 feet for commercial fishing. The refuge was established in 1958 as a sanctuary for waterfowl because of historically heavy hunting pressure around Catahoula Lake. No camping is allowed, but the refuge does permit rabbit, squirrel, and deer archery hunting, and some good antlers have been taken. The refuge also has two fishing areas: 1,200-acre Duck Lake impoundment open March 1–October 31, and 5-mile-long Cowpen Bayou open year-round. Fishing is best for bass, bream, and crappie when the water rises and starts flooding in the springtime. The refuge has a 9-mile circle drive, a nature trail, and an observation tower overlooking the marshy impoundment. The area is popular among birdwatchers, who come to see the up to 100,000 waterfowl that stop there.

The area is known for having produced a fine breed of hunting and herding dog, the Catahoula cur. Legend has it that red wolves, Spanish war dogs, and French hog-hunting dogs eventually produced Catahoulas. When Spanish explorer Hernando de Soto traveled through the area in the 1500s, he and his men lived with the Avoyelle tribe of central Louisiana long enough for his war dogs—greyhounds and mastiffs—to get to know the local red wolf population. In 1700, French explorer Henri de Tonti recorded stories of "strange-looking wolf dogs with white eyes and mottled coats" in Louisiana. Later, French settlers brought Beaucerons—hog-hunting and herding dogs from France—to Louisiana. Don Abney, author of *The Louisiana Catahoula Leopard Dog*, speculates that settlers mixed the Beauceron with the wolf-like dog of the Indians. Catahoulas gained a reputation over the years. Jim Bowie's knife-making brother Rezin reportedly slept with one at his feet. Teddy Roosevelt bear-hunted with them. Governor Earl K. Long collected them and used them at the state prison in Angola, Louisiana. The National Association of Louisiana Catahoulas was formed in 1977, and the Catahoula became Louisiana's official state dog in 1979. Ask someone what one looks like, though, and you'll find there's no simple answer. The classic look is one or two glass eyes, a boxy head, muscular body, mottled coat, and webbed feet. But plenty don't have glass eyes; the coat comes in nearly every color assortment, even solid; and there are three basic body types, thick like a bulldog, stocky, and slender. Their talents are as wide-ranging as their appearance. They're top-notch herding animals. They'll hunt virtually anything, most notably wild hogs. Hog hunters say Catahoulas have the rare ability to stay after their prey for hours. However, they rarely bark until they bay their prey, so hunters outfit the lead dog with a radio-transmitter collar to keep up with them and use walkie-talkies to communicate in the thickets. Typically the Catahoulas bay the hog, then hunters release a bulldog to grab it by the ear or side of the face. Catahoulas make good pets and watchdogs too, though the one I had was bad about digging up my wife's yard plants.

Saline Bayou (Dewey Wills WMA) options

1. Launch at Saline Point Camping Area and explore Saline Bayou and surrounding sloughs. The campground is located off Hunt Road east of Highway 28.

2. Launch at Larto Camping Area and explore Larto Lake, Shad Lake, bayous, and sloughs. Follow Highway 124 south from Jonesville till it ends, then take 3102 to the right as it loops along the east side and south end of the lake. Turn north on Youngblood Road and go about a mile to the campground.

3. Launch at Paul Road and explore Big Saline Bayou upstream toward Catahoula Lake or downstream to Saline Lake. From State Route 115 north of Deville turn east on State Route 1206. Go one-half mile, then continue east on Paul Road for 2 miles to bridge.

Area campgrounds

Saline Point primitive camping area along Saline Bayou.

Larto primitive camping area at Larto Lake.

Bureau of Land Management property on Paul Road along Big Saline Bayou, no facilities.

Maps

For map of Dewey Wills WMA, call 318-757-4571.

High points

Surprising expanse of forest at edge of farm country.

Low points

Large, currentless waterways; some motorboats.

Tips

Explore every small slough you come across.

Bayou Cocodrie

Bayou Cocodrie (pronounced co-CO-druh, unlike the co-co-DREE of south Louisiana) starts at Ferriday and worms its way 50 miles south through a national wildlife refuge, vast stretches of farmland, a state wildlife management area, and a flood control structure before entering Red River a few miles west of the Mississippi River. Though much of the land is agricultural, there are some fine stands of forest that make day trips on portions of this bayou worth the effort, in particular the portions in Red River Wildlife Management Area and Bayou Cocodrie National Wildlife Refuge.

The first stretch of good country is Bayou Cocodrie NWR just south of Ferriday. The bayou forms a figure S as it slices through the 13,168-acre refuge, which according to the U.S. Fish and Wildlife Service contains some of the oldest and least disturbed bottomland hardwood forest along the entire Mississippi River. The land was formerly owned by Fisher Lumber Co., which used selective logging and had an interest in growing big hardwoods. The Nature Conservancy acquired the land from Fisher, then turned it over to the Fish and Wildlife Service. The refuge opened in 1992, and in 1996 the U.S. Fish and Wildlife Service erected a metal building for an office on Poole Road 3.5 miles off Highway 15. The land lies in three tracts and is divided by the bayou. The trees are big throughout the refuge, but the most impressive specimens are found in a 750–1,000-acre swath in the southern part. The area is used for research; for in-

U.S. Fish and Wildlife Service official Jerome Ford uses outstretched arms to convey the size of trees at Bayou Cocodrie National Wildlife Refuge.

stance, Louisiana State University researchers study Neotropical migrant song-birds there.

As with most national wildlife refuges, there is no camping, and at this writing the refuge lacks canoe access. However, there are plans to push a gravel road from Poole Road to the bayou and install a boat ramp in the northern part of the refuge. When that occurs, paddlers will be able to float 10 miles to the old barge landing on Boggy Bayou Road east of Louisiana 129 and another 5 miles to Highway 565 (between Deer Park and Monterey)—or to Kemp's Landing, 1½ miles west of the 565 bridge, on Cross Bayou, which joins Bayou Cocodrie. Or explore the bayou above and below Poole Road, returning to the starting point.

There are also plans to put in hiking trails and an observation tower at the refuge, which would make it easier to enjoy the forest. Four-wheeler trails now provide primary access in the woods, but even so, it's common for hunters to get lost. The refuge is considered one of the premiere hunting places in the state, especially for whitetail deer and gray squirrels. There's plenty of other wildlife too. The area is crawling with cottonmouths, rattlesnakes, and copperheads, devilishly hard to spot among the palmettoes. There are also alligators. The refuge abounds with wild hogs, which may be hunted during any other hunting season. Officials trap hogs in large cages when they become a nuisance from rooting up four-wheeler trails. Black bear sign has been spotted in the area, but officials suspect the bears, which are protected, use the refuge mainly as a corridor between Tensas National Wildlife Refuge to the north and the Atchafalaya Swamp to the south. Peregrine falcons and bald eagles appear seasonally, preying on ducks and geese when they migrate south. The refuge allows cooperative farming on its cleared land, on which farmers devote 20 percent of their crop to wildlife. Plenty of mallards, pintails, and geese take advantage of the green browse, like winter wheat and millet. Scaups, teal, and ruddy ducks are drawn in particular to catfish ponds on neighboring land. The refuge also has a large wood duck roost. Beavers are prevalent, and officials use their efforts to advantage by leaving some of the dams alone over the winter to hold water for waterfowl, then breaking them in the spring to prevent trees dying in the standing water. Officials are converting some of the refuge's cleared lands back into forest, planting nuttall oak, known for its large, long-lasting acorns, as well as water oak, willow oak, overcup oak, ash, cypress, and tupelo gum. The idea is to restore the land to its original status as much as possible. The area, known as Cocodrie Swamp, used to flood until a pumping station was installed on nearby Black River for flood control. Even so, it still holds a lot of water. The refuge is a ridge-and-swale complex, and the swales trap rainwater. The moist land can produce acorns even during drought conditions.

By the time the bayou exits the refuge, it's broad and devoid of shade and usually of current. Less than a mile below the refuge border it splits, with Cross Bayou leading to Cocodrie Lake (locally known as Horseshoe Lake), which in turn connects with Black River Lake, a horseshoe off Black River. This network of lakes, bayous, and river makes for good fishing but is heavily trafficked by motorboats. Meanwhile the still large Bayou Cocodrie winds southeast between farm and woods, all privately owned. The farm fields are miles wide with a medley of crops such as soybeans, cotton, rice, corn, and hay, plus catfish ponds. The bayou is listed as a Louisiana Natural and Scenic River from Cross Bayou to Wild Cow Bayou, which splits off to the south about 10 miles below 565. But the most scenic parts are actually within the national wildlife refuge and in Red River Wildlife Management Area farther down. The reason this part is listed is to protect it from further degradation. The stretches of bayou within the refuges are not listed because they are already protected, a state wildlife official explained to me.

Below Wild Cow Bayou, Bayou Cocodrie zigzags east before turning back south into Red River WMA. For the next 14 miles it winds through big woods, with occasional forays past patches of privately owned farmland, toward its rendezvous with mighty Red River. The WMA contains nearly 40,000 acres, of which 11,717 are owned by the U.S. Army Corps of Engineers. There are numerous options for canoeing in the WMA, from an 11-mile downriver trip to launching, exploring, and returning.

The uppermost put-in within the WMA is the bridge on Yakey Road, a squishy gravel lane that leads west off Highway 15 a couple miles south of the WMA's northern border. The access is rarely used and requires a slide through deep weeds down a mud bank—no great problem for the determined paddler. From here you can set off up the bayou between dense woods of thorny water locust, pecan, overcup oak, and black willow, fringed in the summertime with white and pink blossoms of halberd-leaved rose-mallow, a type of hibiscus. The trees can't compare with those in the national wildlife refuge due to logging in decades past, but they're still impressive. They make me chuckle at people—myself, for example—who go to the trouble and expense to seek adventure in tropical countries when such good places are so close at hand.

In hot weather, gar swarm like piranha in the muddy water, slapping the surface and darting away when you get too close. The predatory fish average about a foot and a half long and hover just below the surface when it's hot, perhaps seeking oxygen. They're a nuisance to fishermen, who typically remove them from the hook by breaking their lower jaw with needlenose pliers to keep from getting bitten. Some anglers shoot them in the head with a .22-caliber bullet. If you want to release a gar unharmed, use two pairs of needlenose pliers to handle the toothy upper and lower jaws. The best fishing is in spring high water when the bayou tops its banks and forms backwaters. Use a worm or a "Double Ugly" spinnerbait with orange head and chartreuse blades for bass. Fish the runouts, or small tributaries and ditches where water runs into the bayou. For crappie, try a chartreuse jig with a pink head. Take plenty of lures since gar will likely steal some.

The northern border of the WMA is located 3 river miles north of Yakey bridge, notable immediately by a shed and farm field on the west side. The top of the bank offers views across miles of beanfields that look more like Iowa than the Bayou State. South of Yakey Bridge the bayou narrows as it runs through a teeming green wilderness crowding the banks of the stream. I was daydreaming on that stretch when my pal, Billy Gibson, in the stern, cried out. He had glanced to the side and found himself staring into the eyes of a big, black wild hog wallowing in the mud in deep shade just a few feet away. The hog vanished without a sound, and I wondered how many other critters we had passed without knowing. There's even a chance of seeing a black bear here since in 2001, wildlife officials transported a black bear and three cubs from Tensas National Wildlife Refuge to the Red River WMA/Three Rivers WMA area.

Bayou Cocodrie winds south for 5 more miles before it widens and enters a narrow "borrow pit" lake against the levee along Highway 15. The borrow pit parallels the road for about a mile; then the bayou shoots west into the woods again, quickly turning back south and winding 5 miles to the water control structure on Acme Levee Road. There's a concrete ramp ¾ mile upstream from the water control structure off Acme Levee Road, and a dirt landing just upstream from the structure. From a ramp on the downstream side of the structure you can also paddle half a mile down Bayou Cocodrie to Red River.

The bayou is log-choked in low water, whereas in high water you can paddle up sloughs and into the woods and explore. The midsection of the bayou runs through private land, but there is talk about the state acquiring some property along Highway 15, which could provide public access to the borrow pit and thus the bayou. Camping is permitted only in designated primitive camping areas located near the Acme Levee Road control structure and off the levee road on the west end of the WMA. The WMA office is at the intersection of Highway 15 and 910. Red River WMA and nearby Three Rivers WMA are popular among deer hunters, who often use pirogues and canoes to get to their hunting spots in the woods. If you go during deer season, wear bright orange.

Another paddling option in Red River WMA is Catfish Bayou, a mile north of Acme Levee Road on Catfish Bayou Road 6 miles west of Bayou Cocodrie. Catfish Bayou stretches southeast for a couple miles, then hooks back for another mile into Whiskey Lake for some good backwoods exploring. After checking out Whiskey Lake, return the way you came.

Trip options

1. Launch at Poole Road in Bayou Cocodrie National Wildlife Refuge and explore the bayou above and below, returning to the starting point.

2. Paddle 10 miles from Poole Road to the old barge landing on Boggy Bayou Road east of Louisiana 129. You can add 5 miles by continuing to High-

way 565 (between Deer Park and Monterey) or Kemp's Landing, 1.5 miles west of the 565 bridge, on Cross Bayou, which joins Bayou Cocodrie.

3. Launch at Yakey Road on the north end of Red River WMA and explore up and down stream. Yakey Road leads west off Highway 15 a couple miles south of the WMA's northern border.

4. Launch at the ramp at Acme Levee Road and paddle up the bayou, then drift back down. To get to Acme Levee Road, at Shaw on Highway 15 (by WMA headquarters) go west on Highway 910. Turn right onto the gravel levee road in about 2.5 miles. The ramp is at the end of a gravel road ¾ of a mile past the water control structure.

5. In high water, paddle 11 miles from Yakey Road to Acme Levee Road.

Area campgrounds

Red River WMA primitive campground by the Acme Levee Road flood control structure, 318-757-4571.

Maps

For a map of Bayou Cocodrie NWR, call 318-336-7119.
For a map of Red River WMA, call 318-757-4571.

High points

Some of the oldest and least disturbed bottomland hardwood forest along the Mississippi River are found in Bayou Cocodrie National Wildlife Refuge, and junglelike forest covers Red River WMA.

Low points

Little to no current.

Tips

For a simple option, launch at Yakey Road or Acme Levee Road in Red River WMA and explore, returning when finished.

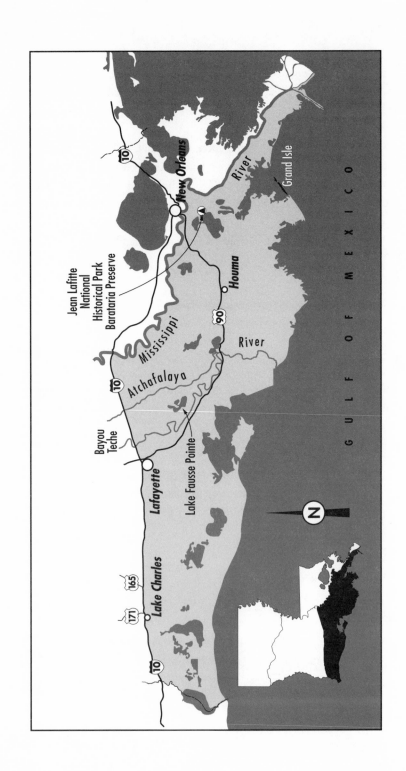

5. South

Bayou Teche

From a geographical standpoint, there are three faces to Cajun country: cypress swamp, marsh, and farmland. In south Louisiana west of the Mississippi River, the greatest swamp lies in or around the Atchafalaya Basin. Marsh, of course, fringes the entire coast. That leaves a huge agricultural swath between Lafayette and Lake Charles, which, while culturally fascinating, doesn't offer much to paddlers. In the flat mudplain between Atchafalaya River on the east and Calcasieu River on the west, bayous squiggle southward like a nest of moccasins. The near-currentless waterways are as muddy as gravy (or roux). That's fitting, I suppose, since they lie in the midst of endless rice fields, and rice and gravy is a southern tradition. One of the prime exceptions is Bayou Teche, which is bordered by live oaks, Cajun châteaus, and parks. Though also muddy and virtually currentless, it is fascinating to paddle. Before I get to that, though, I think it's worthwhile to outline those other bayous.

First, the names. Cajun-country bayous can be hard to pronounce to the non-Cajun: Bayou des Cannes (dez CAN), Bayou Nezpique (NEP-e-kay), Bayou Queue de Tortue (CUE duh tor-TUE), Bayou Plaquemine Brule (plack-MEEN bru-LAY). Tracing out their courses is even more difficult. On a pickup truck sojourn I probably drove 200 miles in several hours checking out more than a dozen bridge crossings. As with a good detective novel, I couldn't stop until all the threads were tied up. On the map, Nezpique—French either for pointed nose, possibly in reference to snapping turtles, or tattooed nose, in reference to an Indian practice of tattooing—seemed to hold the most interest since it's the longest. It heads up west of Ville Platte but doesn't become big enough for a boat until rural Vie Terre Beau Road 10 miles north of Jennings. But there doesn't appear to be any legal public access at this bridge, judging by a bullet-riddled posted sign. The next bridge south, on Highway 97 just north of I-10, has public access provided you've got four-wheel drive to handle the mud under the bridge and don't mind a barge or two on the water. At U.S. 90 at Mermentau 8 river miles south, there's a boat ramp and fishing piers. Here the waterway is called Mermentau River, having absorbed bayous des Cannes and Plaquemine Brule. A wide river with barges and shoreside industry, it meanders south to be joined by Bayou Queue de Tortue before entering Lake Arthur.

Bayou Queue de Tortue, which means tail of a turtle, runs east through deep Cajun country: terraced rice fields, small boxy houses, Cajun music on the radio, a Catholic church and a bar in every town (one sprawling brick bar is named Sin City). There's a dirt landing at Highway 13 north of Kaplan, but the bayou has been channelized into a straight ditch. Highway 91 downstream bears a parish-line sign alerting the public to Acadia Parish's criminal trespass law: You must have written permission to go on anyone's property, and there are no public hunting lands in the parish. You don't have to know French to translate that: Duck-hunt here without permission and you'll get a taste of Cajun cooking, jailhouse-style. Ten miles south of Bayou Queue de Tortue the marsh begins, extending for another 20 miles before it meets the Gulf of Mexico. The marsh is ground that's too wet to plow and too brackish to grow crops. Otherwise I suspect it would be in rice fields too.

Back to the north, Plaquemine Brule, which means burnt persimmon, starts near Opelousas and runs southwest past Crowley before joining Bayou des Cannes and then Nezpique. Bayou des Cannes, which means bayou of canes, is too small even for a pirogue for most of its length, but Bayou Plaquemine Brule is plenty big at Highway 91 west of Crowley, where there's a boat ramp upstream of a pontoon bridge and open dirt banks downstream. The next bridge crossing is Highway 90 at Mermentau about 8 river miles downstream. All told, the best access points are the boat ramps on Mermentau River at Highway 90 at Mermentau and on Bayou Plaquemine Brule at Highway 91 west of Crowley.

It's curious that such featureless countryside produced such colorful Cajun

Drawbridge spans Bayou Teche at Breaux Bridge.

culture, rather like the flat Mississippi Delta gave rise to blues and soul food. Judging by the countless little restaurants I saw, and the radio stations swinging with fiddles and accordions, Cajun culture is alive and well. And the towns are proud of their heritage. Crowley calls itself the rice capital of the world, Gueydan is the duck capital, while Rayne celebrates frogs. (Such titles are debatable: Stuttgart, Arkansas, claims to be both duck and rice capital of the world.)

Now to Bayou Teche. Many people associate Cajun bayous with huge live oaks and cypress trees thick with Spanish moss over rustic châteaus, and Teche fills the bill. It really is lined with huge live oaks, moss-draped cypress, and châteaus both rustic and modern. The 125-mile-long bayou parallels the Atchafalaya River, which lies to the east. Teche stretches from Port Barre (pronounced Barry) just east of Opelousas south past Interstate 10 through such Cajun capitals as Breaux Bridge, St. Martinville, and New Iberia before ending in a network of canals connecting with the lower Atchafalaya River and the Gulf of Mexico. According to Chitimacha Indian legend, the bayou bed was carved out by the death throes of a giant serpent that the tribe fought and defeated in the long-ago. Thus the name Teche, which means snake. When French colonists arrived from the Canadian province of Acadia (now Nova Scotia) after the British took over in 1755, they settled in south Louisiana and turned Bayou Teche into a thoroughfare for transporting timber, furs, sugar cane, and farm produce. A journey from New Orleans to Bayou Teche in those days was quite an adventure.

In the book *Strange True Stories of Louisiana*, a young woman describes such a trip by flatboat in 1795. The group went up the Mississippi River, turned west onto Bayou Plaquemine and proceeded by a circuitous route through the Atchafalaya Swamp to St. Martinville, then an outpost of culture known as Little Paris. "There were many bayous—a labyrinth, as papa said—and Mario had his map at hand showing the way," 17-year-old Francoise Bossier wrote. "Sometimes it seemed impracticable, and it was only by great efforts of our men that we could pass on. One thing is sure—those who traverse those same lakes and bayous today have not the faintest idea of what they were in 1795.

"Great vines hung down from lofty trees that shaded the banks and crossed one another a hundred—a thousand—ways to prevent the boat's passage and retard its progress, as if the devil himself was mixed in it; and frankly, I believe he had something to do with us in that cavern." Once the group arrived at St. Martinville, however, they found counts and countesses, elaborate balls, and much ado over fashion. Civilization was slower to arrive upstream at Breaux Bridge. In 1799, Acadian pioneer Firmin Breaux built a foot bridge across Bayou Teche, and the town of Breaux Bridge sprang up in 1829. The bridge is now a two-lane drawbridge because, though Teche is quite narrow, it's deep enough to accommodate commercial traffic like oilfield vessels and shrimp boats.

The bayou is paralleled for most of its length by highways, dotted with towns, its banks lined with houses, camps, and woods, so put aside thoughts of wilderness such as you might find in the Atchaflaya Swamp. What I didn't expect, when I launched a canoe at Breaux Bridge, was how beautiful the bayou still is, even in an era when urbanization is spreading faster than kudzu.

Probably the most popular canoeing stretch—though few people canoe it—is the 15 miles from Breaux Bridge to St. Martinville, site of the massive Evangeline Oak, named after Henry Wadsworth Longfellow's poem about the Acadian pioneers. There's a town park and boat ramp in both towns. At Breaux Bridge a pleasantly surprising current slides beneath the drawbridge and past gazebos, houses, cottages, and occasional massive live oaks. But it soon dwindles, obliging paddlers to flex their muscles pretty much from then on. Once past Breaux Bridge, woods frequently crowd down to the edge in a tangle of river birch, bald cypress, and non-native Chinese tallow trees. On a weekday there is virtually no boat traffic, but nearly every house on the bayou has a vessel, either johnboat, pirogue, or canoe, and the bayou is no doubt heavily traveled on weekends. At least there are plenty of other places to siphon off some of the pressure, such as nearby Henderson Swamp. Even on a weekday you'll likely pass a few fishermen. One young man angling with a yellow worm said he catches bass up to 4 pounds. A friend of mine told me he used to fish the Teche when he was stationed at New Iberia in the Navy. He used live shad to catch bass around the lock near New Iberia, and caught plenty of 3–4-pound catfish on trotlines. Bayou Teche has elevated levels of fecal coliform, so Department of Environmental Quality officials advise against swimming, but it's considered clean enough to fish.

Halfway between Breaux Bridge and St. Martinville you'll pass Parks, a workaday town with a tumbledown juke joint advertising Jax Beer and a grocery store near the bridge in case you need a snack or soft drink. All along the bayou, woods alternate with houses ranging from mobile homes to brick to white wooden dwellings in the old Cajun style. Even humble shacks often boast enormous live oaks. Elephant ear plants crowd the banks, accentuating the semitropical feel. These plants are not native, and residents often set them out for erosion control, though, as with Chinese tallow trees, they have the noxious habit of crowding out native vegetation and taking over the bank. As you approach St. Martinville you'll pass Magnolia Park, which has a walking track and picnic areas, and Longfellow-Evangeline State Historic Site, which profiles Cajun history, both located off Highway 31 north of St. Martinville. Near the St. Martinville boat ramp, you're likely to be serenaded by local Cajun musicians, who play for a small donation. When we came through we got to hear Lennis J. Romero on the triangle and his brother Ophe J. Romero on accordion singing "Jambalaya."

Bayou Teche might not be wild, much less swift, but it's pleasant enough for easygoing travel, enjoying the Spanish moss, the sultry air, the scent of flowers, perhaps even the sound of a distant accordion. Keep in mind that a canoe trip down Bayou Teche is as much a cultural tour as an outdoor trip, and you'll appreciate it more.

Lake Martin just west of Highway 31 at Parks is another good paddling destination in the area. Protected by the Nature Conservancy, this long, narrow lake is actually an old channel of Teche. It has a bird rookery and some beautiful stands of forest. Area paddler James Proctor tells me it's especially lovely for moonlight paddles—though not in the summer, since the mosquitoes can be unbearable.

Unfortunately, there's not much in the way of camping in the Bayou Teche area. Shoreside camping on the bayou is out of the question since your choice would be between someone's yard and a stretch of muddy, weedy jungle. The nearest public campground is Lake Fausse Pointe State Park, a fine canoe destination in its own right (see below), located 18 miles southeast of St. Martinville. On the other hand, the area abounds in wonderful bed-and-breakfasts, which are more in tune with the Bayou Teche ambience than camping is anyway.

Most paddlers emerge from the water hungry, and this area abounds in fantastic places to eat. Among the most renowned is Mulate's Restaurant in Breaux Bridge. Billed as "the world's most famous Cajun restaurant," the rustic eatery features a blend of traditional and innovative Cajun dishes, typical of restaurants throughout the area. I started with alligator sausage and shrimp gumbo, capped with "Zydeco salad" garnished with andouie sausage, smoked duck, shrimp, and blackened catfish. The music is as spicy as the food. Fiddle, accordion, guitar, and triangle accompany dancers of all ages showing off spirited two-steps, polkas, and waltzes. Prejean's and Randol's restaurants, both in Lafayette, also feature live Cajun music every night, and there are countless other restaurants, from large urban ones to tiny rural shacks with killer gumbo.

There are also plenty of places for those who want to see more of the area's outdoor wonders. Prime among them is Avery Island, 10 miles southwest of New Iberia. The island's low ridge rises like a gator's back from flat sugar cane fields. A toll bridge crosses the bayou onto the island, but a tour of the E. A. McIlhenny Tabasco plant is free. Even outside the sprawling brick factory, the air is piquant with the smell of vinegar and peppers. Workers grind the peppers with salt mined from the salt dome underneath the island. The mash is stored in oak barrels capped with salt, with holes left for gases to escape during fermentation. Three years later, the fermented mash is mixed with vinegar, strained, and bottled. A bottle of Tabasco or one of the other brands made hereabouts is standard equipment for many paddlers. Avery Island is also home to jungle gardens, 200 lush acres of live oaks, cypress, alligators, and egrets. Winding roads and footpaths enable tourists to spend anywhere from half an hour to a day there, with abundant picnicking areas.

A few more of the many other local attractions which might appeal to paddlers: Acadian Village, a restored Cajun village in Lafayette; Vermilionville, a theme park of Cajun culture in Lafayette; Zoo of Acadiana, with everything from gators to giraffes, in Lafayette; Chitimacha Cultural Center in Charenton, showcasing the only Native American tribe in Louisiana still living on ancestral homeland; Live Oak Gardens, surrounding a Victorian mansion near New Iberia;

Shadows-on-the-Teche, an 1834 plantation home with 24 acres of lush gardens on Bayou Teche in downtown New Iberia; Rip Van Winkle Gardens at Jefferson Island on Lake Peigneur, the lake that infamously collapsed when an oil well tapped into an underground salt dome. For full information on touring Cajun country, contact the Lafayette Convention and Visitors Commission, P.O. Box 52066, Lafayette, LA 70505, phone 1-800-346-1958. Ask for the Cajun Country Vacation Guide.

Bayou Teche options

1. Launch at Breaux Bridge and paddle 15 miles to St. Martinville, a good day trip. Each of the two towns has a park downtown on the west side of the bayou with boat ramps and parking areas. You can shorten the trip by taking out, or beginning, at the town of Parks halfway down, or taking out at Magnolia Park a short distance above St. Martinville on the west bank off Highway 31.

Area campgrounds

Lake Fausse Pointe State Park, 18 miles southeast of St. Martinville on West Atchafalaya Protection Levee Road, 1-888-677-7200.

Maps

No topo maps are needed for this straightforward float. A good state highway map or the *Louisiana Atlas & Gazetteer* will suffice.

High points

A grand cultural tour of Cajun country complete with giant live oaks, rustic châteaus, and perhaps even the sound of a distant accordion or scent of fine cuisine.

Low points

Little or no current.

Tips

Don't go in hot weather.

Lake Fausse Pointe

Lake Fausse Pointe State Park, located on the western edge of the Atchafalaya Basin, is an excellent place to sample the south Louisiana swamp environment. The Fausse Pointe area used to be part of the Atchafalaya Swamp when it sprawled between the west bank of the Mississippi River and the east bank of Bayou Teche, but man-made levees cut the lake off from the Atchafalaya floodplain. There's still a huge area to explore, from small sloughs to open lake. The 6,000-acre park has rental canoes and canoe-in campsites, not to mention rustic cabins built over the water with large screened porches. A park map shows area waterways for a variety of day-trip options.

The very remoteness of the park recommends it. To get there, start in St. Martinville and go east on Louisiana 96. State park signs lead you on a winding, 18-mile route through Coteau Holmes and over Bayou Portage onto the West Atchafalaya levee road. After you've driven several miles down the paved but bumpy levee road, glance right for a scenic view of the lake. I happened to be there at sunset and found myself staring across the lake to a sky painted with stunning reds. Camphouses, boats, and moss-hung trees formed a silhouetted image of pure Louisiana.

At the park, there are several camping options: the campground, cabins, and backcountry sites accessible only by foot and/or canoe. Campsites are scattered along the canoe trails at distances ranging from 1 to 3.3 miles from the boat ramp. There are also sites reached only on foot for backpackers. The variety in campsites reflects the variety of experiences available at this fine park. Prime among them are the marked, color-coded canoe trails ranging from 4.5 to 7 miles. The park offers regular guided canoe trips and trail hikes. Whether you go on a guided tour or on your own, be sure and get a map at the entry station.

When you paddle out of the short canal where the ramp is located, you can go left or right. If you go right, you'll soon pass the rental cabins. I was paddling in a cold winter rain when I saw them perched out over the bayou, rain rapping their tin roofs, smoke rising from metal stovepipes. I could hear voices, no doubt from contented campers sitting on screened porches sipping hot coffee. I confess I was envious. Just past the cabins you can continue straight on for the longer route, or turn right for the shorter. Either way, the waterways through the area tend to be long and straight, which doesn't make for the most interesting canoeing, despite the attractive woodland scenery. To enjoy this kind of pad-

Buildings reach out over bayou at Lake Fausse Pointe State Park.

dling, it definitely helps to know a correction stroke so you don't have to switch sides with your paddle all the time. Just get into a steady gait, about like walking. If you're not used to flatwater paddling, the 4.5-mile loop may be sufficient for a day's outing. Otherwise, the 7-miler will make a decent day trip. If you have a sea kayak you can easily go farther afield. The possibilities for detours are enormous. The irregularly shaped lake spans 24 square miles and is surrounded by many more miles of swamp. The canoe trails don't begin to cover the possible routes in this swamp. Canals and bayous branch off every which way, so if you venture off the marked canoe trails, either take a quad map or pay special attention to where you're going. The lake also contains mud flats which can slow progress or even require detours in low water. At lunchtime stop on the bank or at one of the unoccupied backcountry campsites, which have small docks, tables, and fire rings. The isolation of such spots is refreshing. One of the most interesting campsites is Highland Waters, on an island shaded by giant live oaks with a good view of the lake.

Another day trip is possible just down the road in the adjacent Atchafalaya Swamp; I mention it here because it's so close to the park. Follow the levee road just south of the park entrance and turn left; go 3.6 miles to Sandy Cove Landing, which provides access to a canal known as Fausse Pointe Cut. Paddle 2 miles south to find a portage trail on the east side just across from another canal. The trail leads to Bayou Gravenburg, a scenic backwater. Or continue 2.5 miles down the canal to an opening on the left that leads to Buffalo Cove, accessible only in high water. A channel links Gravenburg and Buffalo Cove if there's enough water. Jackass Bay and Charenton are applicable quad maps.

Lake Fausse Pointe park has three hiking trails ranging from 3/4 mile to more than 3, and they are well worth hiking to get a different perspective of this intriguing environment. As you walk along Lake Fausse Pointe and parallel shallow, muddy bayous through the woods, the sense of wildness is palpable. This place reminds me of Baiyer River Bird Sanctuary in Papua New Guinea, which I visited in 1981. I had just completed an arduous two weeks in the jungle, so the sanctuary seemed like paradise: cabins and marked trails in the rain forest, a blend of the wild and the barely civilized. Here at Lake Fausse Pointe there is also wildness all around, yet the park likewise has trails and cabins. While the paddling isn't perfect, I consider this park one of the finest outdoor destinations in Louisiana.

Lake Fausse Pointe options

1. Launch at park boat ramp and follow color-coded marked trails, using park map for reference. The inner loop is 4.5 miles long, the outer loop 7 miles. These can be extended indefinitely by exploring adjacent waterways.

Area campgrounds

Lake Fausse Pointe State Park, 18 miles southeast of St. Martinville on West Atchafalaya Protection Levee Road.

Maps

Simple canoe trail map is available at the park office or by calling 1-888-677-7200.

U.S.G.S. quad maps of the area are Loreauville, Jackass Bay, Jeanerette, and Charenton. Call 1-888-ASK-USGS.

Outfitters

Lake Fausse Pointe State Park rents canoes and provides periodic guided canoe trips.

High points

A picture-perfect swamp setting with everything from rental cabins over the bayou to campsites accessible only by foot or boat.

Low points

Long, straight stretches can make for tedious paddling.

Tips

Try the hiking-biking paths as well as the canoe trails.

Atchafalaya River

The Atchafalaya Basin merits a guidebook all to itself. This huge semi-wilderness is the largest river basin swamp in North America. It embodies what many people expect from Louisiana wildlands: an intricate maze of waterways, wildlife ranging from alligators to bears to bald eagles, Cajuns hunting gators and brewing strong coffee, oilfield equipment, and soul-stilling cypress forests. The paddling possibilities are endless. To simplify things, I'm dividing the topic into two categories: the river and the swamp. While a trip down the Atchafalaya River may include forays into the surrounding swamp, and a trip through Atchafalaya Swamp may include a portion of the river, generally speaking a river trip and a swamp trip are two different experiences and require different planning strategies. While some paddlers may shrink from tackling a river the size of the Atchafalaya, it offers wide views, the relative freedom from disturbances by motorboat wakes (due to its size), and the sense of isolation in knowing you are flanked on both sides by miles of roadless forest.

The Atchafalaya was not always the mighty river it is now. When the first Europeans arrived, it was a logjammed distributary, or offshoot, of the Mississippi, just below the mouth of the Red River. The Red flowed into the top half of a big west-sweeping Mississippi River bend, and the Atchafalaya flowed out of the lower half. But neither nature nor humans could let things be. In 1831 Captain Henry Shreve, of Shreveport fame, dredged a shortcut across the neck of the bend. The upper part silted up, and the Red began running directly into the Atchafalaya. The Mississippi continued to spill water into the lower half of the bend, now known as Old River, and thence the Atchafalaya. However, that flow was stifled by a 30-mile-long logjam in the upper Atchafalaya. In 1839, Louisiana officials managed to break up the jam, which made the Atchafalaya grow even bigger—too big. Since it offered Mississippi River water a 142-mile route to the sea instead of the 315 it traveled past New Orleans, the Atchafalaya seemed destined to become the Mississippi, leaving Baton Rouge and New Orleans on an estuary. In 1954, Congress authorized the U.S. Army Corps of Engineers to prevent that from happening. Several decades and hundreds of millions of dollars later, we have an outlet channel, a dam, a power plant, two flood control structures, and a navigational lock between the Mississippi and the Atchafalaya. During normal flows, the structures are designed to keep too much water from going down the Atchafalaya, but during flood time they're designed to keep too much from going down the Mississippi. The levees at New Orleans can handle 1.25 million cubic feet of water, but a big flood can exceed that considerably, so the Atchafalaya River serves as a bleeder valve during flood time. To contain those waters, the Corps erected levees on both sides of the Atchafalaya River. The Atchafalaya Basin Floodway is a stretch of uninhabited semi-wilderness roughly 100 miles long by 15 miles wide, split down the middle by the now-mighty Atchafalaya, a Native American word for "Long River."

The river begins above Simmesport and is a wide, levee-bordered corridor until just above Interstate 10, where it splits. The main stem continues southeast, while a large branch loops to the southwest. If you've ever driven across the Atchafalaya Swamp on I-10 from Baton Rouge to Lafayette, you've first crossed an enormous waterway called Whiskey Bay, then a slightly smaller one, which a sign identifies as the Atchafalaya River. Whiskey Bay is actually the main Atchafalaya River. What the sign calls the Atchafalaya is the offshoot, called Little Atchafalaya on maps; it rejoins the main river below I-10.

Roads that parallel the river end at I-10 on the east side and at Butte La Rose 5 miles south of I-10 on the west. From there south for many a mile is nothing but swamp. That makes Butte La Rose a prime jumping-off spot for a downriver trip. The next takeout, 34 miles south, is the Myette Point boat ramp on the west bank near Baldwin. This is an excellent three-day trip, longer if you want to explore side bayous. This stretch takes you through the middle of the basin, far from any road, as well as through the 26,300-acre Attakapas Wildlife Management Area. Floats starting above Butte La Rose are possible as well, with boat ramps on both sides of the main river allowing several possibilities. The Atchafalaya Basin map makes planning easy.

The current varies widely in the river according to how much water is being released from the Red and the Mississippi through flood control structures. In low water, such as late summer and fall, the river may be barely moving. In high water, such as late winter and spring, it's rolling, and paddlers should use special caution due to unpredictable currents, undertows, and larger-than-usual wakes thrown by barges battling the current. River stages are published in various newspapers in the region. You can also call the U.S. Fish and Wildlife Service in New Orleans, 504-646-7555, or check the website http://southeastlouisiana. fws.gov/atchafalaya.html. Low-water conditions make for easier camping since mudflats and beaches are sometimes exposed. Be careful to avoid posted property or the proximity of camps. In high water you may have to paddle into flooded woods to find high ground.

As you paddle down Little Atchafalaya, keep a lookout for alligators. If you don't watch carefully, they'll slip away before you know they're there. Scan the banks and the water far ahead. Binoculars help. That log several hundred yards downstream may be a gator, as may be that knobby protrusion in mid-river.

Bayou L'Embarras branches off to the southeast 8 miles below Butte La Rose. This bayou provides an optional route, bypassing the main river, but involves long, straight, channelized stretches. About 5 miles below the entrance to Bayou L'Embarras, the Little Atchafalaya merges with the main Atchafalaya, announced by a stiffening breeze and wide vistas. Entry onto the big river in a canoe is a thrill. You're in the presence of power as well as natural beauty. The Little Atchafalaya may have seemed big until now, but compared to the main river it's a cozy little creek. The waterways meet at a long, round-tipped peninsula, and it's wise to look both ways for towboats pushing barges up or down the channel. As you float down the river, continue to glance occasionally to the rear, because a barge can slide up swiftly and soundlessly. You'll also see fishermen, outdoorsmen heading to their hunting camps, and oilfield crewboats—aluminum johnboats with small cabins. There are nearly as many crewboats as alligators in the basin. On the Little Atchafalaya, motorboats typically throttle down to minimize their wake when they pass. Wake is not much of an issue on the larger Atchafalaya since it's so wide the effects are dissipated. Unlike the Little Atchafalaya, the main river has a bit of a current even in drought conditions. You can stop paddling and drift like Huck Finn and Tom Sawyer if you choose.

Steve Cox steers a canoe from Little Atchafalaya onto main Atchafalaya as a barge glides down the river.

Jakes Bayou comes in from the east just below the mouth of Little Atchafalaya, and Bayou Sorrel appears on the east side about 5 miles farther down. Sorrel may not look large, but don't be surprised to see a line of barges emerge with the hum of engines. Unless they're fighting a stiff current, towboats throw swells rather than waves and are fairly easily handled even by a canoe, especially if you face the biggest swells at a quartering angle. Things are a bit more complicated when two tows meet. Be sure not to get between them, of course, but even if you stay well to the outside, the conflicting wakes create turbulent water that can toss a canoe in a crosshatch of swells. A canoe is more seaworthy than most people think, though, and can bounce over these waves like a truck on a washboarded gravel road. I do like to watch the big tows. The barges slide by with surprising quietness, gently hissing against the water. Behind them stands the towboat, its wheelhouse towering over all, its screws churning the water with a deep hum and a whiff of diesel.

Occasional camphouses stand on the banks, but the view is mainly willow thickets. You can get out of sight to camp if you find a stand of leaning willows shading a long stretch of beach. Though there are virtually no sandbars, camping can be enjoyable on the big river. A breeze minimizes the mosquitoes, and the views are grand. Such places form a postcard scene, except you have mud instead of sand, brown water instead of blue, willows instead of palms. As you eat supper, miles from any road, the sun sets across the river and the moon poses like a bride, with the evening star serving as train-bearer. Fish roll, owls hoot, herons squawk, stars appear. Who needs palm trees, anyway?

About 9 miles below Bayou Sorrel, the Atchafayala enters Attakapas WMA. For the rest of the way to Myette Point you'll be mainly in the WMA. A primitive campground is located on the east bank about 4.5 miles below the WMA boundary, just past an oilfield canal. Accessible only by boat, it consists of a grassy clearing on a high bank, quite pleasant except for mosquitoes that shelter there from the wind. Hog sign is everywhere, and you're likely to hear them crashing through the woods, stomping and grunting.

Attakapas (a-tak-a-POH) was the name of the Indian tribe that inhabited the area. It means man-eater, supposedly because the tribe was cannibalistic. There is evidence that south Louisiana Indians ate human flesh. One 1782 first-person account tells the story of a young Frenchwoman emigrating to America whose ship was attacked by Indians off the mouth of the Mississippi River. She was taken ashore and tied to a stake. "I recall one thing: that is, having seen those savages eat human flesh, the members of a child—at least it seemed so," she wrote in a letter recorded in *Strange True Stories of Louisiana*. The Indians spared her because she was plump, so they could feed her to the chief. However, one impatient brave took his knife and sliced a strip of flesh from the woman's right thigh. She passed out, and revived later to discover soldiers had gotten word of the capture and attacked the Indians. She was rescued but remained a cripple and died three years later.

To get a peek into the swamp, paddle up the oil canal just upriver from the campground on the east side. It's liable to be infested with baby alligators, evident even in daylight. They show little fear, floating on the surface and staring with round yellow eyes slitted by black diamond pupils. Night is the best time to look for wildlife. You can feel the swamp come alive as darkness falls. A good method for spotting creatures is for the stern person to paddle silently while the bow person holds a light. To move silently, don't remove the paddle from the water at the end of the stroke. Slice the blade edge, not the round shaft, gently forward. Thousands of insects will orbit the bowman's light, diving into the boat and dying with a fluttering of wings that sound like a small motor. Raccoons forage along the water's edge. As you ease up, they'll stare at the light suspiciously,

Ryan Hayes of New Iberia keeps a paddle between himself and a 7-foot alligator he caught during gator season.

then make a low, grunting bark and dart up the slope. A strange white shape sliding from the water onto the mud bank and back turns out to be a baby gator feeding on insects. With each assault it turns on its side to get a good bite, revealing its white underside. You can maneuver up beside it until your bow nudges the mud. The reptile may hover, its little legs out to the side. If you're quiet, you can slip your paddle up under its belly. The gator will wriggle out of the way, look back and then, tired of the game, angle downward and disappear into the murk.

Fall is gator hunting season, and during the day you may notice airboats zooming downriver, stopping periodically at the bank. If you hear gunshots, it's probably gator-hunters. We stopped to talk with a pair who had a 7-footer wrapped in burlap in the boat. When I saw it move, I told the man his gator was alive. He claimed it was nerves, but when he reached to lift it, those nerves came to life in the form of snapping jaws and almost took his hand off. He'd already put one .22-magnum bullet behind the eyes; this specimen required another. To catch gators, hunters tie large hooks to limbs and bait them with chickens. When a gator rises to take the bait, it gets hooked. The method isn't foolproof: Some gators get off. Hunters process the hides or deliver the gators unskinned to a processing plant.

Trips such as an Atchafalaya River float often prompt warnings from well-meaning friends and officials. Among the dangers I've been warned about, in addition to gators, barges, and currents, are tough Cajuns who don't like trespassers or outsiders. I'm sure there are some, but the ones I've met are more likely to kill you with kindness. As we paddled, folks waved to us from camps or stopped their boats to chat. At one camp, a Cajun working on a chainsaw shouted, "Want some coffee?" We turned toward shore, naturally. The man, who kept a rifle in a leather scabbard close at hand, and his burly, bearded partner took a break from their work to give us a tour of their camphouse and make a pot of coffee. We sat outside, sipped the strong brew, and talked about hunting, fishing, and politics.

Myette Point is about 2.5 miles below the WMA campground, west of the main river. Take the channel to the right, cross the entrance to West Grand Lake, which stretches northwest, and continue southwest along a tree-lined channel. The ramp is off to the left less than a mile from the river. You'll see the high-rising levee and parking area.

The trip can be extended by continuing beyond Myette Point 19 miles to Morgan City. Below Myette Point the river widens into Grand Lake, about 3 miles long and a mile wide. Then Sixmile Lake branches off to the south while the slightly smaller river channel, Cypress Pass, angles off to the southeast. Below Cypress Pass the river splits around several islands before reaching Morgan City. There are boat ramps on Sixmile Lake, at Wilson's Landing 5 miles above Morgan City, and at Morgan City. The Louisiana Geological Survey map of the Atchafalaya Basin shows all the ramps as well as waterways, levees, and roads. Below Morgan City the river continues to split and widen as it enters marsh country and finally empties into Atchafalaya Bay.

Atchafalaya River options

1. For a 3-day trip, launch at Butte La Rose and paddle 34 miles to Myette Point. Butte La Rose is located 5 miles south of I-10 on the west side of Little Atchafalaya River, which runs into the Atchafalaya. Myette Point is off Martin Ridge Road on the west side of the Atchafalaya River. To get there, follow Highway 87 south of Baldwin and turn left on Martin Ridge Road. Pass WMA headquarters, turn right, and cross the levee to get to the state launch site.

2. Continue south from Myette Point to Morgan City, 19 miles. There are boat ramps along the way on Sixmile Lake, at Wilson's Landing 5 miles above Morgan City, and at Morgan City.

Area campgrounds

Attakapas WMA primitive camping area, accessible only by boat, on the east side of the river 2.5 miles north of Myette Point, 337-948-0255.

Maps

The Louisiana Geological Survey has a full-color map of the Atchafalaya Basin, published in 2000. On one side of the map is a full-color satellite image. The other side highlights such features as boat landings (of which there are many), levees, bayous, lakes, and canals. The map is a product of the Atchafalaya Basin Program of the Louisiana Department of Natural Resources and sponsored by the Louisiana Wildlife Federation and the Sierra Club. Maps are $9 folded, $12 rolled. To order, call 225-578-8590. Or send a check, including $2.75 shipping, to Louisiana Geological Survey, Baton Rouge, LA 70893.

A map of Attakapas WMA is available from the Louisiana Department of Wildlife, Fisheries, and Parks by calling 337-948-0255. It's handy for exploring the WMA.

High points

Magnificent vistas and a real sense of adventure on a Huck Finn–style downriver journey.

Low points

Without sandbars, camping conditions are primitive on the muddy, woodschoked river.

Tips

Check behind you often for the silent approach of barges.

Atchafalaya Swamp

The Atchafalaya Swamp is Louisiana's showpiece, a vast area of natural beauty on a par with the Everglades or the Okefenokee. Covering well over half a million acres, it stretches some 100 miles from Simmesport to the Gulf of Mexico in a strip roughly 15 miles or more wide. And that doesn't take into account adjacent wetlands like Henderson Swamp, Lake Fausse Pointe, and Lake Verret. There are nice chunks of public land in the basin, including Atchafalaya National Wildlife Refuge and nearby Sherburne and Indian Bayou Wildlife Management Areas north of Interstate 10, Attakapas WMA northeast of Franklin and, offshore, Marsh Island Wildlife Refuge and Atchafalaya Delta WMA. A look at the Louisiana Geological Survey full-color satellite image of the basin vividly illustrates the scope of this nature-rich area. On both sides lie pale, chopped-up blocks indicating farmland and urban development. But the swamp itself is mile upon mile of deep green.

The satellite image also hints at some of the problems with the basin. It's raked by oilfield canals and levees that have altered the natural flows and patterns of the swamp, fostering erosion, siltation, stagnation, and saltwater intrusion from the Gulf. Extensive logging has removed most of the old-growth cypress that once sheltered these green mansions. The Atchafalaya was dying the same sort of strangulated death as the Everglades when, in 1998, numerous government agencies joined to create the Atchafalaya Basin Program in hopes of salvaging and promoting this unparalleled natural resource. The U.S. Army Corps of Engineers bought 50,000 acres of old-growth cypress and tupelo forest to increase the amount of public lands and is buying environmental easements on 338,000 acres to restrict development such as agriculture and urbanization. Plans call for building a visitor center on I-10 north of Butte La Rose, interpretive areas, more parks, upgraded boat ramps, boat trails, and picnic areas throughout the basin. Congress authorized $250 million for the project.

From the paddler's viewpoint, the Atchfalaya is magnificent, yet flawed. Though scenic and remote, it's not truly wild. The bayous are heavily traveled by motorboats, especially on weekends during peak fishing and hunting seasons. Oil crews tend growling equipment. Posted signs sprout from tree trunks like poison ivy. Scrawny willow thickets and young cypress have replaced much of the mature hardwood forest that once dominated. As with so much of Louisiana, it's necessary to adjust expectations. Expect the occasional motorboat or even barge, the posted signs in remotest backwaters, the chug of distant oilfield equipment, the stumps of once-huge trees—all that is part of the package. Consider it the price to pay for camping miles from any road, for finding your way down a labyrinth of remote and lonely sloughs, for up-close encounters with wildlife, and for a tour of Cajun culture at its most authentic.

While some impressive forests remain in the Atchafalaya Basin, much of it has been logged, with cypress trees like this one reduced to stumps.

Possibilities are vast for planning your own sojourn, whether for a day, three days, or longer. Probably the simplest way to get acquainted with the area is at one of the tracts of public lands that have campgrounds, taking day trips on nearby waters. The 11,780-acre Sherburne WMA and adjoining 15,220-acre Atchafalaya NWR off Highway 975 north of I-10 on the east side of the Atchafalaya River provide plenty of room to explore. Sherburne has two primitive camping areas and several scenic bayous. The campground on Highway 975 at the north end by the shooting range borders Bayou Close and Big Alabama Bayou, both of which are canoeable. You can launch from the campground. There's also a ramp on the south end of Big Alabama Bayou on Landing Road north of Happytown Road, which runs east from Highway 975 some 5 miles north of I-10. Start by getting a map of the WMA along with the Louisiana Geological Survey map of the Atchafalaya Basin. Stay in a campground and explore the bayous with day trips.

Across the river from Sherburne is 15,610-acre Indian Bayou WMA, operated by the Corps of Engineers. There are no campgrounds in the WMA, but Corps officials tell me there is a possible day trip from Highway 190 to I-10. Launch at Lower Courtableu boat ramp on the east side of the levee just south of Highway

190 some 6 miles west of Krotz Springs. Follow the straight manmade canal south 4 miles until it turns into Bayou Fordoche. Continue southeast some 10 miles to Henderson Lake. The bayou branches occasionally, but the main channel reportedly isn't hard to find and usually contains south-flowing current. Hug the east shore of the lake for 3 miles to the cut-through east to Pelba boat ramp off I-10 by the rest area. Bayou Fordoche runs right through Indian Bayou WMA, passing through cypress-tupelo bottomlands backed by ridges with oak, ash, bitter pecan, and cottonwood. Contact the Corps office in Port Barre (see phone number below) for advice and map.

There are numerous boat ramps throughout the basin from which to make other day trips as well. The Louisiana Geological Survey map of the basin shows most of them and is an invaluable tool for exploration. As an example, launch at the Bayou Pigeon boat ramp on the east side of the swamp, cross the Intracoastal Waterway, paddle west down Bayou Pigeon for about 2.5 miles, turn north onto a small slough, paddle a mile or so north and west until the slough widens into small lake, portage over the narrow high ground on the west side of the lake onto an oilfield canal, paddle north, then turn east on a bayou to get back to the Intracoastal Waterway. Go right to return to the ramp.

Now, I must confess I came up with that itinerary not by careful advance planning but by making my route as I went. Whether you're paddling for a day or a week, that's the method I recommend. If you chart a detailed itinerary in advance, you leave out one of the most attractive aspects of swamp canoeing: exploring. The main information to start with is where you plan to launch, where to take out (often the same place), and how much time you have in between. Then, equipped with the map, compass, and possibly a GPS, take off. If a channel appeals to you, take it. If you don't like the one you're on, find another. There's plenty that a map can't tell you. What looks like a good channel on a map may turn out to be a motorboat alley. What appears to be too small to notice may be an ideal canoe route.

On the evening before the aforementioned day trip, we camped near the ramp, and the lonely wall of cypress jungle looming to the west made me think of the Congo. Under a candy-red sunset slipping into gunmetal-blue clouds, the forest steamed with mist on the far side of the intracoastal canal. Eddie McCalip and I set out for some night paddling, leaving Walter Neil Ferguson to fish from the boat ramp. Crossing the wide canal, we steered down Bayou Pigeon, flanked by forest turning black in the gloomy dusk. Except for a solitary night fisherman

An old canal leads bewitchingly into the interior of Attakapas Wildlife Management Area.

motoring past, the swamp was deserted. Barred owls sounded their nuthouse cries. As night became complete, mosquitoes forced us to spray down with repellent. After a couple miles of leisurely paddling, we decided to call it a night. At the ramp, Walter Neil had lost a lure to a fish and plugged a snake with his pistol. Despite his bottle of repellent, he assured us that mosquitoes were in the very act of lifting him into the air just before we arrived. We turned in to a steambath night with mosquitoes singing at the tent doors.

In contrast with the quiet evening, at dawn a line of motorboats was massed at the ramp. Just getting across the Intracoastal Waterway, with barges bearing down on us, was unsettling. As motorboats roared past us, all we wanted to do was find some quiet slough to escape into. We took the first one we came to. Though unable to locate this slough on the map—which was a smaller, earlier version than the 2000 one—we turned north onto it. As the woods closed behind us, we left the world of motorboats and entered the forest primeval. Like a forest guardian, a cottonmouth snake swam toward us with head raised high. Walter Neil, bemoaning the fact that he had left his pistol in the truck, raised his paddle in preparation for mortal combat. But the snake angled away from us, disappearing under the murky water. Cypress trees draped with Spanish moss arched over our tiny waterway. Sunlight filtered through the branches, barely touching us. A dip of the paddle showed this slough to be scarcely 18 inches deep; it was just wide enough to allow our canoe and pirogue to travel single file. Cranes, egrets, and herons took flight when they detected our presence. A massive owl a good 2½ feet tall flew up to a limb to watch us. Sloughs branched off to the right and the left. I checked my compass. We were turning west. We paddled watchfully. Another slough branched off to the right; compass-check again. Up ahead, more turnoffs. Still unable to locate any of this on the map, I reached up and nonchalantly snapped a limb. "You're breaking that so you can find your way back—not to let your boat through—aren't you?" Walter Neil said. I nodded. Since I was the one with the map and compass, he did not seem very reassured. I immediately heard him and Eddie start breaking twigs. The water fanned out into a green lake, covered with weeds. Our boats hissing as they glided over the half-inch thick layer, we seemed to be paddling through emerald snow. After poking around the shallow lake, I noticed how everything looked the same. I tore a strip off my red bandanna and hung it from a limb. At least we would know how to get back to the slough we came in on. When Eddie and Walter Neil spotted some high ground, we decided to stretch our legs and have a snack. On the other side of the little rise I spotted what looked like a bayou. A check with our map revealed it apparently to be an abandoned oilfield canal running north and south. What the heck? We took it, marking our entry point well. We followed the narrow canal north, then turned east on a small bayou, eventually connecting with a passage that carried us back to the intracoastal canal. From there it was a short jaunt to the boat landing. It was 2 P.M. when we got back. We had covered an estimated 8 miles in 7 hours of leisurely paddling.

Despite the snapped twigs and strip of bandanna, finding our way through wasn't difficult. We started at a north-south levee, went west, then north, so it stood to reason that to get back we'd have to go east, and there were waterways to oblige us. It doesn't take an expert in orienteering to figure that out. Even so, exploring the swamp is trickier on a day trip than on a multiday one. On the latter, since you have gear, food, and water, it's no big deal if you lose your bearings for a while; you'll regain them eventually. But getting lost on a day trip, when you not only lack gear but are probably expected back home by dark, can be unpleasant.

Route options are even greater on a multiday trip. For a sample three-day trip, launch at the Grand River boat ramp south of Ramah, paddle a short distance north on Bayou Maringouin, take the first slough to the west, work your way 2 miles northwest through a dead cypress lake into Upper Flat Lake, explore the lake if you choose, then go about 2 miles to the southeast end where a slough flows out, and follow it a mile or so back to Upper Grand River, towing if the water's too shallow. Turn west onto Upper Grand River, paddle about 3.5 miles, turn south onto Little Tensas Bayou, and go 2.5 miles to the Atchafalaya River. Float 2 miles south, then turn east onto Jakes Bayou, paddle 5 miles to Bayou Sorrel, turn left and paddle 6 miles to Grand River, which parallels the levee. Turn north and paddle 6 miles back to the Grand River boat ramp. The trip totals about 30 miles.

Again, I arrived at this route in hindsight, not through advance planning. The route we took was actually longer. Scott Williams and I inadvertently launched on the north side of I-10 at Ramah, rather than on the south side on Bayou Maringouin as we had intended. As a result, we wound up paddling down a canal 2 miles west under the Interstate—a surreal experience, with huge bridge supports above us marching into the distance to the thunder of traffic—then nearly 10 miles south on a work canal to reach Upper Grand River. Though the work canal was monotonous—a straight ditch lined with willows—it was also deserted and backed by rich swamp. We saw just one motorboat on it. At camp we hiked warily through the woods to a dry lake bed where the mud was riddled with tracks of deer, birds, opossums, and raccoons. The setting sun reddened the cypress trees with their righteous beards of Spanish moss. Nearby, white egrets roosted in stubby trees for the night. Walking back, we passed an auburn beaver sliding calmly into the canal. A browsing armadillo waddled up and sniffed my boot before dashing off in belated fright. After supper we settled back by the campfire for some serious yarning. Owls hooted periodically as if objecting to our exaggerations.

There's something inexpressibly sad about the smell of willows and mud. It's the odor of lonely places more hospitable to reptiles than men. It gets in your marrow and makes you think about how your own bones are going to settle in the mud someday. But morning in the swamp is glorious: blue, green and gold. The light is soft and blurry as you paddle away from camp, still wearing a long-sleeved shirt against the chill. But the day heats up, and the Louisiana sun gets a bit unfriendly, even in late fall. We struck Upper Grand River and turned right, brooking a slight current a few miles till we reached the big, handsome Atchafalaya River, which was growling with barges and lonely with cypress and willow forest. Two miles down it we swung east into narrow Jakes Bayou, where trees leaned over to groom themselves in the smoky mirror of the water. We camped on a high sandbar and, after supper, paddled down the moonlit surface as owls coughed and mumbled from their lofts like winos in a flophouse.

Next day we struck Bayou Sorrel, and the swamp changed character. Oil wells, crew boats, camps, and fishermen replaced the lonely vistas we had been cherishing. This was like a subdivision, with camps instead of houses, motorboats instead of cars. We turned north on the intracoastal canal, made camp in the woods, and paddled on to Maringouin Bayou the next day. It was then that we turned up a narrow slough and entered first a ghostly lake of cypress stumps, then Upper Flat Lake, which was full of alligators. None of the gators was big—none that we saw anyway—but they showed no fear of us. The lake was ringed by posted signs, though, not a good place to camp.

Back on Upper Grand River, we stopped on a sandbar to stretch our legs. "You know this is posted," said an old Cajun from his motorboat. "I just thought I'd keep you from getting into trouble. It's all posted now. There's a few pieces of state land." Posted land can be a problem for paddlers wanting to camp. Scott and I returned to Maringouin Bayou and made camp. Next day we continued north on the bayou, which paralleled the swamp's eastern levee. It was a pretty float but, on a Friday, chockful of fishermen. We ended up back at Ramah. From this roundabout, make-it-up-as-you-go journey, I came up with the sample 3-day route outlined above. For my recommended route, I omit the long canal stretches, though they had their appeal.

The best time to canoe the swamp is spring and fall. Summer is brutally hot, rife with mosquitoes and prone to thunderstorms. Winter, in addition to the chances of cold rain and raw wind, is crawling with deer hunters. Prime paddling times are from mid-February through April (or May in a mild year), and late September through November. In late winter and early spring, rain is fairly frequent, and high water increases opportunities for exploring the swamp. Fall weather tends to be fine—days in the 70s, nights in the 40s are typical—and low water levels make it easier to find your way. I personally favor fall just because it's so pleasant and trouble-free. Crisp, campfire nights and blue-sky days with sweet breezes make for enticing conditions. Whenever you go, take insect repellent, sunscreen, a wide-brimmed hat, and lots of drinking water. Pack warm clothes in fall, winter, and spring because thick swamp mist can make even mild temperatures feel bone-chilling. Canoes and sea kayaks are the best vessels for the

Atchafalaya. Sea kayaks can easily handle the big-water conditions found on the main river and some of the lakes, though it's a chore getting in and out of them in the mud. Canoes can handle nearly all conditions except big lakes in high wind.

There are more controlled ways to see the swamp than charting your own route. The Atchafalaya Basin Program is developing a canoe trail system with downloadable maps, trip descriptions, and GPS coordinates. The Department of Natural Resources website, www.dnr.state.la.us/sec/atchafalaya, is a source of current information, or call 225-219-7516. Outfitters offer guided trips into the swamp in canoes, pontoon boats, and airboats. I took a motorboat tour when visiting Cajun country on a bed-and-breakfast vacation once. Our guide carried four of us out in a 20-foot aluminum skiff for a day trip. He showed us stands of virgin cypress, narrow bayous glittering with buttonbush blossoms and swamp lilies, swallowtail kites and black-crowned night herons swooping among tree limbs draped with Spanish moss. My favorite part was when rain interrupted our outing and he invited us into his houseboat for coffee. He brewed Cafe du Monde chicory coffee in a white enamel French drip pot and served it in big yellow enamel mugs. We sipped the black brew as rain drummed on the roof and speckled the bayou outside while Catahoula hounds dozed at our feet and our guide held forth on such subjects as the origins of Cajun and Zydeco music and how to make gumbo. It wasn't canoeing, but it would do.

Atchafalaya Swamp options

1. For a sample chart-your-own day trip: Launch at boat ramp at Bayou Pigeon, cross Intracoastal Waterway, paddle west down Bayou Pigeon for about 2.5 miles, turn north onto small slough, paddle 1 mile north and west until slough widens into small lake, portage over west side of lake to oilfield canal, paddle 1 mile north, then turn east on bayou and follow back to Intracoastal Waterway, turn right and return to ramp. About 8 miles total.

2. For a sample 3-day trip: Launch at Grand River boat ramp south of Ramah, paddle short distance north on Bayou Maringouin, take first slough to the west, work your way 2 miles northwest through dead cypress lake onto Upper Flat Lake, explore lake, then go about 2 miles to southeast end and follow slough a mile or so southeast to Upper Grand River, towing if necessary. Turn west on Upper Grand River, paddle about 3.5 miles, turn south onto Little Ten-

sas Bayou, follow 2.5 miles to Atchafalaya River, float 2 miles south, turn east onto Jakes Bayou, paddle 5 miles to Bayou Sorrel, turn left and paddle 6 miles to Grand River, which parallels levee. Turn north and paddle 6 miles back to Grand River boat ramp. Total trip approximately 30 miles.

3. For current information on Department of Natural Resources Atchafalaya Basin Program canoe trails, call 225-219-7516.

Outfitters

Pack and Paddle, Lafayette, 337-232-5854.
Louisiana Outfitters, Lafayette, 337-988-9090.

Area campgrounds

Sherburne WMA, Highway 975 southeast of Krotz Springs north of I-10 on east side of Atchafalaya River, has two primitive camping areas off Highway 975, 337-948-0255.

Lake Fausse Pointe State Park, 5400 Levee Road, 18 miles southeast of St. Martinville. In addition to developed and primitive campsites, park has canoe-in-only sites. From St. Martinville, take Louisiana 96 to La. 679, then to La. 3083. Turn right onto Levee Road and go 7 miles. 1-888-677-7200.

Maps

Louisiana Geological Survey maps of the Atchafalaya Basin cost $9 folded, $12 rolled. To order, call 225-578-8590. Or send a check, including $2.75 shipping, to Louisiana Geological Survey, Baton Rouge, LA 70893.

For a map of Indian Bayou WMA, call the Corps of Engineers office in Port Barre, 337-585-0853.

For a map of Sherburne WMA, call 337-948-0255.

For a map of Atchafayala National Wildlife Refuge near Krotz Springs, call the U.S. Fish and Wildlife Service, 504-646-7555.

For a map of Attakapas WMA, call 337-948-0255.

High points

Almost infinite possibilities for exploring.

Low points

Motorboats, posted signs.

Tips

Plan your itinerary as you go.

Jean Lafitte National Historical Park

If you're accustomed to paddling big swamps like Atchafalaya or Honey Island, Jean Lafitte National Historical Park's Barataria Preserve may not seem like much. But if you're new to Louisiana canoeing, perhaps coming from an urban environment, and want to sample the swamp in a controlled setting, the preserve is impressive. Jean Lafitte Park has six units "established to preserve significant examples of the rich natural and cultural resources of Louisiana's Mississippi River Delta region," according to park literature. The site of interest to paddlers is the 8,600-acre Barataria Preserve south of Marrero.

When you turn off busy U.S. 90 onto Louisiana 45, it's hard to imagine you'll be able to launch a canoe into woodland quiet within 15 minutes. But follow the preserve signs left onto Louisiana 3134 and right again onto 45 and you'll find yourself in a beautiful green realm. Stop at the visitor's center for a map, canoe trail descriptions, and other information. Well-marked put-ins allow access to two bayous and several canals, all interconnected. An added bonus: The canoe trails are closed to motorboats.

Bayou des Familles (French for bayou of families, in reference to the Canary Islanders, or Islenos, who once lived here) parallels Highway 45 to the east. You can launch at the Pecan Grove put-in just east of the visitor's center. Bayou des Familles forms a tunnel of greenery as it meanders beneath a canopy of forest. The road is a stone's throw away but not easily visible through the vegetation. You can paddle 3.6 miles northwest to the intersection with Bayou Coquille (French for shell bayou). Turn left, paddle under the bridge and take out at the parking lot, or continue 1.1 mile on to Kenta Canal if you can push your way through the weeds. If you lack a shuttle, paddle back to Pecan Grove.

For canal paddling, launch at the Twin Canals access point off Highway 45. The canal hooks around to the north and south before shooting straight northwest for 0.6 mile to Kenta Canal. A path used by fishermen and hikers parallels the waterway. Side channels lead short distances into cypress swamp and fresh-water marsh for a change of scenery. When you reach Upper Kenta Canal and turn left, you'll immediately see other canals branching off, including the weed-choked parallel "twin" canal. You can paddle southwest down Upper Kenta Canal for 1.25 miles to a foot-bridge, and 2.5 miles southeast down Lower Kenta Canal to a takeout on Louisiana 301, or just return the way you came. Canal paddling can be tedious, so the trick is to pay attention to details. Creep up to the marsh's edge and see what you can see. My wife spotted what she swore was a coconut—brown, round, and hairy. It turned out to be the back side of a nutria rat. It fed placidly until we climbed out of the boat; then it scurried off huffily. Rubber boots are a good choice of footwear; with them you can poke around on shore to stretch your legs. On the marsh you can feel the ground tremble underfoot like a floating mattress. You may see alligators floating shyly in the water with just eyes and nostrils showing, or sunning brazenly on the bank. Great blue herons and white egrets are common sights.

Park employees provide daytime and moonlight guided canoe trips, as do a couple of nearby outfitters. The park also has a number of hiking trails, some of which parallel the waterways. Plus, there's a book shop, nature center, swamp exhibits, and a film that gives an ecological and historical overview of the area. In the late 1700s, for instance, the Spanish imported some 2,000 Canary Is-landers to help settle underpopulated southeast Louisiana, and some lived in this area. In the early 1800s, Jean Lafitte and his fellow pirates headquartered in the Barataria area. In the War of 1812 the British tried to enlist Lafitte, but he turned down their $30,000 offer and threw his assistance to the Americans in exchange for a pardon for his crimes. His men helped General Andrew Jackson defeat the British in the Battle of New Orleans. No camping is allowed at Jean Lafitte Park, but Bayou Segnette State Park a few miles west of Marrero on Highway 90 has campsites; it also offers some canoeing on Bayou Segnette and adjacent waters, though motorboats are permitted there.

Jean Lafitte Park is the sort of place where you're apt to hear tourists talking in French or German; where you'll look up from paddling to see hikers in the woods or fishermen on the bank; where, after you finish canoeing, you can be at a good restaurant within minutes or in the New Orleans French Quarter in less than half an hour. Not surprisingly, the park can get quite crowded, espe-cially on warm-weather weekends. Go on a weekday or in the winter for more solitude.

Jean Lafitte options

1. Launch from Pecan Grove parking lot off Highway 45 onto Bayou Des Familles and paddle 3.6 miles northwest to Bayou Coquille. Turn left onto Coquille and cross under road to takeout on left, or continue on to Kenta Canal.

2. Launch at Twin Canals off Highway 45, paddle 0.6 mile to Upper Kenta Canal, turn left and paddle 1.25 miles southwest, then angle southeast onto Lower Kenta Canal and continue 2.5 miles to Highway 301 for a total of nearly 4.5 miles.

3. Take a park guided canoe trip (provide your own canoe or rent one from a nearby outfitter). Call 504-589-2330 for details and reservations.

Outfitters

Bayou Barn, intersection of Highways 45 and 3134, 1-800-TO-BAYOU (504-689-2663), rents canoes and pirogues and leads swamp tours.

Jean Lafitte Inn Cabin & Canoe Rental, 7040 Barataria Blvd., Crown Point, 1-800-339-8633 (504-689-3271), rents canoes and leads moonlight swamp trips.

Area campgrounds

Bayou Segnette State Park, 7777 Westbank Expressway, Westwego, 1-888-677-2296.

Maps

Basic map of park canoe trails and a separate description of the trails are available at the Jean Lafitte National Historical Park and Preserve Barataria office on Highway 45 south of Marrero, or by calling headquarters at 504-589-3882.

High points

Easy introduction to swamp.

Low points

Bayou Des Familles is close to road, while the canals' straight courses can make for tedious paddling.

Tips

Launch at any of the put-ins, explore, then return to the starting point.

Grand Isle

Let me admit up front that salt marsh does not make for the most scenic paddling. Before I took my canoe to Grand Isle, experienced paddlers told me as much. I doubted their assessment because I had found the Honey Island marsh on the lower Pearl River fascinating. What I failed to take into account was that the Honey Island marsh that I saw was brackish, a different environment than salt marsh. Brackish and intermediate marshes are full of lush grasses rich with variety, loaded with wildflowers, and tall enough to harbor deer and hogs. Unless you stand up in your canoe, visibility is restricted to the immediate waterway you're on, so there's something new to look at around each bend. In salt marsh, on the other hand, the grass is barely high enough to hide a raccoon, and the view extends unchangingly from horizon to horizon. About the only variety is man-made: condos, power lines, cars. Plus there are shallows (which can get shallower when the tide falls), wind, dead-end sloughs, high-speed motorboats on the main channels, and biting insects. And yet, plenty of people paddle the salt marsh. But they usually do so for a reason: fishing.

Whether you're fishing or not, the Grand Isle area is a good place to sample the marsh because of the proximity of a 21,000-acre state wildlife management area, a state park for camping, plus beaches and restaurants for variety. There are other wildlife refuges on the Louisiana coast that provide access to marsh, but most of them lack camping areas.

Just going to Grand Isle is fascinating. Even before you get to Louisiana 1—the only road to the island—you start seeing pirogues on top of pickup trucks, and roadside stands selling satsumas or daiquiris. Turn south onto one of the two highways that flank Bayou Lafourche—Louisiana 308 on the northeast and Highway 1 on the southwest—and the scenery gets even more exotic. (Highway 308 is quicker since most of the development is on the other side of the bayou.) Lafourche (pronounced la-FOOSH) meanders southeast from Donaldsonville to Port Fourchon, an offshoot of the Mississippi River before it was dammed in 1904. It's called "the longest street in the world" since it's a major thoroughfare for an endless sequence of towns. But the traffic on it consists of shrimp boats, oyster boats, barges, even oceangoing vessels. Meanwhile, barely a mile off to either side is pure marsh. South of the town of Golden Meadow—where the speed limit is said to be strictly enforced—the ground becomes too wet for more development. Highway 308 ends, and only Highway 1 remains to soar south across the marsh. Just before it reaches the Gulf of Mexico, Highway 1 turns east toward Grand Isle, while a spur, Highway 3070, continues south to Port Fourchon.

The 10-mile stretch of highway approaching the isle passes through salt marsh, with fishing boats, pirogues, and kayaks often seen in the shallow lakes and sloughs. North of the road lies Wisner Wildlife Management Area, though there's nothing to distinguish it from all the other marsh. A bridge crosses to Grand Isle, a condo-laden fishing resort that serves as a jumping-off place for marsh and saltwater fishing for redfish, speckled trout, and other species. Though it has a resident population of less than 2,000, Grand Isle becomes crowded during fishing season, especially the International Tarpon Rodeo each July.

In the 1800s, the island was home to sugar cane plantations until disruption by the Civil War. Landowners turned to vegetable farming, taking their produce by boat to such outlets as distant Chicago and the nearby French Market in New Orleans, via Barataria Bay and a series of bayous and canals (some of which are now part of Jean Lafitte National Historical Park's Barataria Preserve). Though accessible only by boat then, the isle became a resort in the latter 1800s until the hurricane of 1893, which claimed 2,000 lives. Now linked to the mainland by road, Grand Isle has returned to resort status, with an endless series of condos, motels, and rental cabins, nearly all of them on stilts as a precaution against hurricanes. In addition to tourism and seafood, oil and gas is the main industry these days. A massive refinery at the east end turns the night sky orange, and helicopters routinely ferry crews to offshore oil rigs, whose lights dapple the dark sea at night. The oil rigs have boosted the fish population by providing underwater structure around which they congregate.

In sharp contrast to such development, Grand Isle State Park at the east end offers a peek at the natural island habitat. The park road winds through thickets of wax myrtle and elderberry, then tops a berm and comes out onto the beach, which is also the tent camping area. Rock structures offshore lessen the surf's impact on the beach, but erosion has chewed it back to a relatively narrow strip. Cold, windy weather is the best time for camping as the mosquitoes and no-see-ums can be rapacious other times. Most campsites are on the beach, but there are one or two places to pitch a tent among the bushes for shelter from the wind, though insects are worse there. The beach is popular in the summer even if the water is brown and the sand less than snow-white. Such drawbacks aside, this beach is a wonderful place. My wife, Angelyn, and I camped on a brisk weekend in late December. A cold front was headed our way, but in the meantime the wind was roaring out of the south, so at least the bugs weren't biting, much. We found a site among the bushes to pitch our tent, then went to town for blackened shrimp at a restaurant. We returned to sit on the beach in lawn chairs, bundled up against the cold wind, watching clouds tickle the moon, and listening to the crashing surf. During the night the two fronts collided with thunder, lightning, and rain. We were safe in our cubbyhole, but other campers, who had pitched their tent on the exposed beach, packed up and left—a not-uncommon occurrence when storms hit, I'm told.

Sea kayakers can launch at the park beach or from any of several marinas on the island. However, the park is on the Gulf side, which is often rough and windswept since it's exposed to the open sea, and is so shallow you may have to wade out a good ways to launch. Several marinas provide access to the lee side of the island, which is protected from the wind. Paddling there would be a less turbulent experience. From either the park or a marina on the northeast end of the island, you can paddle a quarter mile northeast to the next island, Grand Terre, to see the remains of Fort Livingston, built by the U.S. Army between 1855 and 1861.

To experience the marsh, drive not quite 3 miles west of the island on Highway 1 and launch at Bayou Ferblanc, the only large bayou that crosses under the road. Paddle north and you'll enter the WMA in half a mile. From there you can branch west onto Bayou Laurier, Bayou Palourde, or any number of small shoots. A WMA map shows a variety of possible routes. Landmarks are obvious, including power line pylons marching northwest into infinity, Highway 1 to the south, and the colorful condos of Grand Isle to the east. If you venture into shallow sloughs, keep in mind that water levels are governed by tides, and you could get stranded if they fall. Local paddlers often wear chest waders. I know some out-of-staters who took a motorboat into that marsh and, when the tide dropped, found themselves stranded for 12 hours, a banquet for mosquitoes. For information on tides, check local newspapers or get the tidal handbook at a local marina or bait shop. You can also access Grand Isle tidal information from the National Ocean Service website, http://co-ops.nos.noaa.gov/tides/gulfGI.html.

The husk of an old boat lies in shallow marsh near Wisner Wildlife Management Area just east of Grand Isle.

Despite the lack of scenery, there are some interesting sights here and there: the husk of an old sunken wooden boat; scurrying redwing blackbirds; beds of oysters; darting fish; wading birds. But the real lure is the fishing. Pirogues and sit-on-top kayaks are the best way to get into the shallow parts of the marsh where the tidal current is running to angle for redfish and speckled trout. Anglers use rods and reels with bright orange bobbers and cocahoe minnows for bait. A stout redfish can pull a lightweight boat around before wearing out, which adds to the thrill of the catch. There are plenty of bait shops in the vicinity for up-to-date information on fishing conditions.

Big as it is, Wisner WMA's 21,000 acres is an infinitesimal part of Louisiana's 3.6 million acres of marsh, of which 1 million are salt marsh. A good way to see more is to drive Louisiana 82, which runs from Port Arthur, Texas, to Abbeville, Louisiana. When you cross the Port Arthur Canal and Sabine Pass into Louisiana, you enter as empty a landscape as you're likely to see. North of the narrow highway lies marsh grass with glimmers of standing water. To the south is more of the same but with the weird silhouettes of oil platforms, as if spaceships have landed in the most out-of-the-way place they could find in preparation for invading earth. Here and there cattle graze unconcernedly. The highway, on which there is scant traffic, takes advantage of the few natural ridges, or cheniers. These are stretches of ground slightly higher than the sodden marsh, with names like Blue Buck Ridge, Salt Work Ridge, Hackberry Ridge, Front Ridge, and Back

Ridge. Less than 20 miles from the Texas border, open Gulf appears to the south, and soon the highway is close to the beach—too close, judging by the piles of rock erected offshore to break the waves and stem erosion. Though this beach isn't the white sand of San Destin, Florida, or Biloxi, Mississippi, the ocean view is enticing, the more so for the lack of development. Five miles later the town of Holly Beach appears, a rustic medley of camps, bait shops, and bars along a grid of narrow streets, some of them sand. Many roads lead to the beach, which is open to the public. A tractor, bales of hay, and a pen of rental ponies indicate this isn't your typical Gulf Coast resort. Nevertheless, Holly Beach is a tourist town, with the tongue-in-cheek nickname of Cajun Riviera. Plenty of the camp houses are for rent, and the area offers standard beach fare of swimming, boating, surf-fishing, or strolling, plus it can serve as a launching pad for kayakers. Despite its mud-brown hue, the beach is sandy, not sticky, and dappled with countless tiny seashells. Louisiana 27 joins 82 at Holly Beach and they run east together, then dogleg north to a ferry across the Calcasieu Shipping Channel. The ferry is quick and efficient, handling everything from local pickup trucks to tourist sedans to 18-wheelers. Across the channel, the highway passes through the towns of Cameron and Creole, where 27 turns back north and Highway 82 continues east, still paralleling the coast, which is now a few miles to the south. Highway 27 is the main Creole Nature Trail Scenic Byway, running in a horseshoe shape from Sulphur south to the coast and back north to Lake Charles. (For more information on the trail and its side shoots, which include Highway 82, call 1-800-456-SWLA or go to the Internet website creolenaturetrail.org.)

After crossing a drawbridge at Mermentau River, Highway 82 glides through the stretched-out town of Grand Chenier, then enters a magical corridor lined with giant live oaks swaying with Spanish moss fuller than Santa's beard. Bordering the highway on the south is Rockefeller National Wildlife Refuge, one of several refuges in these marshes. Others include Sabine NWR north of Holly Beach; Cameron Prairie NWR, and Lacassine NWR northeast of Cameron; plus State Wildlife Refuge and Marsh Island Wildlife Refuge east of Rockefeller and accessible only by boat. These areas consist mainly of open marsh speckled with lakes, ponds, canals, and bayous. Once past Rockefeller Refuge, the highway zips through the town of Pecan Island, then turns north. In about 10 miles you start to reach high ground—high enough, at least, to cultivate rice and some soggy ryegrass. The highway crosses the Intracoastal Waterway and zigzags up to Abbeville. The next road access to coastal marsh is highways branching off U.S. 90 between New Iberia and Louisiana 1, which leads to Grand Isle.

The marsh I describe today may not be the marsh you see tomorrow. Louisiana is losing 25–30 square miles of coastline a year—a football field-size area every 20 minutes—according to the Louisiana Wildlife Federation. Since 1930 the state has lost more than 1,500 square miles of coastal marshes. By 2050, coastal highways and towns such as Port Fourchon are projected to be underwater, and the Gulf of Mexico will have eaten through the marsh to the Intracoastal Waterway, exposing barge and ship traffic to open water. Some $35 million a year is being spent on restoration, but that will preserve and restore only 115,000 acres over the next 50 years, compared to a projected loss of 400,000 acres. Causes of this potential fiasco are complex and much debated. They include the global rise of sea levels; the state's 10,000 miles of oilfield canals, which interfere with the natural ebb and flow of the marsh and allow saltwater to invade fresh and kill marsh plants and creatures; levees, especially those on the Mississippi River, which prevent the natural overflows that replenish the marsh; and flood-control and diversion structures that bar rivers from going where they otherwise would. Some 30 percent of the nation's seafood harvest comes from Louisiana, plus 18 percent of U.S. oil production and 24 percent of natural gas. Also, 70 percent of waterfowl traveling the Mississippi and Central Flyways winter over in coastal Louisiana. Much is at stake.

The most dramatic illustration I've seen of the problem is a map of the coastline as it's projected to look in 2050. The map, which appears in the *Louisiana Almanac 2002–2003* edition, shows the coast as far north as the town of Cut Off, over 30 miles inland from Port Fourchon. Grand Isle will be accessible only by boat, as was the case in earlier times. Wisner WMA and vast areas of surrounding wetlands will be open water. Louisiana's salt marsh may not be the most fantastic place to canoe, but perhaps we should see it while we can.

Grand Isle options

1. Launch at Bayou Ferblanc 3 miles west of the Grand Isle bridge and paddle north into Wisner Wildlife Management Area, exploring bayous and side shoots.

2. For sea kayakers, launch from the beach at Grand Isle State Park on the Gulf side of the island, or at one of several marinas on the lee side.

Area campgrounds

Grand Isle State Park, 1-888-787-2559, on Admiral Craik Drive at east end of island off Highway 1.

Maps

For a map of Wisner WMA, call 225-765-2811.

Quad maps of the marsh west of Grand Isle are Leeville and Caminada Pass. For the east side of the island, see Grand Isle and Barataria Pass. Call 1-800-ASK-USGS.

For a simple map of Grand Isle State Park, call 1-888-677-1400.

Outfitters

At this writing there is nowhere to rent canoes, pirogues, or kayaks on Grand Isle. However, there are plenty of fishing guides. For information on them, plus marinas, charter boats, restaurants, motels, and rental cabins, call the Grand Isle Tourist Commission, 985-787-2997.

High points

Good place to fish from sea kayak or pirogue.

Low points

Monotonous scenery in saltwater marsh.

Tips

Visit Grand Isle State Park.

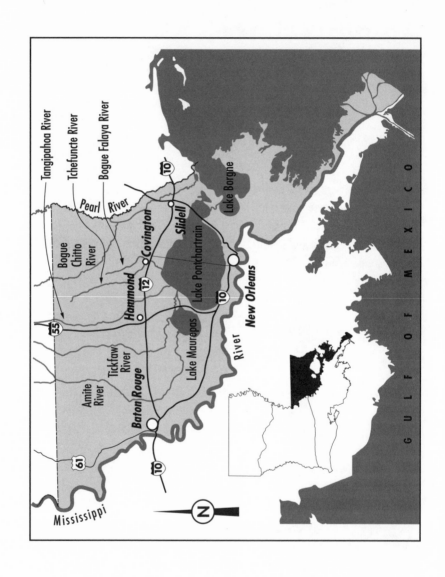

6. Southeast

Amite River

The Amite River begins in southwest Mississippi as two prongs. They join just south of the Louisiana line near Clinton and meander south past Denham Springs to Lake Maurepas. Ironically, in Louisiana the Amite is designated a Natural Scenic River and in Mississippi it isn't designated anything, yet the Mississippi portions are more pristine. They're also virtually uncanoeable due to logjams, though, so the point is mostly moot. Only after the prongs run together does the Amite become wide enough to paddle without inordinate effort, and for about 25 of its ensuing 83 miles it offers good canoeing. Then it succumbs to gravel mining, lined for miles with growling machinery and vast stretches of sand and gravel before reaching the urban sprawl of Denham Springs. Below there it widens and slows, providing an avenue for speedboats of all sorts as it stretches east to Maurepas.

Amite is pronounced a-MEET in Louisiana and a-MITT or A-mitt in Mississippi. According to conventional wisdom, the name came from French for friendship, referring to the fact that the Indians who lived along the river were friendly. But there are other theories. One is that the word stems from the Choctaw "himmita," which means red ant, a symbol of thrift. Another is that it's a short version of the word "sagamite," an Indian corn dish. There's also the notion that Amite refers to a crossroads meeting place, "a meet," which became the site of the town of Amite, Louisiana, to the east. However, the French explorer D'Iberville mentioned the Amite River in 1699, long before there was any settlement in the interior. "Friendly" sounds the most likely to me, and it applies to the current inhabitants as well.

I have a lot of personal connections to this river. In the 1920s when my father was a boy, some big kids threw him in an Amite River swimming hole, figuring he would sink or swim. He sank. Fortunately for him (and me), an older friend dove in and rescued him. When Dad taught me to swim in the Amite, he used more merciful methods—standing out in water just over my head and letting me dog-paddle to him. When my own son was old enough, we took a pirogue down a stretch of the west fork, hauled the boat over approximately 10,000 logjams, caught seven bass, ate them all by the campfire, slept under frosty stars, and the next morning he hooked a 6-pounder—a real lunker for such a small stream.

There's plenty of wildlife on the Amite. You may see a vividly colored male wood duck and his dull brown wife gliding nervously on the water as you approach, then taking off with a squealing flurry of wings. A squirrel scampers along a stretch of grassy bank from one tree to another. A deer crashes into the woods. The percussion of turtles plopping into the river punctuates the water's musical voice. Snakes coiled on bushes slide into the water moments before you come alongside. The upper Amite River valley even harbors Louisiana black bears, a subspecies of American black bears. Late one night in 1998, a 300-pound male collided with a car just south of Liberty, Mississippi, less than 5 miles east of the river. Wildlife officials took the injured animal—dubbed Liberty Bear—to the Baton Rouge zoo, where it was treated for a broken jaw and broken shoulder. It recovered in a few months, and officials released it in the hills of Wilkinson County near the Mississippi River. In 2000, a woman saw a mother black bear and cub cross the road west of Liberty a couple miles west of the river. Mississippi wildlife officials verified the sighting with hair samples taken from the scene, and said it indicated bears are breeding in the area, not just passing through.

Smack between those two bear sightings lies the Ethel Stratton Vance Natural Area, located on the west fork of the river on Highway 24 west of Liberty. When Vance died in 1983 at the age of 100, she willed a 288-acre tract of land to the state of Mississippi for scientific, educational, recreational, and camping purposes. The town of Liberty now leases the park from the state and, thanks to grant funds, donations, tax dollars, and volunteer work, the park has a large multipurpose pavilion with rodeo arena, ballfields, more than 10 miles of nature trail, and prim-

itive and developed camp-
grounds. Yet all that pales
compared to the natural
wonders of the rest of the
park. The area starts with a
piney-woods bluff riddled
with sand-rock and drops off
to a beaver kingdom of winding sloughs and big hard-
wood forest bordering a long
stretch of the river.

It's possible to float the 5
miles—much of it bordering
the park—from Highway 24
to Highway 48, but count on
a log across the river about
every 50 yards. If you can
handle the boot-camp exer-
tion, you'll find yourself
coasting beneath monstrous
oaks, beeches, sycamores,
and hickories. Pawpaw trees
line the bank, dropping their

A pawpaw ripens on a limb in August beside the upper Amite River.

fruit in August. They flourish on riverbanks, with leaves 3 by 10 inches and
trunks rarely more than 4 inches in diameter. Pawpaws, which grow 3–4 inches
long and a couple inches thick, are green mottled with gray and black, with
bright yellow flesh and large seeds. To harvest, pluck the fruit when it's slightly
soft, or shake the trunk gently to make it fall (though that can bruise it). Pawpaws are intensely sweet with a tropical flavor. They don't last long after harvested and must be eaten promptly. Muscadines ripen in late August and early
September. They're most easily harvested over a sandbar; just shake the vines
vigorously, then gather the purplish-black grapes. Persimmons ripen after the
first frost, orange and sweet.

Hardy log-jumpers can continue paddling—and portaging—the west fork on
the 10 miles from Highway 48 to Lower Centreville Road and 4 more to Powell
Road. Both roads run east from Highway 569 south of 48. From Powell Road it's

3 river miles to the state line, less than a mile to the juncture of the forks, and 5.5 miles to Louisiana 432.

An easier float in Mississippi is on the east fork, from rural Mary Wall Bridge to Lindsey Bridge, a 3-mile trip. There are numerous camps along this stretch, and residents periodically clear out the logjams. Since it's so short you might as well take the time to fish, but the fishing when I went was not so great. I did enjoy the sleepy music of cicadas, the dart of a kingfisher, the peek-a-boo of turtles, and a glimpse of something that might have been an alligator. Below Lindsey Bridge are 4 logjammed miles to the state line—nobody clears the obstructions from this stretch—and a mile to the juncture of the forks. To get to Lindsey Bridge, take Highway 1044 north out of Louisiana—it becomes Bean Road in Mississippi—and turn left on Lindsey Bridge Road in about 1.5 miles; the road leads to the bridge in little over a mile. To get to Mary Wall bridge, continue northeast on Bean Road and turn left about 2 miles past Lindsey Bridge Road; it leads to Mary Wall Bridge in about a mile. Both the *Louisiana Atlas and Gazetteer* and the *Mississippi Atlas and Gazetteer* show these crooked, rural roads.

On the upper Amite, I prefer wading to canoeing. Take a rod and reel, small lure box, stringer, and needle-nose pliers. Wade out into the water, wearing old tennis shoes, and ease your way upstream, casting topwater lures or spinners for bass, smaller lures for bream and even crappie. Go upstream so the silt stirred up by your shoes won't spook the fish. If wild fruit is in season, you have the added benefit of emerging with a stringer of fish and bags of pawpaws and muscadines. More realistically, you'll likely come out with briar scratches, mosquito bites, sand in your shoes, and not quite enough fish to justify cleaning them. But it's fun anyway.

Fish and fruit aren't the only collectibles on the Amite. Once I gathered up a canoe-load of garbage on the stretch from Highway 24 to 48. Most of it I found within a mile below the bridge, indicating it came from people tossing their trash into the river. In one disgusting instance I saw a full bag of household garbage. If people treat such a gorgeous stream like that, it makes me wonder if they would litter up heaven itself. The thing about trash hunting is, the more you pick up, the better and worse you feel—better because you're picking it up, worse because it's there to start with. My dog Gabe and I soon discovered that litter pickup from a canoe is a two-man job. I worked double-time manning the boat and reaching for trash. Gabe did his part by chewing up some styrofoam food containers, presumably to prepare them for the landfill. Even though I was keeping my eyes out for trash, I had plenty of time to appreciate the magnificent woodland scenery. By the time I reached the takeout several hours later, the front of my canoe was brimful of glass soft-drink bottles, plastic containers of every sort, and miscellaneous items ranging from a snuff can to a life-sized plastic rooster. It took a good half hour to bag everything up. Picking up trash on a river is no easy affair, but it's uniquely rewarding. And unlike other forms of hunting, you are certain to get your bag limit.

Both east and west prongs are around 25 miles long and remain pretty much the same all the way to their juncture. But there is one possible difference between the prongs: temperature. A woman who grew up on the east fork told me it's colder than the west. When she and her family floated to the junction of the forks, she said, she stood with a foot in each channel and was amazed at the difference. That mystified me. The forks are nearly identical, traveling through similar countryside. Why should one be colder than the other? At my request, a forester friend stuck a thermometer in each one about 2 miles upstream from the junction. His findings: east prong 79.7 degrees Fahrenheit, west prong 78.8—the opposite of the woman's experience. Baffled, I took a darkroom thermometer and went to see for myself. My findings: east prong 81 degrees, west prong 83.5. Then I realized how foolish my quest was. The temperature of the water must vary according to local conditions like sunlight, depth, proximity of springs, and speed of current. Anyone who has swum in a river has found such differences in temperature. A 12-foot-deep hole works like a refrigerator, a long shallow stretch like a heater. Springs well up from the bottom or bubble in from the banks. A mile of shade lowers the temperature; open sunshine raises it. Regardless of minor variations, I've always thought of the spring-fed Amite as ice-cold. But when I got home, I stuck my thermometer in a glass of tap water, which in my case comes from a well. It showed 70 degrees—10 degrees colder than the Amite! With ice in the glass the thermometer, which goes as low as 60, couldn't even give an accurate reading. So the "ice-cold" tag is hyperbole. There's only one thing I'm certain of: When you wade into the Amite River on a hot summer day, it feels cold.

Temperature isn't the only topic of debate on the Amite. Louisiana officials have proposed damming the river for years, in hopes of alleviating floods and providing recreation. Proposed sites have included Felixville, Darlington, and the juncture of the forks. The latter plan, announced in the mid-1990s, called for a 60,000-acre reservoir, most of it in Amite County, Mississippi. At the dam just below the Louisiana line, the reservoir would sprawl 9 miles wide. The idea wasn't too popular in southwest Mississippi since it would have involved submerging houses, churches, cemeteries, farmland, timber, and roads. The Corps of Engineers, whose approval was needed, also didn't go for the idea, and it faded. In 2002 a Louisiana Amite River Basin Commission official told me the dam idea is dead.

The Amite becomes properly canoeable at the juncture of the forks, but there is no public access until Highway 432 several miles downstream, and even there the access isn't great. For years a gravel road leading under the bridge provided an easy way to launch a boat, but a gate was put up across it and even the highway right-of-way was posted. River users later forged a narrow path along the northeast side of the bridge to the river, so it is possible to launch a canoe, though you'll have to park on the road shoulder. The 6 miles from here to Highway 10 east of Clinton provide the best float on the river. Logjams are largely a thing of the past, but the stream is narrow and swift enough to offer good paddling. There are a number of camps along the river, but not enough to dispel the deep-woods feeling. The bass fishing is pretty good too. Topwater lures and spinnerbaits are the best bet. I took a friend on a drizzly day when the fish weren't biting, but during a lull in the rain he tossed a topwater lure in a big, deep bend and hauled out a 5-pounder.

Things begin to change below Highway 10 on the 16.5 miles to Highway 37 at Grangeville. After a pleasant stretch of woods and water, you enter the realm of gravel mining. That means grinding machinery and Saharan vistas of sandbars. I talked to a Louisiana Department of Environmental Quality official, who remembered seeing aerial photos of the river north of Grangeville taken in the 1950s, when there were only one or two gravel pits. Now there are vast expanses of sand and borrow pits on either side of the river. Gravel mines can silt up the river, leave permanent holes near the banks, and cause a normally meandering channel to shorten. But if gravel operations sometimes pour sandy silt into the river, they also pour money into the economy. The Amite River runs through one of the major sand and gravel corridors in Louisiana. Those elements are used in all types of construction, from roads to houses. But as far as canoeing goes, the Clinton-to-Grangeville stretch is problematic.

Gravel mines increase below Grangeville, as do camps and residences. Highways 37 and 16 parallel the river north of Denham Springs, and if you drive Highway 16 you can get a vivid glimpse of the magnitude of the sand and gravel operations. Hemmed in by urban sprawl, the Amite slides past the outskirts of Baton Rouge, then swings southeast past Port Vincent and French Settlement. Having absorbed tributaries like Comite River, Bayou Manchac, and Colyell Creek, the Amite divides, with a diversion canal connecting it to Blind River to the south, which also empties into Lake Maurepas.

Amite River options

1. Louisiana 432 to Louisiana 10 east of Clinton, 6 miles.
2. Louisiana 10 to Louisiana 37, 16.5 miles.

Area campgrounds

Ethel Stratton Vance Natural Area, Highway 24 west of Liberty, Mississippi, primitive and developed sites, 601-657-1001.

Maps

The *Louisiana Atlas and Gazetteer* shows the river and the access roads, including those in southwest Mississippi.

High points

Beautiful deep-woods stream with fairly clear water and nice current.

Low points

Gravel mines.

Tips

In addition to canoeing, try hiking or biking the trails in the Ethel Stratton Vance Natural Area.

Tickfaw River

The Tickfaw River is curiously different from the streams that flank it. Both the Amite River to the west and the Tangipahoa to the east are fairly clear streams

A cypress tree rimmed with knees and draped with Spanish moss captures the sleepy mood of the gentle Tickfaw.

with a decent current and plenty of sand and gravel bars. The Tickfaw is currentless, muddy, and devoid of sand and gravel. Yet its remote, deep-forest setting makes it appeal to anyone who loves undiluted nature. The Tickfaw, an Indian word for "pine rest," starts in the restful piney woods southwest of McComb, Mississippi, and runs through the pastoral landscape of Amite County, Mississippi, and St. Helena Parish, Louisiana. If you take Louisiana 441 south of the Mississippi line, you pretty much parallel the stream, driving past rolling, forested hills and pasture, farmhouses, and cottages. It's delicious countryside, quiet and shady. South of Montpelier, the land flattens out and stays that way all the way to the Lake Maurepas marshes.

The Tickfaw isn't big enough to handle any kind of boat until Springville, and it's just as well since there's no public access at any of the bridge crossings from there north. Even Highway 42 at Springville bristles with posted and no parking signs, ironic considering signs billing it as a Louisiana Natural and Scenic River. But a mile or so south of there on the west bank is a ramshackle deep-woods hideaway known as J&W Campground. For $3 you can launch a boat, or you can rent the campground's sole canoe for $10. About 3 river miles below J&W

on the east bank is 1,200-acre Tickfaw State Park, established in 1999. It's located on Patterson Road off Highway 1037 some 6 miles west of Springfield (not Springville). The park provides canoe rentals and a shuttle to the put-in for a 6-mile float trip from the northern boundary down to Catalpa Canal on the left, marked with a small sign.

Whether you launch at J&W or the park, prepare to be enchanted from the second you leave shore. The Tickfaw flows through a green, shady realm—though flow may be too strong a word for its negligible current. At least that makes it easy to go upstream, a good way to stretch your journey and do some exploring. Even on a hot summer day, the river is sweetened by breezes and shaded by river birch, pecan, water oak, willow, cypress, and spruce pine. Other than an occasional faded posted sign in the woods or an old johnboat pulled up in the shade, for most of the way there's virtually no evidence of humans—no camps or fields, no traffic noises or machinery, nothing but the lazy song of cicadas. You can expect some logjams on the stretch above the state park. Park employees try to keep the logs cut out on their portion. One good strategy for a day float is to launch at the park put-in, paddle upriver as far as you want, then head down to Catalpa Canal. On the other hand, a park official told me many customers simply paddle in the area around the canal, returning to the takeout. The park also has a horseshoe-shaped nature trail, much of it boardwalk, that comes to the river.

The water is never completely clear due to the mostly mud bottom. In spring and summer, bream beds ring the river shallows, with small fluttery bluegill crowding around. The Tickfaw is a good bream and catfish river. A favorite tactic is jug-fishing with catalpa worms, dropping the hooks a couple feet down over underwater dropoffs to catch 7–8-pound catfish; one man even caught a 45-pound flathead farther downstream. Bass and crappie anglers fish the river too. On the upper river you may encounter local fishermen in slow-moving johnboats, angling for bream or running nets or trotlines.

The river gradually widens as it angles eastward, and camps and houses begin to appear on the west bank shortly above the park takeout. Paddling remains enjoyable for a couple more miles downstream from the takeout to a fee boat ramp at Leisure Landing (225-294-3694 or 294-4048) off Highway 1037 on the north bank. Here the river becomes big and deep enough for any kind of vessel. Boats as large as cabin cruisers come up the river to stop at Leisure Landing, which has a lounge, hamburger joint, boat ramp, and camps.

I was curious about the lower river, so Keith Hux and I set out in his 16-foot flatbottom aluminum boat with 50-horsepower outboard down the Tickfaw from Leisure Landing. I'm used to traveling at canoe speed, so I cringed as we rounded bends so fast I expected the flatbottom boat to skid into the trees like a hockey puck—though not nearly as fast as some of the other boats on the water. Conflicting wakes from all these vessels kept us bracing from the impact. I would have hated to be in a canoe here. We slowed as we passed expensive houses and camps, then coasted under the high, arching Highway 444 bridge at the mouth of Blood River. Downstream to the right stands the huge Tin Lizzy Landing restaurant, which gets its name from the fact that it's covered with sheets of rusty tin. More waterside mansions line the river and canals amid young cypress forest, then a boat-access-only bar called the Prop Stop, where speedboats, pounding music, and college-age kids give a Louisiana imitation of *Baywatch*. We zoomed south past the mouth of Natalbany River to wide-open Lake Maurepas, whose far shore was invisible. But we didn't go far. At roughly 8 by 12 miles and shallow, Maurepas can get rough in a hurry, easily upsetting a small open boat. We went far enough out to see the arched bridge to the east at Manchac, 4 miles away. Then we turned back to the relative safety of the river.

The lower Tickfaw is an excellent illustration of a stretch of river that is theoretically canoeable but realistically would be miserable. What with the parade of motorboats—personal watercraft, towering yachts, skiers, even cigarette boats—the wide channel seems more like downtown Malibu than a river. A paddler would have to contend with constant wakes from boats often piloted by folks with beers in hand. That's quite a contrast with the upper river, where peace and quiet reign.

Tickfaw River options

1. Paddle from J&W Campground to the Tickfaw State Park takeout, 9 miles. The park takeout is at the end of Catalpa Canal on the left side of the river going downstream; a sign marks the entry.

2. Do the Tickfaw State Park float, launching at the northern boundary and paddling to Catalpa Canal, 6 miles. A park outfitter shuttles all boats to the put-in, leaving vehicles at the takeout.

3. Continue from Catalpa Canal to Leisure Landing, 2 miles.

Area campgrounds and outfitters

J&W Campground, south of Highway 42 on the west side of the river; signs mark the way; 225-294-8961. When I visited, the campground had one small canoe for rent.

Tickfaw State Park, Patterson Road off Highway 1037, 6 miles west of Springfield, 1-888-981-2020. In addition to campsites and cabins, a park outfitter provides canoe rentals and shuttle.

Maps

Louisiana Atlas and Gazetteer.

High points

Silence and solitude.

Low points

No current or sandbars.

Tips

Lengthen your journey by paddling upstream first.

Manchac Swamp

Manchac Swamp northwest of New Orleans has plenty of open water: Lake Maurepas, Pass Manchac, North Pass, plus lower Tickfaw, Amite, and Blind Rivers. But not even fish can get far into the interior of this big wetland between Ponchatoula and LaPlace. While the water levels in river swamps like Atchafalaya and Honey Island are determined mainly by rainfall, Manchac is a lake swamp. In the low, marshy area around Lake Maurepas, there are few bayous of any length (or depth). River swamps, on the other hand, tend to be chock-full of bayous connecting to a main river. To get beyond the main waters in Manchac, swampers rely on airboats, pirogues, or hip boots. And an unruly wind can shove the water right out of the shallows, making even airboat travel impossible at times. Nevertheless, there are places to poke around in a canoe.

Jimmie Van paddles a bayou in Manchac Swamp.

The 6-mile-long Pass Manchac, a broad channel, connects Lake Maurepas with Lake Pontchartrain to the east. A relatively narrower waterway, North Pass—though still wide by canoeing standards—parallels Pass Manchac to the north. North Pass also connects with bayous branching off to the north. Paddlers can launch onto North Pass at a boat ramp on the east side of U.S. 51. (There is also a ramp on the west side of the highway, plus a ramp at Pass Manchac.) From the ramp, paddle east under the low-slung railroad bridge, pass Port of Manchac buildings to the north, and head down the pass. If you're fighting a headwind, that's good, because it will help you on your return. A stiff tailwind, on the other hand, might push you along like an outboard motor for now but dog you all the way back. And if there's no wind at all, the heat may make you wish there were. As you venture along, explore the short little bayous that shoot off to the north into the marsh, or prairie, as they call it in parts of Louisiana. These bayous begin appearing within a mile of the railroad bridge. Since they rarely extend more than half a mile, they're the kinds of places to go slow and pay attention to detail. White ibises soar overhead, their gray undersides flashing to white like a school of fish when they shift direction in unison. Red-winged blackbirds zip around, filling the air with their chuckles. Bitterns, kingbirds, boat-tailed grackles, Eastern phoebes, cattle egrets, snowy egrets, and great blue herons add to the hustle and bustle. When you stand up, you can see north across the marsh to the woods of Joyce Wildlife Management Area.

Decades ago this windswept, tree-dotted prairie was deep cypress forest. But loggers stripped it bare—many of its apparent bayous are actually logging canals—and saltwater is creeping in, the lake shore is eroding, and half the remaining trees are dead. Huge, ancient cypress stumps remain as a testament to the glory days. Yet Manchac Swamp is still beautiful in a haunted way, especially these cozy little bird-crowded bayous. And there are plans afoot to restore the swamp, as evidenced by the Manchac Project at Southeastern Louisiana University's Turtle Cove Environmental Research Station. There are also plans to redirect water from the Mississippi River through canals in Garyville into the southwestern part of Lake Maurepas, where Mississippi River flood-control levees have long kept overflow from nourishing the swamp.

North of North Pass, the 15,819-acre Joyce WMA offers a half-mile boardwalk and a few pirogue-size waterways leading east off Highway 51. Its canals are even smaller than the sloughs off North Pass, and I found a so-called boat trail so clogged with weeds that at first I thought it was ground. These canals are mainly canoeable in high water. The wooden boardwalk trail offers benches, woods, and a mild breeze. At its end, tupelo and cypress woods give way to open prairie.

The 8,325-acre Manchac WMA lies south of the Highway 51 bridge over Pass Manchac, but is even less accessible to paddling. The ramshackle community of Galva marks the entrance into the area via long, straight Galva Canal. Passages also enter the WMA from Pass Manchac and Lake Pontchartrain, but that requires tackling large, windswept waters in a canoe.

Julia Sims's excellent book *Manchac Swamp: Louisiana's Undiscovered Wilderness* gives a view of this swamp that's almost inaccessible to the outsider, thanks to her photographic skills and her contacts with landowners. The photos are as good as nature shots get: A wing-net shrimp boat comes in at sunrise after a night's work. An owl swoops to its nest with a frog in its beak. A nutria strips tree bark, an otter chomps on a fish, and a gator gulps a bird. A 6-point buck bounds through high water. A gray fox slinks through the woods. And in what may be one of the prettiest photos on the planet, a great white egret stands surrounded by a blanket of purple water hyacinths. Sims's photos are also in display at her Gateway Gallery on Pine Street in Ponchatoula. Yet another way to get a taste of Manchac is to visit the community itself. Eat at Middendorf's Restaurant; buy fresh fish or alligator meat from one of the local seafood markets; or ask old-timers about the construction of I-55, the mysterious death of the cypress trees, and the 1915 hurricane that wiped out everything.

Manchac Swamp options

1. From boat ramp north of Manchac on the east side of U.S. 51, paddle east on North Pass and explore sloughs to the north.

2. In high water, paddle canals leading east off Highway 51 into Joyce WMA.

Area campgrounds

Tickfaw State Park, Patterson Road off Highway 1037, 6 miles west of Springfield, 1-888-981-2020.

Outfitters

Canoe and Trail Adventures, Metairie, 504-834-5257, www.canoeand trail.com. Leads guided trips.

Maps

For map of Joyce WMA call 504-568-7685.
For map of Manchac WMA, call 504-568-5612.

High points

Secluded, bird-filled sloughs in the marsh.

Low points

Most of the swamp is either too shallow to paddle or consists of big, open waterways.

Tips

Take a bird identification book.

Tangipahoa River

The Tangipahoa River is a rarity in Louisiana: a long, relatively clear, flowing river, bordered by abundant gravel and sandbars, offering more than 30 miles of prime downriver paddling, plus many more miles of less-than-prime floating. As with most streams in southeast Louisiana, it begins in southwest Mississippi, to the north. It's dammed early on at Percy Quin State Park near McComb, and below there remains a logjammed creek as it meanders south into Louisiana past Kentwood. Only when it reaches Louisiana 440 east of Tangipahoa does it become wide enough to manage. From there until Louisiana 443 it's a good canoeing river. Below 443 gravel bars give way to mud, banks become lined with camp houses, and motorboats begin to appear. Still, you can canoe on to Lee's Landing, the last takeout before Lake Pontchartrain.

The upper river in Mississippi may not be very canoeable, but it's fascinating in other ways, with a convent, tales of monsters, and a riverside mansion where top officials once retreated. A bizarre testament to this past is a marble bathtub in the middle of the woods not far from the river in the Chatawa community a few miles north of the state line. The tub is long and narrow with tall sides, like a coffin whose corpse has long since escaped into the deep forest. Lacking faucets since it was made before modern plumbing, the tub is the only relic of an old house which was torn down decades ago. Nearby lies the square sandstone foundation of a log cabin, also gone, used as a retreat by students at St. Mary of the Pines Catholic School, who would come to the cabin and meditate.

St. Mary of the Pines, a beautiful retreat with attractive red brick buildings, towering pines, and rustling palm trees, got its start in 1868 when Catholic Redemptorist fathers in New Orleans wanted a country retreat. They bought 80 acres, eventually expanding to 300. They constructed a frame chapel and a three-story brick building. In the 1870s the School Sisters of Notre Dame began operating a Catholic school there, and soon bought the whole thing from the Redemptorists for $9,000. More buildings went up as enrollment grew. Girls made up the majority, and in 1954 the school quit taking boys. In the 1960s some old buildings came down and new ones went up, including a 160-bed dormitory. By 1974, though, enrollment had dropped off and, about 100 years after it opened, the school closed. It is now a home for retired nuns.

Not far away, on a high bluff overlooking the Tangipahoa, stands the privately owned Kramer Lodge, a massive, rustic house that once served as a retreat for former Louisiana governor Huey Long and his cronies. The late X. A. Kramer built both the lodge and the log cabin near the bathtub, which he filled with goldfish.

The deep woods of Chatawa have given rise to monster legends, which may contain an element of truth. The so-called Chatawa monster, long rumored to be a Mississippi version of Bigfoot, may have been a black panther. In the 1930s, old-timers say, a circus truck overturned on Highway 51 and two black panthers escaped. Though circus officials claimed they recaptured the animals, people reported seeing a panther later.

Weird animal sightings continue to occur at Chatawa. In the late 1990s, a local woman said she saw a monkey swing out of a tree, land in the road, stand up, and eat something. When she slowed her car, it ran off. The woman insisted it was not a squirrel, raccoon, or other monkeylike creature. She described it as 2½ feet tall with a long tail. Kramer Lodge had various exotic pets including monkeys in the 1930s, but a wildlife biologist told me he doubted a population of monkeys could have survived in the wild there that long, especially without having been reported. Someone later told me a tractor dealer bought a load of monkeys cheap in New Orleans and gave one away with every tractor purchased. When the idea didn't go over well, he allegedly released the monkeys. I can't vouch for any of that.

The Chatawa woods have a sinister side as well. In 1993 I got a call at the newspaper where I work about a body floating in a small creek that runs into the Tangipahoa. An Amite, Louisiana, man was found with a bullet hole in his back. A bridge inspection crew had spotted the body floating face-down one February morning and called the sheriff's department. A bridge inspector, who had a pair of waders, waded into the waist-deep creek and looped a rope around the man's chest. The coroner and others pulled the body ashore. The man, who wore a short-sleeved shirt, blue jeans, brown boots, and a belt with a first name engraved on it, lacked any identification, but it didn't take authorities long to identify him. They concluded he was shot elsewhere and dumped in the creek. Three people were arrested in the case, which lawmen described as a love triangle.

The main problems on the Tangipahoa are considerably more prosaic than murder and monsters. They consist of bacterial pollution, gravel mines, logging, and the proximity of towns and highways. It's ironic that a river whose Choctaw Indian name means "cornstalk gatherers" has been so damaged by a four-legged type of cornstalk gatherer—cattle. The plight of Girl Scouts at summer camp without a place to swim helped bring the Tangipahoa River into the public eye in 1987 and 1988. Tests showed the river was heavily polluted with cattle and human fecal bacteria, directly affecting the girls at Camp Whispering Pines near Ponchatoula. State officials declared the river a public health threat and posted advisories closing it to most recreation, including swimming and tubing. The bad publicity forced the closing of three campgrounds and canoe outfitters on the river.

How could such a scenic, pastoral stream be polluted? It passes through no large cities. There are no oil refineries or smokestack industries pumping wastes into it. Percy Quin State Park has a sewage lagoon, but officials say it doesn't pose a significant problem. As the Tangipahoa runs south and east through Mississippi, it merges with Little Tangipahoa River and picks up runoff from municipal sewage lagoons and small industries in Pike County. But the worst problems don't start until the river reaches Louisiana, where pollution comes from more sewage lagoons, fishing camps, and dairy farms. Gorgeously green Tangipahoa Parish contains probably the largest concentration of livestock in the state, and Louisiana Department of Environmental Quality (DEQ) officials estimated that dairy farms were causing 50 percent of the river's problems. The contaminant is fecal coliform bacteria, produced by humans and cattle alike. Contact with polluted water can cause ailments ranging from common diarrhea to eye or ear infections. Officials said eating properly cooked fish from the river was safe, but swimming or tubing was not.

Pollution from municipal sewage lagoons may be obvious, but dairy farm pollution is more subtle. Problems come when farmers hose down the areas outside their milking barns. The semi-liquid runoff flows into the pasture, eventually making its way to ditch, creek, and river. In the 1990s, farmers took advantage of government programs designed to help clean up the Tangipahoa. Funded by state and federal agencies, the programs paid as much as 75 percent of the cost of constructing lagoons to treat cattle wastes. Agencies also helped towns along the river find funds to upgrade their sewage lagoons, and health officials sought out camp owners who weren't treating their sewage. When progress lagged, the organization Citizens for a Clean Tangipahoa (CFACT), which monitors the river for the DEQ, joined with the Sierra Club Legal Defense Fund in threatening to sue the towns of Kentwood, Amite, Roseland, Tangipahoa, and Independence over their sewage systems. The upshot was a gradually cleaner river.

Meanwhile, if the bacteria didn't make you sick, the litter would. From Tangipahoa to U.S. 190, beer cans twinkled on every sandbar. CFACT members periodically floated the river, picking up hundreds of bags of litter. Within a month, though, the river was typically trashed again. Part of the problem is access. From Kentwood to Ponchatoula, the Tangipahoa, running roughly parallel to Interstate 55, is stitched by bridges, and nearly every bridge features a swimming hole with fine sandy beaches. Such places make it easy for crowds to tube, float, picnic, swim, and sunbathe. Unfortunately, some of these folks think their mothers are going to clean up after them, leaving heaps of cans, bottles, and bags on the beach. Ironically, the health advisories improved the litter situation, keeping away some of the people who were leaving their trash. All these problems brought lots of media attention and increased public awareness, hopefully leading to better care of this lovely stream.

Some people float the stretches above the town of Tangipahoa, mainly to fish (in particular, the 5 miles from the railroad service road at Chatawa, Mississippi, to the Osyka-Progress Road bridge east of Osyka, Mississippi; 3.5 miles from Osyka to Louisiana 1054 at Greenlaw; 5 more to Louisiana 38 east of Kentwood; and 6.5 more to Highway 440 east of Tangipahoa). But even locals run into problems, like the pair of college lads who got lost in the upper Tangipahoa swamps in July 2001. The young men, both in their early 20s, set off to canoe from U.S. 51 to Chatawa, about 6–7 miles. In theory, that would be 2–3 hours of paddling or 5–6 hours float-fishing. But logjams changed the equation drastically. In places logs blocked the river entirely, and the pair had to portage around through the woods. Within an hour or so they realized they weren't making much progress; they could still hear traffic on Interstate 55. They quit fishing and paddled but by 6:30 P.M. knew they were in trouble. They unloaded everything but paddles, insect repellent, and a cell phone and began paddling as fast as they could. By 8:45 P.M. the pair realized there was no hope in making Chatawa, so they turned around, trying to get back to a spot where the river passes against the railroad track. Unfortunately, in the dark, they mistook a slough on the east side for the main river and wound up even farther off-course. The phone didn't want to work either. At 9:15 they succeeded in contacting one of their mothers and asked her to call a wildlife conservation officer. It took a few hours for the officer and a civil defense director to get there and drive their trucks along a service road by the railroad track that parallels the river to the west. On the fading phone, the officer advised them to leave the canoe, keep the moon to their backs, and walk toward the tracks. Using the dim light of the cell phone as a flashlight, the young men banged their way through the woods and waded through the swamp and across the neck-deep river. They finally reached the rescuers, but they weren't out of the woods yet. One of the trucks got stuck on the muddy, rocky service road, and then the headlight of a train appeared. The officials got on the phone to try to stop the train but it barreled past less than 10 feet away. Finally they got in touch with railroad officials and told them to stop train traffic between New Orleans and Jackson. They winched the truck out and eventually made it to Chatawa—where the hapless paddlers discovered the keys were in the other truck at Highway 51. The wildlife officer gave them a ride, and when they finally got back to Chatawa in the wee hours, the young men were so exhausted and thirsty that they sat at the artesian well by the railroad tracks there and drank their fill.

Things aren't much better for a considerable distance south of the state line. Let me give you a comparison. In Homer's *The Odyssey*, Ulysses must pilot his ship between two monsters: Scylla is a six-headed dragon who plucks sailors from ship's decks; Charybdis is an underwater beast who churns the sea into chaos. Well, if Ulysses had had to steer his little ship down the upper Tangipahoa, *The Odyssey* would have been a short story. I started one float at Greenlaw—the first put-in below the Mississippi line—with a weight lifter, Billy Gibson. Shortly below the put-in, Billy had to put his muscles to work: A log lay across the river, directly in our path. We pulled alongside it, climbed out, and heaved the heavily-loaded canoe over. We didn't realize at the time that we would perform this feat until we were doing it in our dreams. When not hauling over logs, we tried to maneuver the 17-foot canoe around hairpin bends in fast water among sticks and stumps. We zipped through one set of stobs, and as we struggled to make a 90-degree turn, I saw a stump about the size of a hand, smack in our path. We gave a mighty effort but, like Charybdis, the stump got us. It grabbed the boat and flipped it, giving Billy his first canoeing baptism. He remained stoical as we dried our gear on a sandbar, but as we resumed paddling, he thought up a nickname for the upper Tangipahoa: the House of Horrors. And we had only just begun. "You know," I told Billy as we relaxed by a campfire that night, "a real nightmare would be one giant logjam that just went on and on as far as you can see downriver." Next day the nightmare came true. One river bend contained so many logs that I stopped counting at 20. I learned later a tornado had passed that way, flattening the trees. Give me Scylla and Charybdis any day. Unsheathing my machete, I hacked a path through the branches. Then Billy and I got to work pulling the canoe over, under, in between, and around. The logjam was so thick we didn't see how the water could get through. When we got past the bend, we felt like we had just passed Marine Corps basic training. But a short distance above the Highway 440 bridge at Tangipahoa, we

Bobby Funderburk of Baton Rouge uses a 10-foot flatbottom boat to get down Tangipahoa River.

emerged from the jungle onto a wider, shallower, sandier river, enlarged by tributaries and no longer barricaded with fallen trees. The creek had become a river at last.

Below 440 there are wide-open views. Oaks and sycamores tower on high bluffs overlooking vast sandbars. Birch, cypress, and willows loom behind swaths of emerald swamp grass inscripted by S-shaped white egrets. Birdwatchers can have a field day sorting out the egrets, cormorants, ducks, ospreys, herons, and countless smaller birds. In many ways this is classic Louisiana, but with the added bonus of a fun current for paddling. The Tangipahoa runs fast, clear, and tricky, keeping a paddler alert as it sifts among downed trees and over shoals. A small canoe with a bit of rocker is a good choice of vessel, as are pirogues and kayaks—anything that can maneuver the swift turns and dance among the logs. Local anglers use small flatbottom boats to drift the river, angling for bass.

Highways 440 east of Tangipahoa, 10 east of Arcola, 16 east of Amite, 40 east of Independence, and 442 east of Tickfaw all have access, adjoining beaches used by the public. Highway 443 has the most difficult approach, down a steep bank on the northeast side of the river. With distances between these bridges ranging from 4 to 8.5 miles, there are plenty of options for trips. It's 8.5 miles from Tangipahoa to Arcola, 5 more to Amite, 8 to Independence, 5 to Tickfaw, and 4 to Highway 443. Typical canoeing speed on this river is 2–3 miles per hour, 1 if you're fishing.

Although the wide river bed is welcome after the narrow, log-choked stretches, it reflects another problem: headcutting. As on the Amite, gravel mining has spurred erosion, resulting in collapsing banks, shallower water, and ever-growing gravel bars. Officials say this headcutting is moving slowly upstream.

Four miles below Highway 443, Chappepeela (which means hurricane) Creek runs in from the northeast. U.S. 190 crosses the Tangipahoa 2.5 miles below that, Interstate 12 in 2.5 more miles, and Highway 22 in 3 more. There is no access at those three bridges. By I-12 sandbars have vanished, the river has narrowed, big trees overhang the water, and the water is deep enough to support motorboats. To a paddler, the sight of teenagers popping wheelies in flatbottom boats with high-powered outboards is not cheering. Riverside camp houses proliferate around Highway 22 east of Ponchatoula, so even finding a secluded place in the woods to camp is difficult. But camp houses thin out as the river continues south in serpentine fashion, at times doubling back on itself. Some 5 miles below Highway 22, Lee's Landing on the east bank offers the last takeout before Pontchartrain. Below Lee's, the Tangipahoa continues for 7 miles to Lake Pontchartrain, with Bedico (pronounced BEE-di-co, a corruption of the name Bethencourt, an early French settler) Creek entering from the northeast about 2 miles before the lake. There is no takeout on Lake Pontchartrain.

The only public campground near the river is Percy Quin State Park, one of Mississippi's most popular parks. You can rent canoes to paddle the 700-acre lake and venture a mile up the tree-arched upper Tangipahoa River, or walk trails and boardwalks alongside it. While Louisiana's Tangipahoa Parish lacks a state park near the river, there are plenty of private campgrounds in the parish. Hidden Oaks Family Campground off Highway 445 north of Robert is the only one on the Tangipahoa and provides half-day canoe trips. It also boasts a variety of festivals including Native American powwows the first weekend in May and on Thanksgiving, a Memorial Day Swamp Pop Fest, a crawfish boil in the spring and pig roast in the fall, a fireworks display July 4, and a snow machine providing real snow in December.

Some 10 miles east of Independence on Highway 40 is Zemurray Gardens. It's open only in early spring when azaleas are in bloom and is well worth a visit by anyone who loves natural beauty, as most paddlers do. This 150-acre rhapsody in flowers has 250,000 azaleas, 10,000 camellias, as well as countless white dogwoods, red-berried ardisia, fragrant lavendar wisteria, yellow and purple irises, yellow daffodils, white canterbury bells, pink native azaleas, tulip trees, giant bamboo, and more. An easy walking trail wends among lofty pines through avenues of sheer, intoxicating color around a 20-acre lake garnished here and there with classical statues, like the bowhuntress Artemis, the houndsman Actaeon and the beautiful young mother Daphne with child beside her. Admission is $4 for adults, $3 for children and senior citizens. There's a large picnic area out front, or combine your trip with a visit to one of the great restaurants in nearby towns. The gardens are open from 10 A.M. to 6 P.M. daily in season. For more information call 504-878-2284. For more information on other parish destinations, contact the Tangipahoa Parish Tourist Commission at 1-800-542-7520.

Tangipahoa River options

1. Tangipahoa to Louisiana 10 east of Arcola, 8.5 miles.
2. Arcola to Louisiana 16 east of Amite, 5 miles.
3. Amite to Louisiana 40 east of Independence, 8 miles.
4. Independence to Louisiana 442 east of Tickfaw, 5 miles.
5. Tickfaw to Louisiana 443, 4 miles.
6. Highway 443 to Lee's Landing on Louisiana 445 south of Louisiana 22, 17 miles. There is no access to the Tangipahoa at U.S. 190, Interstate 12 or Highway 22 east of Ponchatoula. Lee's Landing is at the end of Louisiana 445 on the east side of the river.

Area campgrounds and outfitters

Percy Quin State Park, Highway 48 West, McComb, Mississippi, 601-684-3938. Rents canoes for use in park.

Hidden Oaks Family Campground at Robert provides half-day canoe trips, 1-800-359-0940.

Maps

Louisiana Atlas and Gazetteer.

High points

Nice current, lots of gravel bars.

Low points

Litter, history of fecal coliform pollution.

Tips

The 13.5-mile stretch from Tangipahoa to Amite makes a delightful day trip.

Bogue Falaya and Tchefuncte River

Tchefuncte River starts in the piney woods and dairy farm country between Tangipahoa and Franklinton. It glides south in the narrow corridor between the Tangipahoa River to the west and Bogue Chitto to the east. The Tchefuncte remains a creek almost until it reaches the town of Covington, where it quickly swells to a size large enough to accommodate yachts. At Madisonville it's big enough to host the flotillas of the annual wooden boat festival. Two miles below there it enters Lake Pontchartrain.

For a paddler, the Tchefuncte becomes dependably floatable below U.S. 190 northwest of Covington, though local residents canoe upper stretches when there's sufficient water, dragging over logjams when necessary. There's no public access at 190, but Covington provides access to the Tchefuncte and its main tributary, Bogue Falaya River. The two rivers converge just south of town, Tchefuncte from the northwest and Bogue Falaya from the northeast. On the Tchefuncte, there's a ramp at the west end of East Second Avenue, 2 miles above the convergence. On Bogue Falaya, you can launch at Bogue Falaya Wayside Park off North New Hampshire Avenue 3.5 miles above the convergence, or Menetre (pronounced MEN-e-tree) Park at the end of East Fourth Avenue 1.5 miles downstream. Bogue Falaya Wayside Park is only open from 8 A.M. to 5 P.M. daily, so if you plan to launch before or after then, pick a different spot. From any of these launch sites you can leisurely explore the two rivers, up and down, as well as Abita River, which runs into Bogue Falaya from the east across from Menetre Park.

The word "Tchefuncte" is the name of an Indian tribe and came from the Choctaw word "hachofakti" for chinquapin, a nut-bearing tree. Bogue Falaya is

Choctaw for long creek: Bogue means creek or swamp; falaya means long. Despite the name, Bogue Falaya is remarkably short. While it can hold large motorboats at Covington, in dry season it is inches deep and logjammed just above the Highway 190 bridge on the east side of town. Below Menetre, Bogue Falaya joins the Tchefuncte River in less than 2 miles, which means the navigable portion of Bogue Falaya is barely 5 miles in low water. But what a gorgeous 5 miles! Leaving the park and heading upstream on Bogue Falaya, you can dip your paddle into a mirror image of blue sky and rich green live oaks, cypress, beech, hackberry, and pine, splintered now and then by the poised figures of great white herons. Here and there grassy lawns reach back to beautiful houses. Assorted vessels shelter under trees and in boathouses: pirogues, canoes, johnboats, personal watercraft, party barges.

When Covington resident Brian Moore and I paddled up Bogue Falaya one late-summer day, our paddles began to stab sand after we passed Highway 190. Schools of fish fled in the shallows, and trees closed in overhead for a remarkable sense of woodland seclusion, considering how close we were to town. How far you can go above Highway 190 depends on the water level and your willingness to climb over logjams or tow the boat over sandy shoals. We paddled a mile and crossed two logjams above 190 before the creek grew too shallow to continue. But the water level was low, and you can no doubt go farther when it's higher. We returned to the park for lunch, then continued down to Bogue Falaya's juncture with Tchefuncte. We turned right and paddled up the Tchefuncte, this time skirting the west side of town, which has a similar mix of woods, houses, and moored boats. First Avenue Park borders the river with a high, covered wooden deck over the water. The ramp at the end of East Second Avenue is shortly above there. It's about 8 miles upriver to the Highway 190 bridge, and current is slight. Above 190, both the Bogue Falaya and Tchefuncte extend well upcountry in the form of creeks. Unfortunately, they're prone to fecal coliform pollution due to dairy farms, small towns, camps, and houses.

From the juncture of Tchefuncte and Bogue Falaya, it's 7 miles downriver to Fairview-Riverside State Park on a wide, slow river lined with woods and houses and traversed by big boats. You can take out at the park, on the east side of the river, or on the northeast side of the Highway 22 bridge a mile downstream. The final takeout on the river is a ramp at the end of Louisiana 1077 on the west side near the mouth, a couple miles below Highway 22. (Launching is free unless you have a boat trailer, in which case you must pay a $12 annual fee at town hall in Madisonville; call 504-845-7311 for details.) You can get to a nearby scenic bayou here by paddling east across the river and along the shore of Lake Pontchartrain about 50 yards, then portaging north over into Bayou Chinchuba, which parallels the lakeshore.

The 99-acre Fairview-Riverside State Park offers 81 developed campsites plus a tent camping area. With its pine trees, live oaks, and riverfront, the park is undeniably beautiful. Unfortunately, nearby industry makes for noisy camping. On the plus side, the river yields bass, white perch, and bream near the park, which has a fishing pier, and channel catfish, speckled trout, and redfish where the river meets the lake. Crabbing in the lake and river is also popular. So is skiing, so it's wise to avoid summer weekends. The stretch below the park provides views of condos and marsh. Upriver yields a mix of cypress woods and wealthy houses. There is little current to impede progress, and the industrial noise fades after a few bends. A few ancient, stranded boats add charm. But as a reminder that this area lies within the grip of modern development, an interesting-looking cypress slough to the west leads not to deep swamp but to a sewage treatment facility.

Such facets are partly redeemed by the town of Madisonville across the river from the park. Attractive old houses line shady streets; children play ball in the town park; a drawbridge leads east out of town; narrow Highway 1077 winds south through the marsh to the windswept lake. Madisonville, with a population around 1,000, though growing fast, has the good fortune to lie off the beaten path. Its relatively isolated location north of Pontchartrain, south of Interstate 12, and west of the Lake Pontchartrain Causeway has helped preserve its small-town beauty. Founded in 1811, the historic town is proud of its heritage, and rightly so. There's the Madisonville Museum, located in the old courthouse, plus old houses like 1807 Bayou Cottage. And there are riverside restaurants where you can sit outside and eat po-boys as sunlight dances on the breeze-brushed water. For more information on Madisonville, call the Greater Madisonville Area Chamber of Commerce at 504-845-9824.

By far the most appealing thing about Madisonville, from a paddler's standpoint, is the annual wooden boat festival held the last weekend of September each year. People reportedly come from as far off as Alaska and New England for

A team builds a pirogue in the "quick and dirty" boat-building contest at the wooden boat festival by Tchefuncte River in Madisonville.

the event, which is well-known in wooden boating circles. At a typical festival, small boats like canoes, pirogues, rowboats, punts, and yawls are displayed on shore, some of them for sale. Even more vessels float in the river, lined up gunwale to gunwale or standing offshore. There are long, sleek bateaux with old-timey motors, wood-toned runabouts, classic round-bellied sailboats, and huge yachts. In addition to boats on display, there are old motors and nautical equipment along with booths selling fine cigars, T-shirts, books, photography, art, and jewelry as well as jambalaya, po-boys, and other regional treats. Live music may include blues, Cajun, bagpipes, and Caribbean steel drums. The highlight of the weekend is the "quick-and-dirty" boat-building contest. On Saturday, teams of competitors are given plywood, boards, sailcloth, wire, screws, nails, and rope, with 12 hours in which to construct a vessel from scratch. They work feverishly just north of the drawbridge over the river, with a roped-off path allowing spectators to stroll by and observe. On Sunday the boats race, using oar and sail. Proceeds from the festival go toward the Lake Pontchartrain Basin Maritime Museum, which is open 10 A.M. to 4:30 P.M. weekdays at 133 Mable Street in Madisonville. For more information call 504-845-9200.

Tchefuncte, Bogue Falaya options

1. Launch on Bogue Falaya River at Bogue Falaya Wayside Park at the south end of North New Hampshire Street in downtown Covington. The park is open 8 A.M. to 5 P.M. weekdays. Call 985-898-0333 for details.

2. Launch on Bogue Falayala at Menetre Park at the east end of East Fourth Avenue in Covington on Bogue Falayala 1.5 miles downstream from Bogue Falaya Wayside Park, and explore Bogue Falaya, Abita, and Tchefuncte Rivers. East Fourth is in the south end of town off South Jahncke Avenue.

3. Launch on Tchefuncte from public ramp at the west end of East Second Avenue in Covington. The juncture with Bogue Falaya is a couple miles downstream. East Second is in the south end of town off South Jahncke Avenue.

4. For a downriver trip, paddle 9 miles from Menetre Park in Covington to Fairview-Riverside State Park on Louisiana 22 just east of Madisonville; another mile to a takeout on the northeast side of Highway 22; and 2 more miles to a ramp at the end of Highway 1077 near the river mouth on the west side.

Area campgrounds

Fairview-Riverside State Park on Highway 22 just east of Madisonville on Tchefuncte River, 1-888-677-3247.

Maps

For a map of Covington, which is useful in locating access points in town, call the Covington Downtown Development Association, 1-866-892-1873.

High points

Gorgeous scenery around Covington lends itself to leisurely day paddling.

Low points

Most of the canoeable portion of the river is also large enough for big motorboats due to its estuarylike nature.

Tips

Visit Madisonville's wooden boat festival held the last weekend of September each year.

Lake Pontchartrain

Lake Pontchartrain, the 41-by-25 mile brackish lake whose south shore is occupied by the city of New Orleans, hardly seems a sensible canoeing destination at first glance. It's vast, windswept, and marshy-shored. But the lake is ringed with bayou-laced parks and wildlife refuges, providing good paddling along with an easy way to sample the 630-square-mile lake. The disk-shaped Pontchartrain sprawls between Interstates 55 on the west and 10 on the east, with the towns of Madisonville and Mandeville on the scenic north shore and Slidell to the east. In 1718 French explorer Sieur Jean-Baptiste LeMoyne de Bienville founded New Orleans on the saddle of land between Pontchartrain and the nearby Mississippi River to the south for strategic reasons, guarding ingress from both sides. Nowadays visitors can go to the French Quarter and admire riverboats and ocean vessels in the Mississippi River, then drive across town to feel the breeze and listen to the gulls at Pontchartrain.

Some canoeing is possible within the city. On the east side of town, 23,000-acre Bayou Sauvage National Wildlife Refuge forms the largest urban national wildlife refuge in the nation, lying entirely within New Orleans city limits. A boat ramp on Louisiana 11 about 4 miles north of Highway 90 provides access to miles of canals, ponds, bayous, and marsh. No camping is allowed in the refuge, but it offers a number of daytime activities in addition to paddling: hiking on Ridge Trail boardwalk, which leads to Madere Marsh and an observation deck; bicycling on the Maxent Canal levee, on roadways within the refuge, and on a bike trail on the Lake Pontchartrain hurricane protection levee; wildlife watching, with the possibility of spotting alligators, bald eagles, peregrine falcons, wood ducks, and wintering waterfowl; and fishing from boats and shore along Maxent Canal and off Highway 11. The U.S. Fish and Wildlife Service provides free guided canoe trips at Bayou Sauvage and at Big Branch Marsh NWR (see below) on the north side of the lake. The day trips are conducted on weekends year-round and include one evening trip per month. The Service provides canoes, life jackets, and paddles. Make reservations well in advance.

An excellent canoeing spot on the lake is Cane Bayou on the north shore east of Mandeville. The bayou, listed as a Louisiana Natural and Scenic River, forms the boundary between 11,000-acre Big Branch Marsh NWR on the east and 2,900-acre Fontainebleau State Park on the west. There's a gravel boat launch on U.S. 190 a half mile east of Fontainebleau park, leading south through a mix of cypress swamp and marsh to the lake just over a mile away.

When you launch onto Cane Bayou from 190, at first the sounds of the swamp seem to consist mainly of roaring traffic and heavy equipment. But after a little paddling down the muddy bayou, natural sounds take over: the hum of crickets, trill of songbirds, wind in the cypress. Tensions fade as the bliss of nature sets in. To the right lies the state park, to the left the refuge. The woods give way to marsh, and you may spot a massive osprey nest in a dead tree, with a pair of the majestic birds soaring overhead. After about a mile you'll see what appear to be flocks of low-flying birds wheeling just over the surface of an open lake. A closer look shows those flocks to be an optical illusion: They're waves. As you emerge onto Lake Pontchartrain, the hazy silhouette of the New Orleans skyline limns the horizon 20-odd miles south. To the right stretches the Lake Pontchartrain Causeway like a dinosaur's backbone. Everywhere else is water, sky, and marsh. A right turn will take you along the park shoreline. In a little over 2 miles, if you venture that far, you'll see the park beach and brick buildings on the right. In the park, a gated grass road to the left of the shoreside bathhouses leads to the beach; ask for the combination to the lock at the park entrance. To paddle the national wildlife refuge shoreline, turn left from Cane Bayou onto the lake.

Either way, the view is mainly of marshy shore leading back to a dark wall of forest. The water close to shore is around 2 feet deep and often clear as an aquarium. But exercise caution on the lake since wind and waves can get up in a hurry. Even light, gusty breezes can pose problems, especially if you make the mistake I did and paddle a big, empty, two-man canoe solo. At times the puffs skittered my vessel sideways, forcing me to drop to my knees and manhandle it back in position. But during lulls I tried standing and using my long paddle as a pole. It's not hard to imagine Native Americans poling dugouts through the shallows, spearing fish, collecting shellfish, picking wild greens, and plucking tubers. Their modern-day counterparts angle for fish from motorboats anchored in the channel. When you get tired of fighting the wind, return to Cane Bayou, which has several narrow side-channels to explore. You can probe clearwater chutes little wider than a canoe as panicked fish torpedo away from you. Some passages dead-end; others widen to small lakes and marshy mazes punctuated by cypress trunks. Purple Louisiana irises bloom by the acre in the spring. East of Cane Bayou, a channel runs through a pretty stretch of woods to a residential area on Lemieux Road.

The adjacent Fontainebleau State Park offers majestic live oaks draped with Spanish moss along park roads, plus a nature trail that leads to Cane Bayou, and campgrounds with 127 improved campsites, 39 unimproved campsites, a separate primitive camping area, group camps, swimming pool, beach, and lodge. Modern visitors can thank a 7-foot tall blacksmith for all this. In the early 1800s, wealthy plantation owner Bernard Marigny challenged a hefty blacksmith to a duel, a common way to settle disputes in that era. The gentle giant didn't want to fight, but finally agreed to choose his weapons: sledge hammers in 6 feet of water. His humor defused Marigny's anger, and the two men had a good laugh together. Had Marigny fought the big man and not have survived, a 2,900-acre chunk of his north-shore plantation may never have been set aside as Fontainebleau State Park. As it was, Marigny went on to develop the town of Mandeville and establish a ferry service to New Orleans, precursor to the causeway. The live oaks in the park were probably big when Marigny was a lad. The brick remains of an old sugar mill stand among them. Nearby, the loop hiking trail crosses the route of an old dummy line—a narrow-gauge railroad used for logging—and winds through big woods full of weird reptiles and amphibians, like the fat brown skink with a red head I saw perched on a log.

Big Branch Marsh NWR has a more recent history. Assisted by conservation groups, the U.S. Fish and Wildlife Service purchased 3,300 acres in 1994 and has continued to acquire land. The refuge now encompasses 11,000 acres. There is a visitor center on Highway 434 just north of Lacombe, open 9 A.M. to 4 P.M. Mondays through Saturdays. While Cane Bayou is the most popular destination, paddlers can launch at a ramp that gives access to Lake Pontchartrain and Bayou Lacombe at the end of Highway 434 (Lake Road) south of Lacombe. There's also a launch site on an old pipeline canal on Bayou Paquet Road; turn south off Highway 190 onto Transmitter Road a couple miles east of Lacombe, then west onto Bayou Paquet Road. This area provides marsh paddling, and only nonmotorized vessels are permitted. The canal leads a couple miles through the marsh to the lake; if the water is high enough you can paddle out into the marsh among wading birds. Hikers and mountain bikers can drive west on Bayou Paquet Road to the old Boy Scout Road, which has been converted into a 4.5-mile trail with a quarter-mile boardwalk and observation tower.

West of Fontainebleau lies Fairview-Riverside State Park on Highway 22 just east of Madisonville on the Tchefuncte River. Both Fontainebleau and Fairview-Riverside State Parks are a short distance east of Hammond, with signs on I-12 pointing the way. There's also a ramp at the end of Highway 1077 south of Madisonville on the west side of Tchefuncte near its outlet into Pontchartrain. (See Tchefuncte River section above). West of the ramp, accessible only by boat, stands a 30-foot lighthouse originally built in 1838 and rebuilt in 1868. A group is working to restore it.

A sea kayak is an obvious choice for paddling on Lake Pontchartrain. Not many people care to venture far onto the lake in a canoe, but one notable exception is Arthur Hebert of Gretna. In 1990 Hebert, a construction supervisor by trade, paddled a canoe 49 miles west to east across Lake Pontchartrain in 15 hours and 45 minutes. In 1992 he circumnavigated the lake, 108 miles in 50 hours. Both trips were fund-raisers for Covenant House, a shelter for homeless and runaway children. Those trips were just warm-ups for much longer sea kayaking journeys. In 1993 Hebert and a partner kayaked 480 miles of Louisiana coastline from Mississippi to Texas. In 1997 he paddled 200 miles from Pensacola, Florida, to Madisonville, Louisiana. Then, in 1998, Hebert did the near-impossible and crossed the Gulf of Mexico in a sea kayak, paddling 720 miles in 19 days across the open Gulf, from Isla Mujeres, Mexico, to Southwest Pass on the Mississippi River, without an escort boat. Compared to that, Lake Pontchartrain is a pond.

Lake Pontchartrain options

1. Launch at Cane Bayou on U.S. 190 east of Mandeville and paddle 1 mile to Lake Pontchartrain between Fontainebleau State Park and Big Branch Marsh National Wildlife Refuge, exploring bayous and marshes along the way, then the lakeshore.

2. Launch directly onto lake at Fontainebleau State Park. Take gated road to the left of the shoreside bathhouses. Ask for the lock combination at the park entrance.

3. Launch at old pipeline canal on Bayou Paquet Road. To get there, turn south off Highway 190 onto Transmitter Road a couple miles east of Lacombe, then drive west onto Bayou Paquet Road. The canal leads a couple miles through the marsh to the lake.

4. Launch at ramp that gives access to Lake Pontchartrain and Bayou Lacombe at the end of Highway 434 (Lake Road) south of Lacombe.

5. Launch at ramp at the end of Highway 1077 south of Madisonville on the west side of Tchefuncte near its outlet into Pontchartrain.

6. Take a free guided canoe day trip on weekends year-round at Big Branch Marsh NWR and Bayou Sauvage NWR. Call 985-882-3881 for reservations.

7. On the east side of New Orleans, launch at boat ramp on Louisiana 11 and explore canals, ponds, bayous, and marsh in Bayou Sauvage National Wildlife Refuge.

Area campgrounds

Fontainebleau State Park on Lake Pontchartrain, U.S. 190 just east of Mandeville, 1-888-677-3668.

Fairview-Riverside State Park on Highway 22 just east of Madisonville on Tchefuncte River, 1-888-677-3247.

Outfitters

Canoe and Trail Adventures, Metairie, 504-834-5257, www.canoeandtrail.com. Leads guided trips.

Maps

Maps of Big Branch and Bayou Sauvage National Wildlife Refuges are available by calling 985-646-7544.

High points

Marsh and bayou paddling along edges of lake, with several parks and wildlife refuges.

Low points

Wind can be a problem on the lake itself.

Tips

From a starting point, like Cane Bayou, paddle a short distance along the lakeshore to get acquainted with this impressive realm.

Bogue Chitto River

The Bogue Chitto River presents two distinctly different paddling experiences. One is a downriver float trip with nice current and good scenery. The other is a deep-swamp journey with sloughs branching off into the unknown. One is carefree and easy, while the other requires a bit of planning.

The Bogue Chitto (Choctaw Bogue for creek, Chitto for big) begins near Brookhaven, Mississippi, meanders southeast some 100 miles past Franklinton, and merges with the vast swamps of the Bogue Chitto National Wildlife Refuge along Pearl River. The Bogue Chitto River is canoeable for more than 30 miles in Mississippi and more than 50 in Louisiana. For most of its length it's just the right size for a canoe—too small for most motorboats but big enough to obviate excessive logjams and shallows. The water is fairly clear and there are sandbars galore.

The Bogue Chitto enters Louisiana near Warnerton. The last bridge in Mississippi is on Dillons Bridge Road, which runs east from Mississippi 27 a couple miles north of the state line. Dillons Bridge itself lacks decent access, but there are two canoe rental companies with good landings. Mississippi's share of the Bogue Chitto is more pleasant than Louisiana's because of the number of gravel mines in Louisiana. Between the state line and Franklinton, heavy machinery growls almost without pause at the huge sand and gravel pits next to the river. Gravel mining has been a longstanding source of controversy in Louisiana. It can silt up the water and foster a type of erosion called headcutting, which works gradually upstream, rendering a stream wide and shallow. Mines are usually located just adjacent to the river, and landowners have the legal right to do the work on their own property. The noise and sight of machinery definitely detracts from the aesthetics, but the river remains beautiful anyway, with purling water, white sands, and leaning sycamores and birches.

Not too aesthetic but nevertheless interesting on this part of the river are the plentiful black and turkey vultures. If you see buzzards early in a float trip, it's a clear omen that you'll never make it out alive; the big birds foresee your fate and are waiting to pick your bones clean. At least that's what I tell people who float with me for the first time. Actually, I don't recall any Deep South float without vultures wheeling overhead. They like the remoteness of rivers and often roost on big dead trees nearby. The easy way to tell the difference between the two species is the head: black buzzards have a black head, while turkey vultures have a head like a turkey's.

It's 3.5 miles from Dillons Bridge to Louisiana 438 at Warnerton, 6 miles from Warnerton to Louisiana 38 west of Clifton, and 9 more to Louisiana 10 just west of Franklinton. Plans are in the works to establish a state park on the river 5 miles south of Franklinton, which is great news for paddlers. The park will include RV and tent camping sites, cabins, a visitor center, trails, picnic areas, and lakes converted from old gravel borrow pits. The Office of State Parks may also work with a canoe outfitter to provide convenient river recreation for visitors. As for camping, some canoe rentals along the river also have campgrounds.

From Franklinton it's 13 miles to Louisiana 437 southwest of Enon, 7 miles to Isabel, and 10 miles to Louisiana 21 between Sun and Bush. Highway 21 is the last takeout on the river proper. However, you can continue 3 miles to the West Pearl barge canal, turn north, and paddle less than a mile to Lock 3, where there's a boat ramp. The lock is at the end of a narrow road east of Sun off Louisiana 21.

Louisiana 25 parallels the river from the state line to Franklinton; then Louisiana 16 continues to do so down to Sun, forming a pretty much continuous river road. It stays on the river's east side for its entire length, with roads leading west (or southwest) to bridges across the river at Warnerton, Clifton, Franklinton, Enon, Isabel, and Sun. There's some sort of access to the river at every bridge, though at Isabel and Enon it's via canoe rental companies only. If number of canoe rental companies is an indicator of popularity, the Bogue Chitto is right up there with Whiskey Chitto. I count around three rentals in Louisiana and five in Mississippi. An obvious reason for the Bogue Chitto's popularity, aside from its current and sandbars, is its ideal size, which remains pretty much the same from Pike County to Pearl River.

For the most part, canoeing the Bogue Chitto isn't difficult. In places it's moderately demanding as it shoots among logs, over shoals, and around bends. In other places the water barely moves. Most any canoe will work well on the river, though one with slight rocker is at an advantage since it can handle both swifts and flatwater. Pirogues and river kayaks also work well on the Bogue Chitto. Bass fishing is good with topwater lures and spinnerbaits. Just drift along and cast around logs and against the bank. For bream, crappie, or catfish, stop in a bend with a large, deep pool and angle with crickets or worms. Droplines baited with worms or other live bait will catch catfish at night.

The Bogue Chitto changes from river to swamp at the West Pearl barge canal, which forms the western boundary of the Bogue Chitto National Wildlife

Lawrence Pitcairn of Winnipeg, Manitoba, gets a taste of the Bogue Chitto
River during high water.

Refuge. The 37,000-acre refuge extends some 21 miles along both sides of
Pearl River from just south of the St. Tammany Parish line. To follow the Bogue
Chitto River through the swamp: When you get to the barge canal, turn right,
paddle a short distance, portage around a lowhead dam to the left, and follow
the river some 10 miles to Wilson Slough (which becomes West Pearl River).
Turn right and paddle 14 miles, passing the mouth of Holmes Bayou on the
east, to the intersection with the barge canal. Turn right onto the canal and go
half a mile to a boat ramp at Lock 1, located off Louisiana 41. To continue down
the Pearl, see Pearl River section below. Bogue Chitto NWR allows primitive
camping within 100 feet of Bogue Chitto River, Wilson Slough, West Pearl
River south of Wilson Slough, East Pearl River, and Holmes Bayou. Camping
conditions aren't great, but there are strips of dry ground, even a few small
sandbars. The refuge is closed to camping when the Pearl reaches 15.5 feet on
the Pearl River gauge.

The lower Bogue Chitto is plied with motorboats, and the most interesting areas lie off the river on the convoluted sloughs and bayous. That's where things
get tricky. I recommend taking the U.S.G.S. quad maps Industrial and Hickory,
which show the river and swamp, plus a compass and GPS. Either that or take a

carefree spirit and plenty of provisions, like Scott Williams and I did when we ventured into this swamp.

Scott and I started canoeing the Bogue Chitto at U.S. 98 in Mississippi, and after nearly a week we reached the swamp. I already knew this area was formidable, having read a newspaper article about a man lost for a week, and having talked to others who had also gotten turned around. Even so, we took only a highway map. Chalk it up to bravado, laziness, or youth. We crossed the West Pearl barge canal and followed the slow, muddy Bogue Chitto through deep, dark forest, making camp in the woods where a cypress-kneed stream coursed past a small shaded sandbar. We didn't get lost until the next day. That's when we turned off the main Bogue Chitto, following a mysterious wooden sign with an emblem of a canoe. We soon passed even odder canoe signs bearing numbers with no apparent significance. We wound up on a swift, curving, log-jammed stream under huge trees. Such currents make it hard to retrace your steps. Our canoe slammed into fallen logs as we struggled to keep from turning over. There were no more canoe signs. I kept an eye on my compass as our stream led us east, north, south, and occasionally west. At last we emerged onto a wide river. Scott and I nodded as though we had planned it this way—though we weren't sure if we were on the West, East, or perhaps even the Middle Pearl.

A strong south wind whipped the wide river into swells and whitecaps, battering our canoe and taxing our strength as we paddled downriver. We took refuge on a rare sandbar and made camp. Next day we passed under an interstate highway. Then a branch of the river split off to our left. It was smaller and thus more enticing to a canoe than the big river, so off we went. The muddy stream promptly divided again, with branches angling off to the north and east. We saw signs indicating we were in Louisiana, though by our reckonings based on studying the highway map we should be in Mississippi. I shrugged and concluded that whoever put the signs up was simply in error. Our stream continued to split until it was narrow and swift. "As long as we keep going downstream we'll be all right," I opined. Almost immediately, the river ran into a wide, sluggish bayou with no apparent current. "As long as we keep headed south we'll be all right," I declared. The bayou promptly angled northeast. "Wonder where we are?" I said. The bayou branched and branched again, spreading into wide channels as we entered marsh country. The Pearl River had disappeared. We had to face facts: We were flat-out lost.

Mind you, we weren't concerned enough to ask a passing fisherman for directions. Rather, we tried to discern currents by the angle of lily pad stems and the pattern of the waves. Then we noticed surer signs—a utility pole, and a small bridge that by our calculations had no business being there. At the bridge, an old-timer told us this was Highway 90 over the Middle Pearl. Scott's truck was parked on Highway 90 on the East Pearl at Pearlington, so we weren't too far off. We found an east-west bayou connecting the various Pearls, so off we went, arriving at the truck on schedule.

Since then I've acquired all kinds of maps and have a pretty good idea where we went (I think). And I admit if I made the trip again I'd take better maps. But there's an appeal to that sort of devil-may-care travel, if you're prepared for it. After all, if you have a canoe full of gear, several days at your disposal, and the desire to explore, getting lost is part of the fun. However, there are safer ways to explore the swamp. Forge your own route with detailed maps and GPS. Sign up for a guided trip. Even take a motorboat tour, of which there are many. But this wild, wonderful country is worth a look.

Bogue Chitto River options

1. Mississippi 570 to Mississippi 44 east of McComb, 4 miles.
2. Highway 44 to Holmesville, 7 miles. The Holmesville bridge is located on Pike 93 Central north of U.S. 98.
3. Holmesville to ramp at U.S. 98, 4 miles.
4. Highway 98 to ramp at Bogue Chitto Water Park, 2 miles. The water park is located on the west side of the river off 98.
5. Bogue Chitto Water Park to ramp at Walker's Memorial Water Park just south of Mississippi 48 (Walker's Bridge), 5 miles. To get to the park, take the first road south on the west side of the river. There is no sign, so watch for the paved drive among several residences about half a mile from Highway 48.
6. Walker's Park to Stallings Bridge Road west of Lexie, Mississippi, 6 miles.
7. Stallings Bridge to Dillons Bridge west of Mississippi 27 south of Lexie, 3 miles. Magee's Creek, a good floating stream, enters from the east a half mile above Dillons Bridge.
8. Dillons Bridge to Louisiana 438 at Warnerton, Louisiana, 3.5 miles.
9. Highway 438 to Louisiana 38 west of Clifton, Louisiana, 6 miles.
10. Highway 38 to Louisiana 10 just west of Franklinton, Louisiana, 9 miles.
11. Highway 10 to Louisiana 437 southwest of Enon, Louisiana, 13 miles.

12. Highway 437 to rural road at Isabel, 7 miles.

13. Isabel to Louisiana 21 between Sun and Bush, Louisiana, 10 miles.

14. Highway 21 to Lock 3 on West Pearl barge canal east of Sun, Louisiana, 4 miles. Turn left, or north, at barge canal 3 miles below Highway 21 and paddle less than a mile to Lock 3, where there's a ramp.

15. Lock 3 to Lock 1 via Bogue Chitto and Pearl Rivers, 24 miles. When Bogue Chitto enters barge canal, turn right onto canal, then portage around lowhead dam to left. Go 10 miles to Wilson Slough and turn right. It becomes the West Pearl River. When it intersects with the lower end of the barge canal in about 14 miles, turn right and go half a mile to a boat ramp at Lock 1 located off Louisiana Highway 41. To continue down the Pearl, see Pearl River section below.

Outfitters

Bogue Chitto Choo Choo, near entrance to Bogue Chitto Water Park, 601-249-3788.

Dogwood Rentals, near entrance to Bogue Chitto Water Park.

Ryals Canoe and Tube Rentals, near entrance to Bogue Chitto Water Park, 601-684-4948.

Canoe and Trail Outpost at Dillons Bridge, 601-876-6964.

Sweetwater Park and Canoe Renting, Dillons Bridge, 601-876-5474.

Wayne's World, Enon, 504-795-2004.

Bogue Chitto Canoeing and Tubing Center, Isabel, 504-735-1173.

Canoe and Trail Adventures, Metairie, 504-834-5257, www.canoeand trail.com. Provides guided trips.

Area campgrounds

Bogue Chitto Water Park, Dogwood Trail east of McComb, Mississippi, off U.S. 98 just west of river, 601-684-9568.

Bogue Chitto River State Park, to be located off Louisiana 16 south of Franklinton, 1-888-677-1400.

Maps

To float the river prior to its entry into Bogue Chitto National Wildlife Refuge, the *Louisiana Atlas and Gazetteer* is sufficient.

For a not-too-detailed map of the refuge, call the U.S. Fish and Wildlife Service at 504-646-7555.

U.S.G.S. quad maps of the lower river are Industrial and Hickory; call 1-888-ASK-USGS.

Fishing Map Center maps of Bogue Chitto NWR are available at area sporting goods stores.

High points

Clear water, nice current, abundant sandbars.

Low points

Gravel mines.

Tips

Get quad map or equivalent for the swamp portion of the river.

Pearl River

The Pearl River is more than 400 miles long, with the upper 300 in Mississippi and the lower 100 forming the border between Mississippi and southeast Louisiana. It got its modern-day name from French explorers who discovered pearls near the mouth of the river. The river begins in northeast Mississippi, spreads behind a dam at Ross Barnett Reservoir near Jackson, Mississippi, then runs south through the middle of the state until it reaches the Louisiana line northeast of the village of Angie. By this point the Pearl is a wide, muddy river traveled by fishermen in johnboats. Below Bogalusa, it splits into numerous channels, made more complicated by a man-made canal, sills, a weir, and so on. Despite these difficulties it passes through some fabulous cypress swamp and marsh and thus is of interest to paddlers.

Some of the best, and least complicated, paddling is in the 34,000-acre Pearl River Wildlife Management Area, which stretches south from Interstate 59 for 18 miles to the coast. At U.S. 90 in particular, a host of options present themselves for day trips. By that point the Pearl has split into five channels, each with its own bridge. While you can launch at any of the five bridges, the middle one is best-positioned for exploring. From there you can paddle north into the cypress swamp, looping back around or returning the way you came, probing into side shoots that appeal. Or venture south into the marsh, where the interconnecting waterways provide all sorts of options. Since they connect, you can make loop trips without retracing your steps. The Pearl River WMA map makes it easy to find your way.

An example of a leisurely 9-mile circuit through the marsh: Launch at the middle bridge, paddle half a mile south on Middle River, turn left onto Old Pearl River, go a mile, and take the left fork onto broad East Pearl. Turn right and paddle 2 miles south to a big sandbank made by the dredging of a ship channel. Watch for ships as you cross the channel to the sandbank, which is a good place to stretch your legs. Half a mile south of there, turn northeast back up the Old Pearl. In a quarter mile take the narrow channel to your left. Follow as it swings west and then north back to Old Pearl. Bear immediately left on Old Pearl and enter Grassy Bayou. Travel a mile west on it till you reach West Middle Pearl. Go north 1.5 miles, passing Black Bayou and West Middle Pearl on the left, and stay right as the channel swings back around to the east. Then reconnect with the Middle Pearl and turn left to get back to the bridge. It's actually very simple, especially if you have the WMA map in front of you.

Typical first impression of this marsh environment is monotony. After all, what is marsh but grass, water, and sky? The channels look the same too: broad avenues of water bordered by grass. But as you paddle down Middle River to Old River toward the East Pearl, the sense of monotony evaporates. First there's the alligator or two floating a few feet away, staring. Even if they're only 5-footers, they'll make you wonder where their mama is. Then there are the wildflowers. Seen up close, the marsh isn't just grass at all. It's an unbelievable profusion of plants, aglow with wildflowers. Embroidering the grasses, sedges, and canes are wild displays of blooms. In late summer, for instance, you'll see the white blossoms of bunchflower, swamp lily, false asphodel, and hog-fennel, the pinks of morning glory and seashore mallow, the yellows of sea ox-eye, seaside goldenrod, partridge pea, and rattlebox, the purples of sea lavendar and purple gerardia. A guide to wildflowers is well worth taking along.

On the broad East Pearl, you'll probably encounter motorboats—skiers, fishermen, joy riders. But the river is wide enough that their wakes shouldn't bother you as they would on smaller passageways. Ships are a possibility as you cross the channel to the sandbar on the East Pearl. The sight of a massive, towering vessel is impressive, especially from a canoe. The sand bank provides an eleva-

An oceangoing vessel dwarfs a canoe in Pearl River Wildlife Management Area. Most of the area is not accessible to ships, of course.

tion from which to look out across the shimmering marshes to distant piney woods, billowing smokestacks, bridges, a train moving along a rail trestle, and open water. South of here the Pearl Rivers empty into Little Lake, a bay that gives way to Lake Borgne, a much larger bay in the Gulf of Mexico. To the southwest, out of sight, sprawls New Orleans, and to the southeast the Chandeleur Islands.

When you turn back north onto Old Pearl and enter the narrow channel, you get a close-up view of the marsh. The variety of plants is incredible, not just the flowers but the stems, leaves, roots—the scene easily tops the Impressionists exhibit in the National Museum of Modern Art. As you paddle quietly along, you may startle something big—like the wild hog we spooked in a side slough. It plunged into the weeds, its progress easy to trace by the shaking of the weed tops and the sound of grunts. We kept pace in the canoe, and when the hog realized it was being followed, it increased its speed. But it couldn't shake our canoe. Finally the beast plunged into the water several yards in front of us and swam across. When it emerged on the opposite bank it looked as big as a hippo crossing an African stream. It stared back at us, and for a minute its scowl made me wonder if it might turn on us. But it vanished into the bush without a trace.

I was surprised a hog could get around out here, but when we pulled over to shore, we found a strip of near-dry ground and flattened weeds. There was some footing out here, even if it was squishy.

As you paddle north up Middle River past Black Bayou, on your left lies Honey Island, for which Honey Island Swamp is named. The term Honey Island Swamp is used to describe the entire area of swamp and marsh on the lower Pearl River. But the "island" itself is a patch of marsh bounded by bayous. According to the *Louisiana Atlas and Gazetteer*, it was named for its thriving population of bees. Its wildflowers are different from other areas, with yellow predominating. Maybe they draw more honeybees.

Back at the launch, you may meet local fishermen angling from shore. Anglers use crankbaits and spinners for bass, live bait for catfish. They may throw a cast net to gather shiners for bait, or hook a giant black and yellow locust plucked from a nearby weed. Just about any bass lures will catch bass here, along with redfish and speckled trout.

That's one of many possible trips. A sea kayak enlarges the possibilities since it can cover more miles and handle rougher water than a canoe. With it you can easily get out to Little Lake, Lake Borgne, and the Rigolets (the passage between Lakes Borgne and Pontchartrain). Unlike Bogue Chitto NWR to the north, which allows camping along the main waterways, camping in the WMA is only permitted at Crawford Landing. The primitive campground makes a possible base of operations for day trips in the swamp and marsh. It consists of a grass field with port-a-johns next to a parking area where buses discharge passengers for Honey Island Swamp tours, and I-10 lies just to the south, so traffic noise is constant. Another option is Buccaneer State Park on Beach Boulevard west of Bay St. Louis, Mississippi, some 15 miles east of the river. The 80-acre piney-woods park has 149 developed campsites plus a large primitive campground and group camp areas.

For downriver paddling on the Pearl, you can launch at Lock 1, located off Louisiana Highway 41, paddle 6 miles to a ramp on the east bank under I-59, and another 6 to Davis Landing. These stretches feature a host of side bayous to explore. If you want to continue down the West Pearl, paddle 3 miles from Davis to Crawford Landing, 5 more miles to Indian Village, and 2.5 more to the westernmost bridge on U.S. 90. The west bank of the river is private land and includes camps and residential areas. However, one popular Nature Conservancy-owned area, Maple Slough, lies midway between Indian Village and Highway

90. Take the oxbow to the west and thence go into the mile-long scenic slough, which has a good alligator population, fine cypress trees, and lots of water birds, including bald eagles. If the West Pearl current is slack you can paddle upstream from Highway 90 to Maple Slough, or paddle down from Indian Village and then back up when you're through. The downside of Maple Slough is its popularity with motorized tour boats.

To get into more remote waters, branch off to the east 1.5 miles below Davis Landing. Here things get really interesting as the Pearl splits first into two and ultimately into five rivers, with numerous offshoots. Shortly below the turnoff, you can veer north into Peach Lake. Or continue south 3 miles, pass under I-10, then decide whether you want to take West Middle or Middle Pearl. Both come out close to one another at U.S. 90, and side bayous connect all the Pearl channels except the West just north of the bridge, so if you arrive at the wrong bridge it's no problem. Equipped with the Pearl River WMA map or quad maps, you can explore to your heart's content. Unlike the West Pearl, which receives most of the flow, current on these other Pearl channels is normally slight, so it's usually easy to backtrack. Indeed, they're subject to tides and periodically flow backward, though not with enough force to pose a problem.

Pearl options

1. Launch at any of the bridges on U.S. 90 except the one over the West Pearl, explore the swamp to the north or marsh to the south, and return to starting point. The West Pearl does not connect easily to the other rivers here, plus it has a stronger current.

2. Paddle 6 miles from Lock 1 to ramp under I-59 on east side of West Pearl. Lock 1 is located east of Louisiana Highway 41 between Hickory and Talisheek; a wooden Corps of Engineers sign marks the entrance from the highway. The I-59 ramp is located off Old Highway 11 at the exit 5 miles north of the intersection of I-59 and I-10; approach exit slowly due to a sharp curve.

3. Paddle 6 miles from I-59 to ramp at Davis Landing on West Pearl River. Davis Landing lies at the end of an unmarked residential road off Louisiana 1090 just over a mile north of I-10. The Pearl River WMA map is useful in driving to the landings.

4. To continue down the West Pearl, paddle 3 miles from Davis Landing to Crawford Landing, 5 more miles to Indian Village, and 2.5 more to the western-

most bridge on U.S. 90. Crawford Landing lies at the end of Crawford Landing Road off Louisiana 1090 just north of I-10. The Indian Village ramp lies at the end of Indian Village Road off U.S. 190 between White Kitchen and Slidell.

5. To get into remoter waters, launch at Davis Landing, take the east branch 1.5 miles down, and paddle roughly 11 miles down the West Middle and/or Middle Pearl to U.S. 90.

Outfitters

Mr. Denny's Voyageur Swamp Tours, Highway 98 East, Slidell, 985-643-4839. Provides canoe tours of Honey Island Swamp.

Canoe and Trail Adventures, Metairie, 504-834-5257, www.canoeandtrail.com. Provides canoe tours of Honey Island Swamp.

Area campgrounds

Crawford Landing, primitive campground in Pearl River WMA at the end of Crawford Landing Road off Louisiana 1090 just north of I-10, 225-765-2360 or 504-646-6440.

Buccaneer State Park, 1150 South Beach Blvd., Waveland, Mississippi. Travel east on I-10 into Mississippi. Exit on Highway 607 and go right. Either drive into Waveland, following the Buccaneer signs, or take a shortcut by turning right on Lakeshore Road, driving to the coast and turning left on the beach road which leads to the park entrance. For more information call 228-467-3822.

Walkiah Bluff Water Park west of Mississippi 43 north of Picayune. The park is located on Pearl River and is operated by Pearl River County, 601-798-1339.

Maps

For a Pearl River WMA map, call 225-765-2360.

U.S.G.S. quad maps of the lower river, starting from Bogalusa and going south, are Nicholson, Haaswood, Rigolets, and English Lookout. Call 1-888-ASK-USGS.

For a map of Bogue Chitto National Wildlife Refuge, call 504-646-7555.

High points

250 square miles of virtual wilderness.

Low points

Complex navigation.

Tips

Using a Pearl River WMA map, launch at U.S. 90 and explore bayous and sloughs north and south for loop day trips.

Recommended Reading

Abney, Don. *The Louisiana Catahoula Leopard Dog*. Doral Publishing, 1996.

Bass, Rick. *Oil Notes*. Houghton Mifflin, 1989.

Cable, George W. *Strange True Stories of Louisiana*. Pelican Publishing, 1994.

Calhoun, Milburn, ed. *Louisiana Almanac: 2002–2003 Edition*. Pelican Publishing, 2002.

Davis, Edwin Adams, ed. *The Rivers and Bayous of Louisiana*. Louisiana Education Research Association, 1968.

De Caro, Frank, ed. *Louisiana Sojourns: Travelers' Tales and Literary Journeys*. Louisiana State University Press, 1998.

Dobie, J. Frank. *The Ben Lilly Legend*. Little, Brown & Co., 1950.

Estes, Chuck, Elizabeth F. Carter, and Byron Almquist. *Canoe Trails of the Deep South*. Menasha Ridge Press, 1991.

Feibleman, Peter S. *The Bayous*. Time-Life Books, 1973.

Herndon, Ernest. *Canoeing Mississippi*. University Press of Mississippi, 2000.

Klier, Betje Black. *Pavie in the Borderlands: The Journey of Theodore Pavie to Louisiana and Texas, 1829–1830, Including Portions of His Souvenirs atlantiques*. Louisiana State University Press, 2000.

Kniffen, Fred B. *The Indians of Louisiana*. Pelican Publishing, 1998.

Leeper, Clare D'Artois. *Louisiana Place Names: A Collection of the Columns from the Baton Rouge Sunday Advocate, 1960–1974*. Legacy Publishing, 1976.

Lindahl, Carl, Maida Owens, and C. Renee Harvison, eds. *Swapping Stories: Folktales from Louisiana*. University Press of Mississippi, 1997.

Lockett, Samuel H. *Louisiana As It Is*. Louisiana State University Press, 1969.

Lockwood, C. C. *Discovering Louisiana*. Louisiana State University Press. Baton Rouge, 1986.

Martin, Gay. *Louisiana Off the Beaten Path*. Globe Pequot Press, 1993.

Parker, Amos. *Trip to the West and Texas*. Arno Press, 1973.

Pitre, Glen, and Michelle Benoit. *Great River*. Pelican Publishing, 1993.

Read, William A. *Louisiana-French*. Louisiana State University Press, 1963.

——. *Louisiana Place-Names of Indian Origin*. University Bulletin, Louisiana State University and Agricultural and Mechanical College, vol. 19 n.s., no. 2, Feb. 1927.

Robin, C. C. *Voyage to Louisiana*. Translated by Stuart O. Landry Jr. Pelican Publishing, 1966.

Sims, Julia. *Manchac Swamp: Louisiana's Undiscovered Wilderness*. Louisiana State University Press, 1996.

Streever, Bill. *Saving Louisiana? The Battle for Coastal Wetlands*. University Press of Mississippi, 2001.

Trail Guide to the Delta Country. Delta Chapter, New Orleans Group of the Sierra Club, 1997.

Walton, Richard K., and Robert W. Lawson. *Birding by Ear: A Guide to Bird-song Identification, Eastern and Central North America*. A Peterson Field Guide set of three cassette tapes. Houghton Mifflin, 1989.

Wilds, John, Charles L. Dufour, and Walter G. Cowan. *Louisiana Yesterday and Today: A Historical Guide to the State*. Louisiana State University Press, 1996.

Williams, Dr. and Mrs. Richard. *Canoeing in Louisiana*. Lafayette Natural History Museum and Planetarium, 1985.

Index